THE MUNCHKINS of OZ

ALSO BY STEPHEN COX

The Beverly Hillbillies

The Munsters

The Abbott & Costello Story (with John Lofflin)

The Addams Chronicles

Here's Johnny!

The Hooterville Handbook: A Viewer's Guide to Green Acres

Here on Gilligan's Isle (with Russell Johnson)

Cooking in Oz (with Elaine Willingham)

Dreaming of Jeannie: TV's Prime-Time in a Bottle

THE MUNCHKINS of OZ

Revised & Updated

STEPHEN COX

CUMBERLAND HOUSE
NASHVILLE, TENNESSEE

*This book is dedicated
to my little friend with a big heart:
Mickey Carroll—one of the Munchkins.
Without him, I couldn't have
written the book.
. . . and for all the Munchkins
and their descendants.*

Portions of this book were published earlier in *The Munchkins Remember the Wizard of Oz and Beyond,* copyright © 1989 Stephen Cox.

Grateful acknowledgment is made for permission to quote lyrics from "Ding Dong! The Witch Is Dead" by Harold Arlen and E. Y. Harburg. Copyright 1938, 1939 (renewed 1966, 1967) by Metro-Goldwyn-Mayer Inc. Rights assigned to SBK Catalogue Partnership. All rights controlled and administered by SBK Feist Catalog Inc. International copyright secured. Made in U.S.A. Used by permission.

Published by
Cumberland House Publishing
431 Harding Industrial Drive
Nashville, Tennessee 37211
www.cumberlandhouse.com

Cover design: Unlikely Suburban Design
Interior design: Harriette Bateman

Library of Congress Cataloging-in-Publication Data
Cox, Stephen, 1966–
    The Munchkins of Oz / Stephen Cox.—Rev. & updated.
       p. cm.
Includes index.
    ISBN 1-58182-269-3 (alk. paper)
  1. Motion picture actors and actresses—United States—Biography. 2. Midgets in motion pictures. 3. Wizard of Oz (Motion picture). I. Title.

    PN1998.2 .C68 2002
    791.43'028'092273—dc21

                                        2002004866

Printed in the United States of America
1 2 3 4 5 6 7 8—07 06 05 04 03 02

CONTENTS

FOREWORD

I was too young to perform in *The Wizard of Oz,* but it is a great pleasure to write this foreword because I feel this motion picture opened a window to the real world for Little People.

For the first time, an opportunity was afforded Little People, or midgets as they were called, to act independently as people, not freaks. Most Little People were told when, what, and how to dress, eat, act, and talk—essentially how to live. Of course, there were exceptions, but very few.

This movie gave the actors a chance to run the gamut of emotions, from slapstick comedy to pathos. Steve Cox has done an excellent job of following the lives of the Munchkins during and after *Oz.*

Even today, thousands of Little People are still searching for the independence that is every citizen's heritage. In 1957 I founded Little People of America, Inc., to help persons of small stature attain that goal and accept the unique challenge of being a Little Person.

In 1975 I augmented this endeavor by founding the Billy Barty Foundation. Through such fundraising events as the Billy Barty Little People Celebrity Golf Classic (now in its twenty-fourth year), we raise money that is channeled into medical research, educational scholarships, and

the breaking down of attitudinal and architectural barriers that affect Little People.

Let freedom ring!

Billy Barty

ACKNOWLEDGMENTS

The author is beholden to the following people and organizations, who gave of their time and energy for this book:

The Academy of Motion Picture Arts and Sciences, the Associated Press, Mary Balzer, Clare and Robert Baum, Diana Brown, Jodie Carn, Willard Carroll, Tina and Andy Cassimatis, Mark Collins, Elizabeth Cottonaro, Lindsey Cunningham, Eric Daily, Ray and Phyllis Erickson, Linda Fitts, John Fricke, Cindy Glick, Joanne Gregorash, Steven Harvey, Robert Japs, Pat Jordan, John Kelsh, Mary Lou Kirkendall, Jane and Ted Kondrak, Marcella Porter Kranzler, Allen Lawson, Scott Maiko, Patty Maloney, Jeanne Martinet, Elizabeth Maren, Dona Massin, Roger Mayer (president of Turner Entertainment), Doug McClelland, Scott Michaels, Mary Ministeri, Anna Mitchell, Gloria Nelson, Jean Nelson, Betty Lou Nevin, Tim Nicholson, Rita Nissenson, Melvin O'Docharty, Vicki Profitt, Marie Raabe, Patty Reeder, Alice Reppe, Dorothy Sadue, Ray Savage, Marion and Jimmy Slover, Mary Ellen St. Aubin, Beverly Smith, Greg Smith, Patty Smith, Judy Sweeney, Myrna Clifton Swensen, Carolyne Thiessen, Dan Thome, Pat Thome, Marilyn Thompson, Turner Entertainment, Annabelle Bump Waldman, Olive Brasno Wayne, Edna Wetter, Don Williams, Dottie

> "We thank you very sweetly, for doing it so neatly."

Williams, Phyllis Windle, Anne White, Jean Wood, and Max Zimmerman.

Great big thanks to two very special friends, Elaine Willingham and Tod Machin—both of whom have provided a precious source of friendship, professional advice, and support over the years. Elaine, my hometown pal, prodded me to write this book and nurtured my love for this classic motion picture. As webmaster of the *Beyond the Rainbow* website (www.beyondtherainbow2oz.com) and owner of an Oz collectibles mail-order business of the same name (P.O. Box 31672, St. Louis, MO 63131), she has unselfishly provided an invaluable source for multitudes of *Oz* and Judy Garland fans in their quest for knowledge and personal collections of their own.

Of course, a big round of applause for the thirty-two Munchkin actors who I have interviewed during my long trip down this yellow brick road. I thank them for proudly opening up their lives. And for their trust. Anna Cucksey Mitchell and Margaret Pellegrini were both instrumental in preserving for posterity many of the wonderful, rare images found within these pages. History will thank them. Cheers to all of the little people who cared enough to document their lives and their participation in *The Wizard of Oz* in such a manner. The ages will be grateful to them as well.

Others who were of enormous help in preparing this book for publication include Ron Pitkin, Mary Sanford, and the rest at Cumberland House.

And many thanks to my parents, Gerald and Blanche Cox, for their assistance and support in a variety of ways. Also to my older sisters, Bernadette and Michele, and my brother, Brian, all of whom rooted for me years ago when *The Wizard of Oz* aired opposite *Little House on the Prairie*—our dad's choice. He gave in.

INTRODUCTION

In 1988 I began a nameless quest to locate a group of little people who appeared in the masterpiece motion picture *The Wizard of Oz*. I was fresh out of college when I began preparing the original manuscript of this book. The book was aimed for the golden anniversary of the timeless MGM film, which I had mysteriously loved since I first watched it as a child. Simply, I grew up with it, counting on a reunion every year on television.

The inception of this book took place in St. Louis. My search for these people was sparked by my favorite Munchkin right in my own hometown. His name is Mickey Carroll, and we've been the best of buddies since I was, well, let's just say when we saw eye to eye. Like a lot of the Munchkins, he still receives fan letters from all over the world. A wide range of age groups has an unending fascination with his involvement in the movie. I thought surely other people from the film must be alive as well. Mickey had stayed in contact with only one other.

With a Munchkin in my own backyard, the book's starting point was obvious. But tracking down the rest of the surviving Munchkins from this 1939 Technicolor dream was more impenetrable than I imagined. Here, five decades after the fact, I knew this was going to be a chore that required some commitment, some support, and a lot of investigative energy. Thankfully, a few new friends who were fervent fans of the film generously passed along some leads.

Then something clicked. I pitched my problem to a local reporter at the Associated Press who seemed drawn to this strange, nationwide probe. The journalist took the story and ran with it. Within weeks an amusing story about my hunt for Munchkins went across the wire and was reprinted in newspapers and periodicals all over the country. Morning radio show hosts were cracking jokes, all the while helping me in this search. Somewhere in there it occurred to me that the whole thing resembled Leo Singer's original search to locate midgets for the film back in 1938.

Probably what advanced me most was the Associated Press newspaper stories. Headlines such as these were common: COME OUT, COME OUT, WHEREVER YOU ARE or AUTHOR SEARCHES HIGH AND LOW or TRACKING DOWN MUNCHKINS NO SMALL TASK. In rapid succession the feedback hit. I was acquiring more leads, addresses, and contacts of deceased Munchkins and phone calls from some of the little people themselves. The Associated Press was receiving letters, and cryptic messages were filtering in to my publisher.

Strangely, I had to weed out a few impostors. ("These things must be done delicately.") In this book I did as much as humanly possible to assure that only the individuals who actually participated in the production are given credit for their contribution to film history. Munchkins, as it turned out, seemed to live in clumps. (There is such a thing as a peck of flour, a flock of geese, and yes, that's right, a clump of Munchkins.) There were about eight living in the Los Angeles area, another group in the Phoenix area, and a third assembly in Florida retirement communities. The rest, as it turned out, were scattered around the United States. All well-integrated human beings, some remained in show business, and some had more conventional careers and lives. After *The Wizard of Oz* it seemed as though they all took Aunt Em's advice and found themselves a place where they wouldn't get into any trouble.

After spinning the wheels of the Munchkin network, I found that some of the little people kept in touch with others, and thus my yellow brick road was ahead—albeit in desperate need of paving.

One Munchkin led me to another and so on. I consulted countless phone directories in an effort to contact even a distant relation to some names I had been provided. With the aid of some very patient little people such as Margaret Pellegrini—who has the memory of a wizard—hundreds of phone calls, and a few favors begged here and there, I met as many of these wonderful little people as possible. My only disappointment is that I couldn't have begun this book years prior; if I had, I would have been able to interview so many more.

I was off to see the Munchkins, the wonderful Munchkins of *Oz.* And what a delight it was to meet such a conglomeration of people, with many views of the film, their scene, and its success. In the interim, the loving friendships I've made along the way are the experiences that make life worth living. The Munchkins are inspiring to me.

Because of *The Wizard of Oz,* these people had the unforgettable opportunity to converge—a summit of epic proportions. It will probably never happen again in the history of human-kind: Proportionately correct midgets are a rarity today because of advances in hormonal treatments.

Moviegoers for the last half century have labeled *The Wizard of Oz* an ultraclassic—not only the original book but also the MGM film

phenomenon as well. With the sixtieth anniversary of the motion picture in 1999 and the one-hundredth annniversary of the publication of L. Frank Baum's book the following year, the Munchkins became virtually the only surviving cast members of the movie to have witnessed the making of the grandest movie of all time. It's finally their turn to bask in some of that applause.

A book about a ten-minute scene in a movie? Preposterous, you might say. Why would anyone want to read a book just about the Munchkins? I hope you come away with a bit more than just the answer to that question.

So get ready to take a trip that will bring you into the late 1930s, when show business was not a snow business. It was what Munchkinland was all about—fantasy. And it *was* no small task.

Munchkinland is a spectrum of colorful imagination embedded in the minds of young and old as one of the most enchanting sequences ever encased in celluloid. Indeed, affection for the Munchkins hasn't diminished. The actors who appeared in these roles deserve recognition. This is why I undertook the writing of the Munchkins' memoirs. I was thrilled to be able to revise and update this book and publish, for the first time, some photographic gems that surfaced after this book was originally published.

When the first edition of this book was published in 1989 (under the title *The Munchkins Remember*), I had located thirty-one surviving midgets who played Munchkins. Since then one additional person sprang from anonymity. Today only ten survive.

It's very sad to realize that an era will vanish when the last Munchkin goes to that Emerald City in the sky.

I wonder who it will be.

Stephen Cox
Los Angeles, California

POSTSCRIPT: 2002

The sixtieth anniversary of *The Wizard of Oz* did not go unrecognized with fans around the country, and it seems the Munchkins, once again, carried the torch. In the interim between 1989 and 1999, the film entertained even more generations with its annual television broadcasts, and, of course, millions of viewers can watch it anytime courtesy of videotape. Although the alumni of Munchkins is dwindling, they remain outspoken and undaunted in their praise of *Oz*. In the past few years the little people have been featured in a *Life* magazine photo spread, a *TV Guide* feature story, a brilliant new documentary produced by Turner Classic Movies, and extensive *Washington Post* and *New York Times* stories. What more can be said about *Oz*?

There is something to discover, if you haven't already. It's a must. If you really want a thrill, take a long, loving look at the stunning digitally remastered version of the movie offered on DVD from Warner Brothers, the film's current distributor. You will experience the movie like never before—with greater clarity and depth, more brilliant color, and a rich, glorious texture that puts you right there in Oz. The image is so advanced and improved, it takes no effort to notice the long black hair stemming from a mole on the chin of the Wicked Witch. And I had never before noticed the Scarecrow brandishing a handgun when the four characters enter the Haunted Forest. (No joke.) And finally, I hope this book will serve as a nice addition to your *Oz* collection.

This revised and expanded edition includes newly discovered biographical and photographic elements, hopefully sprouting some dimension to the story of the Munchkins. I have attempted to correct errors from previous editions, and thanks to some invaluable research assistance from *Oz* enthusiast Vicki Proffit, this edition features a comprehensive Munchkin register found at the conclusion of the book.

In December 2001, my pal Billy Barty (author of this book's Foreword) died at the age of seventy-six. Besides being damned good at his chosen field, Billy, at three feet nine, was blessed by becoming one of the entertainment industry's most famous dwarf actors, having appeared in more than 150 feature films and scores of television shows. I think my favorite was his role as the mystical High Aldwin, a bearded little sorcerer in Ron Howard's fantasy film *Willow* (1988). Although Billy did not work in *The Wizard of Oz* (many people assumed he did), Billy did portray a Munchkin in the 1981 parody flick *Under the Rainbow*. Billy's career went way back to the late 1920s when he was a child actor. He portrayed Mickey Rooney's little brother in the short-subject *Mickey McGuire Comedies*. Rooney once said of his longtime little pal, "We almost grew up together." Probably more than any other diminutive actor, Billy strived to raise awareness of the problems of those with dwarfism, and to improve the quality of life for other little people around the globe. And if for nothing else than this, he should be fondly remembered.

At the time of publishing, regrettably just ten midgets from *The Wizard of Oz* survive; only five are able to travel and make personal appearances. Some of these individuals are more active than ever, gladly involved with *Oz* promotions throughout the country—and abroad. Last year, Margaret Pellegrini became the first Munchkin to travel from America to Australia when she was named the celebrated ambassador at an *Oz* festival. Annually, festivals, parades, and themed events continue to attract record crowds around the United States, and hopefully the presence of a real-life Munchkin will continue to grace these gatherings for years to come. It really is a unique occasion when you meet a Munchkin. See for yourself.

—S.C.

THE MUNCHKINS of OZ

"But If You Please, What Are Munchkins?"

In mid-November of 1938, a special group of people ambled their small-scaled statures through the mighty gates of Metro-Goldwyn-Mayer studios in Culver City, California. These petite people, nearly a hundred and a quarter in count, were blatantly staring at the massive studio surroundings as much as the actors, technicians, directors, and studio employees were gawking back at them.

"Acquired from twenty-nine cities in forty-two states," as an MGM press release stated, this historical gathering of diminutive people converged on the movie lot to participate in a motion picture that would mark their lives forever—although none of them had an inkling at the time.

This was no ordinary motion picture. It was *The Wizard of Oz*. And they were about to become Munchkins.

The truly American fable involving Dorothy Gale and her adventures was the inventive product of writer L. Frank Baum back in 1900. Baum decided to drop Dorothy into a land called Oz after glancing at his file cabinet, which had drawers marked "A–N" and "O–Z." The result of that little peer over his shoulder became an obsession for many readers, as well as viewers of what is now a bona fide movie classic in every sense. It has become the stuff of legend.

Since the movie's original release in 1939, *The Wizard of Oz* has climbed to such status

munch • kin (munch' kin) *n.*
1. A very small person, especially one with an elflike appearance. 2. *Informal.* A child. 3. *Informal.* A minor official. [After the Munchkins characters in *The Wonderful Wizard of Oz* by L. Frank Baum.]

—*American Heritage Dictionary of the English Language*

Many of the midgets walked to work in the morning since their hotel was just blocks from the studio. An unusual sight—even for Hollywood. (Courtesy of Margaret Pellegrini)

that it can honestly be labeled the most-watched film of all time. This is mainly due to an astonishing forty consecutive annual airings on prime-time network television (predominantly CBS), beginning in 1956. It didn't matter that for nearly ten years viewers suffered with it in black and white.

Oz has been called America's favorite fairy tale. Some say it is timeless, others claim its appeal is in the underlying theme: "There's no place like home." Whatever the reason—and there are many—children everywhere have grown up loving one particular portion of the movie.

The colorful entrance into the fantasy world of Oz, which introduces the Munchkins, seems to be for children the most enchanting, exotic, and cherished scene. It takes place beyond the rainbow, and it's what dreams are concocted from. Strategically, Munchkinland is the first glimpse of color in the film. Focus is intention-

ally zeroed in on the whirlwind music and the bizarre little dwellers who, to the delight of the children, match the height of young ones.

With equal intensity, children's emotions shift to fear in the same scene when the most horrid of evil entities—the Wicked Witch of the West—makes a blasting intrusion. The striped legs and remains of the deceased Wicked Witch of the East that poke out from under Dorothy's displaced farmhouse are a frightful sight for youngsters. No exposed, hemorrhaging severed body parts of today's horror films can match the simple, gruesome sight of the striped legs curling up into oblivion. For children, this is a tense moment. For most adults, it's a memory of their discovery of the enjoyment of movie magic.

For decades prior to the video age, viewers anxiously anticipated the movie's arrival on prime-time television. New generations caught the fever each time. And as the decades

A rare photograph taken December 27, 1938, of the Munchkins outside the studio soundstage, at the close of their filming. (L–R): Prince Denis, Margaret Nickloy, Hildred Olson, Ethel Denis, and Johnny Winters. (Courtesy of Margaret Pellegrini)

marched on, the major stars of the motion picture died one by one. Actor Ray Bolger, known best as the Scarecrow, was the last to go. First Frank Morgan, then Bert Lahr passed away, Judy Garland, even the beloved Tin Man, Jack Haley. A tearful Bolger said at Haley's funeral, "Jack, it's going to be very lonesome on the Yellow Brick Road."

But whatever happened to the Munchkins? Nobody knew. For a time, they were the flotsam and jetsam in a sea of nostalgia, waiting to be rescued at just the right moment.

The word *Munchkin* seems to be instilled in our minds as denoting something tiny, wee, or miniature. This term, coined by Baum, has been with us for so long now its meaning doesn't even require association with the movie to be recognized: little people. What isn't little is the appeal of these tiny charmers from *Oz.*

Ironically, just months before the convergence of more than one hundred midgets in

Culver City for the production of *The Wizard of Oz,* many of the very same people acted in a "terror-ble" motion picture, *The Terror of Tiny Town.* It was a tiny success of an idea that did more to make fun of midgets than it did to genuinely entertain. An all-midget musical western produced by Jed Buell in May 1938, the movie has in fact been cited many times in lists of the all-time worst films. Today it is an amusing oddity that has fallen into the public domain; thus countless video companies have released the title in a variety of forms.

Between the two films, the little actors traveled the spectrum, appearing in the same year in both one of the worst and one of the best films ever produced. All the while, these little people carried on much the same lives as any other individuals. A small portion went on to careers in the entertainment industry. Others retreated to their homes and followed in family footsteps. Still others met their spouses on the set of *The Wizard of Oz* and rode into the Munchkin sunset.

What an achievement this was, to assemble such a group of pocket-sized performers from all points of the globe. It was the duty, by contract, of an impresario by the name of Leo Singer. He organized the Munchkin search and finalized the details surrounding the collection of the little people for filming. It was a job that, although it paid him handsomely, was a test of Singer's patience and was his full-time employment for many months.

Singer was the impresario who held the master contract with Loew's Incorporated (Metro-Goldwyn-Mayer) and who was in charge of locating the little people and offering the roles to them. Of course, the Singer Midgets, his famous troupe of performers, constituted his core group and were the first to be hired. Singer's responsibility was to sign approximately 125 proportionately correct midgets for the movie, and this he accomplished with nearly complete success. It is not known whether precisely 124 midgets, as reported over the years, walked onto the set. But records do confirm 122, plus nearly one dozen children.

Collectively, they were just about 135, with one or two midgets leaving the production for differing reasons. (MGM memos show Munchkin Elsie Schultz of New York leaving midway through filming because of an automobile accident. An underage member of Singer's troupe, Margie Raia, was found out by MGM officials and asked to exit *Oz*.) Unfortunately, MGM's complete records and paper trails for such productions have since been destroyed, leaving only bits and pieces of documentation for even their most successful motion pictures. These important and varied remnants detailing the daily production process are now scattered across the country in many private collections, as well as the archives of Turner Entertainment. (Ted Turner's corporation acquired the motion

Shooting Technicolor footage required the use of a "lilly," a hand-held card that helped ensure proper color balance in the shot. (Courtesy of Tod Machin)

picture when he purchased the massive MGM library, *The Wizard of Oz* and *Gone With the Wind* being the flawless diamonds among the lot.)

This much is clear: For nearly seven weeks between November 11 and December 28, 1938, this group of little people spent their daytime hours on a massive, beautifully decorated soundstage of unmatched opulence. They spent Thanksgiving and Christmas in southern California, away from home, writing to their families of their experiences.

It was an adventure that can only be dreamed of now. But the unpolluted legend left behind is in the minds and memories of a privileged few. Luckily, for the most part, the "little ones" have big hearts and are happy to share.

"We got a call to make a movie at a studio," says Munchkin Jerry Maren. "Not just any studio. It was the biggest studio in the world! Just to go through the gate was a thrill. I thought, Wow! I'm a movie star!"

This would not be the last time young Gerard Marenghi, who simplified his name to Jerry Maren, would walk through studio gates. He became one of Hollywood's most successful midget actors. Now semi-retired, he has a long career on which to reflect. But on that cold November day in 1938, he was just one of many.

For more than one hundred midgets to assemble in one place—for almost two months—marks history in and of itself. It is highly unlikely that a grouping of this nature could, or will, ever occur again because 98 percent of these little people had a rare genetic makeup. They were midgets, not the commonly known dwarfs, semi-short people, or youngsters. There is a difference, and MGM knew it.

Here's the story, and it has a twist: The studio specifically wanted their Munchkins to be proportionately correct little people, commonly known as midgets. (Clinically speaking, any individual with an undersized, tiny stature is medically classified as a dwarf.) The politically correct call it "vertically challenged."

The defect causing unusual lack of height lies in a few different areas of the body. For midgets, the pituitary glands malfunction at some point in gestation. Rarely is it genetically transferred to offspring. For dwarfs, the flaw can be caused by defective cartilage growth (achondroplastic dwarfism). In more cases than not, this condition is genetically transferred. Reportedly, there are more than one hundred different defects that cause the bone dysplasia resulting in less than average height.

Although all adults of such size (no more than four and a half feet) are politely called little people, dwarfs differ from midgets because of their disproportionate body makeup.

Munchkin Margaret Pellegrini (located near Judy Garland's hand, wearing a flowerpot hat) remembers this particular photo shoot very well. "While we were taking pictures I started to get a nosebleed," she recalls, "and all of a sudden Mervyn LeRoy came over and picked me up right out of the bushes and took me over to first aid." (Copyright © 1939 Loew's Inc., renewed © 1966 by MGM)

Sometimes dwarfs' heads are somewhat over-sized, or their trunks or arms are smaller or unusually large. In many cases, dwarfs are afflicted with detrimentally bowed legs. Dwarfs are shaped differently from proportionately correct midgets, but one thing both groups have in common is their height. There were actually a handful of dwarfs used in *The Wizard of Oz*. Ruth Smith, Jack Glicken, Nels Nelson, Johnny Pizo, and Elmer St. Aubin were all dwarfs, though under their elaborate costumes and makeup they were not readily distinguishable from the rest of the Munchkins.

Leo Singer was used to working exclusively with midgets, so he ultimately chose certain little people. Because midgets have bodies that are proportionately correct, only miniature, they are physically more adept at dancing and moving exactly as average-sized people do. So if a prospective little person was brought to Singer's attention during his nationwide search, he extended an offer to participate in the motion picture, with one proviso: He or she had to send him a snapshot. That was the deciding factor in whether Singer would pursue an offer to the individual.

Pure imagination inspired one little person to put the difference between midgets and dwarfs into a unique motion picture perspective: "The Oompa Loompas in the movie *Willy Wonka and the Chocolate Factory* are dwarfs," he said. "And the Munchkins in *The Wizard of Oz* are midgets."

Today midgets are, in effect, antiques.

Because of advances in hormonal treatment, proportionately correct midgets are now very rare, and they may cease to exist in the future. Many midgets can be activated to grow with hormone injections, even into their twenties and thirties. Oddly enough, many of the midgets who performed in *The Wizard of Oz* grew several inches when well into adulthood, without the aid of hormones.

For many years, midgets have aided science in laboratories all over the world. They have submitted to experiments that have enabled doctors to control the growth to some degree. Midget offspring of midgets is extremely rare, although some cases have been recorded. There are many cases, however, of multiple midgets born to average-sized parents.

In 1934, years before *The Wizard of Oz*, authors Walter Bodin and Burnet Hershey posed a question in their now-classic study of midgets titled *It's a Small World*: "Will midgets continue timelessly? Or will they, with their curious cousins, the giants, become extinct, as have countless small and large creatures which roamed the earth with the beginning of time and which also were victims of their glands?"

Therefore, the extraordinary group assembled at MGM was remarkable not merely because of its visual impact. Most likely, this special sector of the human race will never reappear. The Wizard clearly made the best of the little people's juncture; it is captured on film for posterity.

MORE THAN
A HANDFUL

L egend has it that MGM wanted nearly three hundred midgets to portray Munchkins in their tale of a little girl bewildered in a Technicolor dream. Whether this idea was actually attempted is not known. What is known and verified by contracts is that MGM's agreement with an agent named Leo Singer was to "procure and supply" the services of 124 midgets for their "photoplay" *The Wizard of Oz.* Singer put

his little clients in show business and in one of the film classics that has captured generations of audiences.

"For more than forty years Singer has made the little things count," read the headline of a 1939 feature story about the agent in the *San Francisco Chronicle.*

Baron Leopold Von Singer was the leader of the midget entertainment world in the days of

A unique, behind-the-scenes glance at a proud Leo Singer among the little people.

Artist's rendering of Papa Singer with two of his midget troupe, which appeared in the *San Francisco Chronicle* on August 2, 1939.

Singer's Midgets pose for a gag shot inside a normal-sized refrigerator. (L–R), back row: Christie Buresh, Nita Krebs; middle row: Freddie Retter, Eddie Buresh, Jackie Gerlich; front row: Karl Kosiczky, Jeannette Fern.

While on tour, a few of Singer's troupe pose on the "California Limited" of Santa Fe.

vaudeville. A German Jew born in Vienna, he traveled with fifty European-born midgets throughout Europe and on to South America, Asia, and Australia, finally landing the group in the United States. In North America they toured most of the states, including Hawaii, and performed in many provinces of Canada. During their travels the troupe of entertainers attracted other little people, so Singer eventually recruited a melting pot of the small performers.

To further clarify Singer's intentions, it must be mentioned that, unfortunately, midgets born in Europe in those days were very much scorned. According to one foreign little person, back in the 1920s and 1930s Europe had many farms, and if a son or daughter couldn't work, he or she was considered somewhat of a family nuisance or an outcast. The United States, the land of opportunity, seemed to have much more to offer little people.

Singer recognized this fact and gathered midgets to work for him in the entertainment world—many times regardless of their talent or lack thereof. In some instances, Singer literally "purchased" the little person outright from the parents. One newspaper reporter who wrote about Singer's Midgets in 1959 noted, "By today's standards these agreements would seem precariously close to bond servant arrangements, as the diminutive performers were completely dependent upon their employer."

In fairness to Singer it must be said that he supported these little people, provided education for them, and for some, professional music training. He provided his little people a salary, ample custom-tailored clothing, food, housing,

The little rustlers of *The Terror of Tiny Town.*

The cast of the ultra-flop *The Terror of Tiny Town,* an all-midget western musical, traveled forty miles daily from Hollywood to the Lazy A Ranch in Santa Ana to shoot their movie. This was just months before they would film *The Wizard of Oz.* (L–R), top row: Crawford Price, Johnny Leal, Joe Herbst, Sandor Roka, W. H. O'Docharty, Johnny Bambury, Clarence Swensen, Johnny Winters, Jakob Hofbauer, George Ministeri, Little Billy Rhodes, Josefine Balluch, Freddie Retter, Mike Balluch, Eddie Buresh, Carlos Manzo; bottom row: Lida Buresh, Billy Curtis, Charlotte Sullivan, Christie Buresh, Charlie Becker, Jackie Gerlich, Nita Krebs, Nona Cooper, Marie Winters, Karl Kosiczky, and Jeannette Fern.

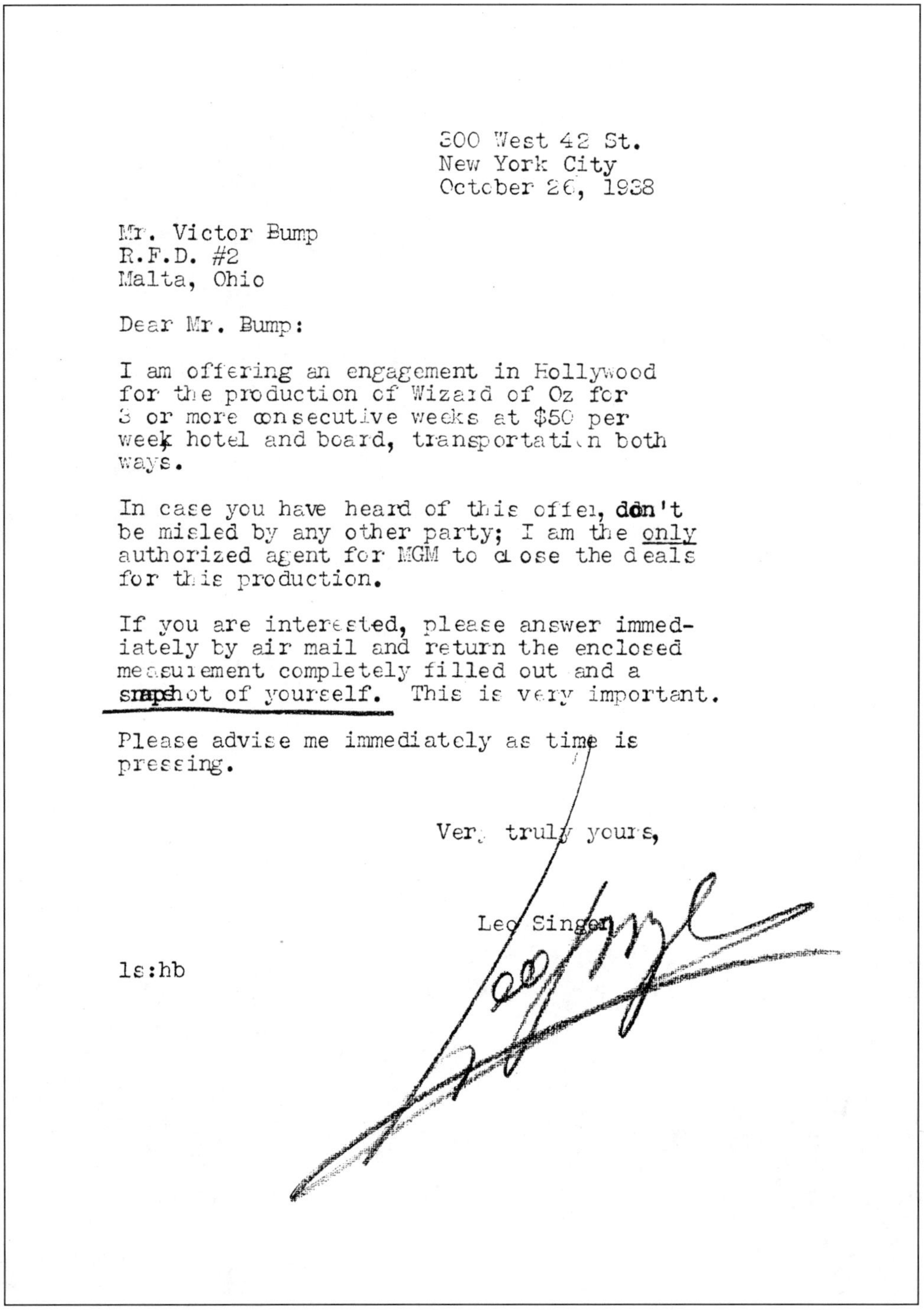

300 West 42 St.
New York City
October 26, 1938

Mr. Victor Bump
R.F.D. #2
Malta, Ohio

Dear Mr. Bump:

I am offering an engagement in Hollywood
for the production of Wizard of Oz for
3 or more consecutive weeks at $50 per
week hotel and board, transportation both
ways.

In case you have heard of this offer, don't
be misled by any other party; I am the only
authorized agent for MGM to close the deals
for this production.

If you are interested, please answer immediately by air mail and return the enclosed
measurement completely filled out and a
snapshot of yourself. This is very important.

Please advise me immediately as time is
pressing.

Very truly yours,

Leo Singer

ls:hb

Leo Singer's invitation to *Oz.* Midget Victor Bump and his wife (the former Gladys Farkas) both declined. (Courtesy of Annabelle Bump Waldman)

and gifts. Still, the midgets lived a nomadic lifestyle traveling from city to city, existing in hotels and theatre dressing rooms.

During this period, little people also performed in circuses, and it was acceptable to display midgets just for the sake of viewing them. They were exhibited as freaks in a carnival sideshow. Singer had minimal involvement with circuses or any form of freak show-type atmosphere. His little people played every theater on the Orpheum and Keith circuits. He also provided midgets for many early Worlds Fairs and events such as the Golden Gate Exposition in San Francisco in 1940 and 1941. Some of these extravagant fairs featured a Midget Farm or Midget Village in which a large group of little people moved about a tiny, specially constructed village and greeted fairgoers all day long.

On November 5, 1938, twenty-seven little people departed New York City for a cross-country trip to Hollywood in a chartered bus. (Courtesy of Jerry Maren)

"PAPA SINGER"

To his midgets he was known as "the boss," "Mr. Singer," or "Papa Singer"—titles he delighted in. He loved commanding their respect. On October 1, 1938, Papa Singer signed the master contract with Metro-Goldwyn-Mayer to supply the Munchkins for its film. He was also employed by the studio to assist in the managing ("handling," as MGM's contract stated) of the midgets during the term of their own contracts.

This was not the first film endeavor for many of the Singer Midgets. Although primarily stage performers, his midgets appeared in more than a dozen films before the crowning moment in *Oz*. Occasionally one or two of his little people were cast in films, including Laurel and Hardy's *Block-Heads* (1938) and Spencer Tracy's *They Gave Him a Gun* (1937). Just a few months before *Oz*, many of Singer's little people, and additional independent performing midgets, worked in an all-midget musical western film, *The Terror of Tiny Town* (1938). For this pro-

ject, Singer supplied nearly twenty of the forty midgets, who earned approximately $150 each for twelve days of shooting.

Singer began his work on MGM's Oz project in early September when he scouted for midgets with the aid of several agents throughout the country. Singer's own contract with Loew's Incorporated paid him $100 per week until October 3, after which he was to receive $200 per week until the full contract and his duties came to term. In early October Singer was to travel from Los Angeles by train to the East Coast and then gather his little performers while trekking back to the West Coast.

On October 1, 1938, Loew's vice president, Eddie Mannix, signed his name in green ink while Leo Singer penned his signature in black on three copies of an eight-page contract. The notary public impressed a seal on each page while Singer and Mannix shook hands, and the official agreement was final. The Munchkins were to arrive November 11 ready to work. Two-thirds of the little people arrived on schedule; the rest trickled in daily until the last one expected, Bill Giblin, arrived on November 24. Those disembarking from a train that had brought them from all sections of the country were greeted at the depot by Singer's private limousine, his chauffeur (a black man named Oscar Long), and a midget representative.

"When me and another midget, Leona Parks, stepped off the train, there was little Freddie Retter waitin' for us," says Munchkin Margaret Pellegrini. "He was all dressed up and had Singer's limo there for us. I thought that was great treatment."

Twenty-seven midgets and four average-sized people (including Walter Paul and Mervin Rogers, managers to some of the little people) boarded a chartered bus from All-American Bus Lines in New York. The bus began traveling the primitive roadways on the morning of November 5, en route to Los Angeles, and stops were made along the way to pick up three additional little people. As stipulated in the agreement with the bus line, meals and lodgings were provided, "not to exceed 25 cents for breakfast; 30 cents for luncheon and 40 cents for dinner . . . hotel accommodations for 5 nights at an average estimated at $1.00 per night, per person."

In the personal scrapbook of Munchkin Jerry Maren is pasted a yellowed and brittle clipping from an unidentified Oklahoma City newspaper. The article describes the arrival of the midgets to the midwestern hotel:

> The coterie of minute humanity which came to Oklahoma City in a chartered bus Monday at 9:30 p.m. had no press agent, but it needed none. The laughing, pranking little fellows were their own press agents as they romped about the lobby, took candid camera pictures of the normal-sized human beings who gaped at them, gave their dogs an airing, dangled their feet from tall stools in the Kingkade coffee shop, and rode the elevator,

Miniature Paychecks, Too?

Dorothy's dog, Toto, was paid more than the Munchkins. For the little female Cairn terrier named Terry, MGM cut a weekly check of $125, made out to her owner and trainer, Carl Spitz. Quite an expensive bark.

The highest salaries of the film went to Ray Bolger— $3,600 per week for twenty weeks' work. Frank Morgan and Bert Lahr earned $2,500 per week, and Jack Haley received $2,250 a week. Judy Garland made a mere $500 weekly, while the Munchkins, in comparison, made peanuts. And after Singer took his cut, a mere shell was left.

The preliminary compensation designated by MGM for each Munchkin was fifty dollars a week from November 11, 1938, until the first day of rehearsal or no later than November 22. After that Singer was allotted one hundred dollars per week for each of the midgets until the expiration of the term. In addition Singer was contractually obligated to hold the entire group of midgets in Los Angeles for two weeks after completion for possible retakes, added scenes, or changes in the film. If MGM needed the services of the midgets for retakes, they would be paid normal weekly wages or prorated wages for work rendered daily, according to the contract. Despite amounts allotted by MGM, Singer thought he'd be pretty foxy and had plans of his own regarding salaries for the midgets.

During the few weeks that Singer crossed the country rounding up midgets through every lead he could grasp, the number just wasn't adding up to the 124 he had promised. He regularly checked in with his agents, such as a Mr. Springer, Johnny Simons, E. W. Latendorf, and Robert Brandies, who were probing leads and roaming the country placing ads in some of the larger metropolitan newspapers. Singer would consult his girl Friday, Frances Schmeisser, to see if any new little people had been found. In order to reach the total in time, he had to strike a subcontract with the managers of two smaller groups of midgets: The Harvey and Grace Williams group and the Henry and Dolly Kramer Troupe. Combined, the ensemble brought in fewer than thirty midgets, but they raised the total closer to what was expected of Singer.

An older midget from New York named James Doyle (aka "Major Doyle"), who walked with a cane, thought he could handle the whole deal for MGM much more efficiently than Singer; however, he did not receive the contract, as reported in accounts over the years. Doyle did bring a few midgets with him, but signed independent contracts with MGM, as did additional little people. Manager Fred LaReine brought in four midgets from New York: Colonel Casper, Howard Marco, Albert Ruddinger, and George Suchsie. LaReine also bypassed Singer for a direct contract with the studio. Besides his own nucleus of little people, Singer knew he could not magically produce the remainder of the little people, and he acquiesced, allowing the front office to sign walk-ins.

Singer's secretary of twenty years, Frances Schmeisser, told reporter Michael Mok in 1959 that "talking pictures finished everything," referring to the death of vaudeville and the near-extinction of Singer's traveling troupe in the late 1930s. "But we had a few encores. . . . When they filmed *The Wizard of Oz* there wasn't a midget out of a job. They needed them all for Munchkins, and we were together again."

"Any little person who showed up at the front door of MGM got a job as a Munchkin," confirms Meinhardt Raabe, who was awarded the memorable role of the robed coroner Munchkin who pronounced the wicked witch "really most sincerely dead."

"I went out purely on a will-o'-the-wisp," Raabe explains. "The midget grapevine went around the country that MGM needed little people for a picture. On the basis of that, I took leave of absence from the Oscar Mayer Company, where I worked, and headed out to California."

Raabe signed a contract to be paid by Singer, as did most of the little people, over whom Singer hovered like a parent over a newborn. But some of the independents, among them Mickey Carroll and Johnny Bambury, already had existing contracts with MGM.

Mickey Carroll, whose real name was Michael Finocchiaro, dealt directly with Fred Datig, one of the heads of the studio's casting department. "My brother Bud did all the talking for me," he said. "My job had absolutely nothing to do with Singer." Naturally, because Singer had failed to fulfill his original contractual obligation to supply the complete miniature population for the film, MGM adjusted his payment accordingly. The total number of midgets was nearly complete.

If you rely solely on surviving MGM records, 116 midgets worked in the movie; however, after much research, documentation has surfaced proving that at least 122 midgets worked in the film, and possibly one or two more.

In addition, nearly a dozen children of approximately eight to ten years of age were auditioned and chosen to fill the background of Munchkin City. They were pretty little girls who had some dancing experience (the number of male midgets was almost double that of the female). The children's finances were handled directly through the front office at MGM. The parents or guardians of the little girls were paid daily, the same as movie extras.

For various reasons, many of the independently signed midgets chose not to negotiate with Singer and were handled directly by MGM's offices. For these performers, autonomy paid off, as their compensation was the same as MGM allotted Singer for his midgets: a hundred dollars a week.

Singer's tiny clients were unaware that they were receiving only half of what was allotted by MGM, although many of them were suspicious. Most got fifty dollars a week, and Singer kept the other fifty. Some of the little people who were given lines received a bonus; Jerry Maren, one of the Lollipop Guild, recalls that he earned seventy-five dollars a week. But the actors rarely complained about their salaries or fought over who was paid more. Everyone was happy to be working during the close of the Depression. In light of the nation's delicate economic condition, fifty dollars a week was considered handsome earnings. Many of the Munchkins wired much of their income home to help their families. Moreover, Singer had the right to terminate nearly any of the midgets from the film if he so wished, so financial arguments rarely occurred.

It is not known whether Singer openly discussed these dubious financial arrangements with the midgets prior to their signing a contract. No one recalls. But it would have been out of character for Singer—considered a shrewd businessman—to explain to the midgets that he was pocketing half their weekly salary for his position as their manager. He was known for duplicitous dealings, according to some of the little people who worked for him.

On the other hand, many of his little employees felt he was just. "Singer always treated his people fine; he was a peach," said Nita Krebs, who left Europe in 1928 and joined Singer's troupe. "He also bought us things . . . wardrobes and such." According to Munchkin Jeanette Fern (aka Fern Formica), "He was a moneymaking man, but he took care of his little people. He was like a father. He was a good man."

15 at a time, to the bewilderment of James Hunch, the Negro bell boy.

Joe Hicks, the room clerk, had the hardest job, assigning rooms to the small guests. Most of them bedded up two to a room, with single bed, but a few, such as Charles Ludwig (48 years old, 43 inches high) took an entire room, while one group, consisting of the Rogers brothers, slept three to a single bed.

The transcontinental drive landed them in Los Angeles late in the evening of November 10; some of them were dropped off at the Adams Hotel, and the remaining little people (most of the group) unloaded at the Culver Hotel, both residences being near the studio. The bus driver, J. D. Crabtree, helped the excited little people handle their baggage. (Crabtree was quoted about the midgets in the Oklahoma newspaper, saying "They're the most fun you ever saw.")

The lobby of the Culver Hotel suddenly came alive, and the register on the counter became crammed. "We were so tired, most of us went to bed right away," remembers Jerry

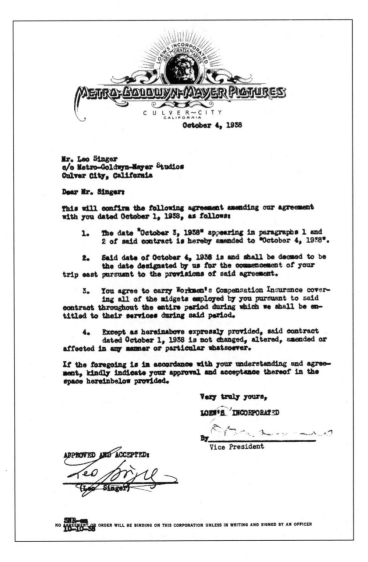

In this contract amendment between Loew's Incorporated and Leo Singer, notice that Singer was to supply workmen's compensation for all the midgets. Eddie Mannix, vice president, signed for Loew's. (Reprinted by permission of Turner Entertainment Company)

Maren, the youngest of the bunch. Maren recalls being awakened early the next morning by the sound of crowds and a parade marching down the street.

"I heard a big band playing, and I looked out of the window and yelled to the other fellows in my room. 'Hey! Look! They're havin' a parade for us! Come on, look out the window!'" Maren says. "After closer observation I noticed it was for Armistice Day. You know—Veteran's Day. And I thought it was for us."

When Leo Singer gathered all of the little people he had recruited, he had them all sign a contract promising to work exclusively with him as his employee, not the studio's. Besides the expense-paid round-trip, the agreement included workmen's compensation and lodgings during their expected stay. Unbeknownst to the midgets, however, Singer was claiming half of the salary MGM allotted for each of them.

Each Munchkin under Leo Singer's employ had to sign a stock contract such as this one signed by Charlie Becker, who portrayed the mayor of Munchkinland. (Reprinted by permission of Turner Entertainment Company)

Culver City, California
October 1, 1938.

Loew's Incorporated,
Culver City,
California

Gentlemen:

I hereby warrant to you that I have entered into a contract of employment with Leo Singer, whereby I have agreed to render my exclusive services for you in connection with the production of your photoplay "WIZARD OF OZ". I agree that in rendering such services I will carry out such instructions as you may give me, and will perform all services which may be required by you conscientiously and to the full limit of my ability and as, when and wherever you may request. I further agree to observe all of your studio rules and regulations.

I agree that I will look solely to Leo Singer for all compensation for the services which I am to render for you, and will not look to you or seek to hold you liable or responsible for the payment of any such compensation.

I hereby confirm the grant to you contained in the agreement between you and Leo Singer dated October 1, 1938, of all rights of every kind and character in and to all of my acts, poses, plays and appearances and in and to all recordations of my voice and all instrumental, musical and other sound effects produced by me, and in and to all of the results and proceeds of my services for you, and the right to use my name and likeness and reproductions of my voice and sound effects produced by me in connection with the advertising and exploitation thereof. I agree that you may use such photographs and recordings in said photoplay "WIZARD OF OZ" or in any other photoplay or photoplays and otherwise as you may desire.

All notices served upon Leo Singer in connection with the aforesaid agreement shall for all purposes be deemed to be notice to me of the matters contained in such notice.

Very truly yours,

Charles Becker

IHP%em

Lady Munchkins at MGM during a break in filming in December 1938. (L–R), back row: Gladys Allison, Ruth Smith, Lida Buresh, Josefine Balluch, Lillian Porter, Gladys Wolff; front row: Leona Parks, Margaret Nickloy, Freda Betsky, Jeane LaBarbera, Margaret Williams, Christie Buresh, Helen Royale. (Courtesy of Margaret Pellegrini)

Actor Victor McLaglen visits MGM's Lot 2 and poses with some of the midgets making *Oz*. (L–R): Billy Curtis, John Ballas, Daisy Doll, McLaglen, Charles Silvern, Gracie Doll, Alta Stevens, Robert Kanter, and Dominick Magro.

Some of the Munchkin men group together for a snapshot at MGM. (L–R), back row: Joe Herbst, W. H. O'Docharty, John Bambury, unidentified, Charles Kelley, George Ministeri, Clarence Swensen, Carl Stephan, Walter Miller (wearing glasses); front row: Little Billy Rhodes, Charley Royale, Jerry Maren, Harry Klima, Freddie Retter, Henry Boers. (Courtesy of Pat Jordan)

An early portrait of Singer's Midgets in the United States, circa 1929, with an unidentified dignitary. (Courtesy of Tod Machin)

Big Moment: In a highly publicized marriage ceremony, thirty-four-pound little performer Jack Glicken wed four-hundred-pound Mildred Monte in New York on December 4, 1934. Glicken later played one of the Munchkin mayor's entourage in *The Wizard of Oz*.

Miss Hildred Olson of Dassel, Minnesota, was a microscopic Munchkinette . . . one of the tiniest of the ladies in the movie.

His name was Clarence Chesterfield Howerton, otherwise known as "Major Mite." One of the smallest midgets in *Oz,* he was an American-born midget who stood just above two feet tall when he played one of the Munchkin trumpeters. This was not his only film appearance; he and midget Tiny Lawrence appeared in an Our Gang short titled "Free Eats" (1932). Major Mite was the smaller midget crook dressed as a baby, swiping jewelry. The Our Gang short marked the debut of Spanky McFarland and can be remembered for Stymie's references to the little men as "the fidgets." Below: The tallest human in the world, Robert Wadlow (eight feet eleven) compares shoe size with Major Mite in 1937. Wadlow was just under twenty years old and Major Mite was twenty-four when this photograph was taken in New York City. Wadlow's custom-made patent leather shoes measured a whopping size 36, while Major Mite fit into a tiny pair of size 4 dress shoes.

On May 14, 1967, Judy Garland made an appearance on a television special hosted by Jack Paar called *A Funny Thing Happened on the Way to Hollywood*. Most of the Munchkins took umbrage at the ridiculous way Judy Garland described them that evening. Even in jest, her comments had lasting impact. Interestingly, the special was produced by none other than Jack Haley Jr.

TAINTED YELLOW BRICKS

During their six-week sojourn in southern California, outlandish rumors about the midgets became commonplace. Around the studio and even in the print media, bizarre midget anecdotes were popular. Most of the wild tales involved odd situations and behavior described as less than civilized.

The late Mervyn LeRoy, who has stated he was enamored of the little actors, was one of the prime culprits. He and many of the technicians and studio employees found it amusing to go to the studio in the morning and hear the latest about the midget adventures during off hours.

Unfortunately, many of the rumors that have come to haunt the Munchkin actors were perpetuated by Judy Garland herself. In 1967 the singer was interviewed on television by Jack Paar. Audiences howled, and Garland herself laughed aloud as she delivered this whopper:

Paar: What about the Munchkins?
Garland: They were very tiny.
Paar: They were little kids?
Garland: They were little drunks.
Paar: Little drunks?
Garland: Well, one of them who was about forty asked me for dinner. And I couldn't say, "I don't want to go: I can't go out with you because you're a midget." I just said, "My mother wouldn't want me to." He said, "Bring your ma, too!"
Paar: How tall was he?

> "They had sex orgies in the hotel, and we had to have police on just about every floor."
>
> —Producer Mervyn LeRoy

METRO-GOLDWYN-MAYER PICTURES
CULVER-CITY
CALIFORNIA

INTER-OFFICE COMMUNICATION

To Mr. Hendrickson - cc to Mr. Chic, Mr. Busch

Subject WIZARD OF OZ

From Keith Weeks   Date Dec 30 1938

Mr. Singer has made a personal request this morning that he be allowed to receive carfare for and send home immediately the following people:

Mr. Kelly - a midget
Mr. Powell - an adult manager - and his two midgets, Gus Wayne and Leo Polinsky.

The reason Mr. Singer gives is that he anticipates a great deal of trouble from these people. He stated that Mr. Kelly tried to kill Mrs. Kelly last night, and that one of Powell's midgets tried to knife his assistant, Mr. Torelli, in an altercation last night.

Pleasant little fellows.

Will you please notify me as to whether or not I should allow them to go?

Keith Weeks.

In a memo from production manager Keith Weeks, the possibility of releasing a few midgets was discussed. However, it is doubtful that any action was taken, as this was the final day of shooting. Note: "Mr. Powell" refers to Walter Paul, manager to Munchkins Gus Wayne and Leon Polinsky. According to Wayne, Singer's real problem was that Paul was getting the commission for these midgets. (Reprinted by permission of Turner Entertainment Company)

Garland: About two inches high.
Paar: What could you do with him?
Garland: I don't know. They evidently did a lot.
Paar: There were lots of them.
Garland: Oh yeah. Hundreds. Thousands! They put them all in one hotel room—no, not in one room, one hotel. In Culver City. And they all got smashed every night and they picked them up in butterfly nets. They'd slam a tulip in their nose, the poor things. I imagine they get residuals.

Judy Garland was a pro at playing to an audience—of one or one thousand. It was a well-known fact that the legendary entertainer loved to exaggerate and twist a story a bit, to get a laugh. "Everything became an epic," recalls Garland's daughter, Liza Minelli. In a 1970s *60 Minutes* segment Minelli talked about how Garland felt compelled to stretch stories, even for her personal psychiatrist. (Interestingly, at the time Garland joked with Paar of the little people's inebriation, she was battling alcohol

An extraordinary behind-the-scenes snapshot of the cast and crew setting up the shot for Munchkinland. Look closely and you'll spot Bert Lahr visiting the set (far left). (Courtesy of Jerry Maren)

and drug dependency herself. Judy Garland died just two years later at the age of forty-seven, from what is described as an accidental overdose.)

LITTLE MISNOMER

If the Munchkins were intoxicated, it was with the pure electricity and frenzy that accompanied the thrilling experience of movie production. For some of the little actors, their weeks at MGM remained the highlight of their lives, and many were infuriated by the bloated stories that shadowed them. Whatever trouble did occur was probably aggravated by the treat-

ment they received from the studio and the public who met them.

For example, MGM naturally had interoffice memos that circulated from one executive to another and from one technician to another. In some of this surviving correspondence, references to the midgets are less than respectful.

One such memorandum refers to "Mr. Powell—an adult manager and his two midgets . . ." thus implying that little people were not adults. Another memo states: "Bus left New York this morning with twenty-eight midgets and two adults." Ironically, many of the Munchkins were older than the studio employees who worked behind the scenes.

The Culver Hotel

✴

Ninety-four hundred Culver Boulevard, Culver City, California—the infamous site of alleged late-night Munchkin mischief. Originally built in 1924 as the Hunt Hotel (also housing the offices of Mr. Harry Culver, the city's founder), this six-story landmark structure is within walking distance of MGM Studios. In 1938 the complex became the six-week living quarters for most of the little people during production of *The Wizard of Oz.*

The exterior of the hotel can be seen in the backdrop of a few early Hal Roach shorts such as Laurel and Hardy's silent *Putting Pants on Philip* (1927), and the Our Gang short *Honky Donkey* (1934). Joan Crawford made it her home and headquarters for a few months while filming at nearby Metro during the early 1930s.

Long after the Munchkins had come and gone, actor John Wayne owned the hotel sometime in the 1960s. (Legend has it he won it in a poker game.) It was later sold, and for many years the building served as low-income apartments. In 1994 the hotel was purchased, renovated, and refurbished, restored to a quaint lodging, now rich in historical significance.

Care was taken to maintain a decorative period elegance true to the thirties, with both European antique furniture and completely modern facilities. Although the Munchkins' rooms were standard and charming for the day, the hotel's new mini-suites—each equipped with a wet bar, refrigerator, and modern marble bath—are plush compared to what the little people encountered fifty years ago. (Totally new plumbing had to be designed and installed; each floor originally had only one bathroom at the end of each hallway.)

Fifty-nine years after *Oz,* a group of six surviving Munchkins reunited for a Halloween splash held in the lobby of the renovated Culver Hotel. Costumes were optional. Advertised as the "Munchkin Rendezvous '97," the event drew great crowds and press to the newly restored inn, and a city councilman even presented the little people keys to the city. "We're too old to trash the place this time," joked Munchkin Mickey Carroll.

Jerry Maren stayed at the quaint hotel while making the film, recalling "we were three to a bed for a couple of nights," he says, "but don't believe the BS about drunken parties. We were too tired for that stuff."

The Culver Hotel was refurbished in the late 1990s and resumed operation as a first-rate hotel. It is listed on the National Registry of History.

Yet another document, referring to a partial list of the little people, notes, "Don't know whether these twelve include any adults, or whether they are all midgets."

Of course, MGM was new at employing such an immense group of little people; it had never happened before, and some unusual things were bound to happen. In one reported incident the studio teacher attempted to round up some of the midgets for school, mistaking them for children. To top that, a wardrobe mistress reportedly attempted to help one shy little "boy" with his costume.

She coaxed him in a motherly tone, "C'mon now . . . I have a little one just like you at home." Embarrassed, she realized he was a mature adult when he undressed.

Some of the little actors did not appreciate being treated like children, and they let it be known. Others shook it off.

"In the beginning," remembered Gus Wayne, a Munchkin soldier, "they put us through some rehearsal and talked to us like we were kids. 'Left foot, right foot. . . .' Ya only got two feet! Very difficult," he said sarcastically.

Leo Singer lingered on the set during much of the filming to make sure that the little people had everything they needed and that their work was running smoothly. "After we got to the studio, they told us Mr. Singer was in charge of all the little people," Jerry Maren remembers. "He attended to our eating and any other activities and such, to take the headache away from MGM."

For the most part, recruiting the midgets and making their stay comfortable was not too painful for Singer, although the job was not without confrontations—just as the studio expected. One such incident was with a gun-slinging man named Charley Kelley. During the whole *Oz* production Kelley was estranged from his wife, Jessie, and rabid in his personal struggle to handle their separation.

"One day in the studio, Kelley came in with guns on his side," remembers little Karl Slover, one of Singer's troupe. "They were real guns. Two of 'em. The director spotted him and told Singer. Singer said, 'Oh boy, I better take care of this,' and he found that the guns were real. He asked Charley what the guns were for, and Charley said, 'They're for the protection of my wife.' I think Singer threw him out of the movie."

According to many of the Munchkins, Charley Kelley was a jealous, unpredictable midget with personal problems. Remembers Munchkin actor Margaret Pellegrini, "When I got to Hollywood, I was assigned to stay with Jessie Kelley. She had been in show business, and she was like a little mother hen, since she was older. Jessie was a very sweet person.

"On a Sunday morning, I was sitting at the desk writing out Christmas cards, kind of blue and homesick. It was the first time I'd been that far away from home. And I remember this perfectly, like it happened yesterday.

"All of a sudden we get a knock on the door, an' here it is Jessie's husband, Charley, and he had a knife. He was holding it straight out from his belly. He comes walkin' in. I stepped back. Then I said, 'I'm going outside. I'll leave you two alone.' He said, 'No you don't,' and shuts the door. I think he said, 'You sit down,' and I started crying, and I was shaking. Jessie got him over to the side of the bed and started talking to him, 'cause he had been drinking. Finally he put the knife down, and she got him to leave.

"Jessie and I had to move to anther hotel, the Vine Manor in Hollywood. Jessie reported it to Singer, and he didn't want us hurt."

Pellegrini and a few of the other little people distinctly remember when Charley Kelley came into the main restaurant one morning during breakfast and abruptly grabbed his wife by the hair. "He threw her down and started rasslin' with her when a few of the little ones grabbed him," Pellegrini says.

Certainly stories such as this did not aid attempts to squelch the rumors. Fact is, there were a few disruptive moments during production. In spite of voluminous rumors of violence

One predicament in *Oz* was that there were twice as many male midgets as female. Here, a group of the fellows pose at the MGM studio lot on a cold December morning.

pinned on the little people, Charley Kelley's escapades were probably the extent of the physical mischief. As with any group, much like participants at any given convention, stories get exaggerated. In this realm the male midgets seemed to bear the brunt of the gossip. Tall tales about the little men surrounded their whole existence in Culver City. Stories of the Munchkins' drinking, whoring, and pimping were rampant. It is doubtful that most of these things actually took place; however, there were a select few of the midgets who enjoyed an occasional tip o' the bottle. Some enjoyed more tips than others.

"There were two little men named Mike and Ike Rogers [also known as the Matina twins]. God, they were lush-hounds," Karl Slover

recalls. "One of them came in the studio drunk one day, and Singer had to send him home."

Munchkin Nels Nelson also remembered the baby-faced, chubby midget twins. "We used to pit them against each other for laughs," said Nelson. "We'd say, 'Hey, your brother's drinkin' your booze when you're asleep!' and so on. We'd sic them on each other 'cause they argued about their liquor all the time."

Singer, who stayed at his residence with his group of veteran midget performers, wound up getting a few late-night phone calls from the Culver Hotel manager. There were complaints about a few of the guests being loud and uncontrollable. (In no way did the disturbances resemble the chaotic scenes depicted in Orion Pictures' 1981 film *Under the Rainbow*, which displayed dwarfs wildly swinging from chandeliers and trashing the Culver Hotel like it was a playground.)

"Singer went over to the hotel one night and was still in his nightshirt," Karl Slover recalls. "He walked up the steps and down the hall, and he heard someone yelling 'Help!' He got mad. Johnny Pizo also got up and met Singer in the hallway. They looked in the bathroom at the end of the hall, and here was Charley Ludwig with his face in the toilet bowl, his face all black and blue. He had fallen in! Singer made Ludwig stay at his house from then on so Mrs. Singer could look after him."

Veteran MGM makeup men Jack Young and Louis LaCava, both of whom worked on the film, added that some of the crew would join the parties at the hotel or gather a group of little people in their car and drive to a club in Hollywood. "The little people didn't come in to work any more drunk than a couple of the boys who went out with them," said Young. "A lot of the crew came in drunk, too. Really, it was not that unusual. The midgets were new people in a new town."

Louis LaCava, in an interview with this author in 1989, related a funny story about an unidentified Munchkin who was frequently plastered:

There was one man, one of the principals, who came out in the scene dressed in a costume with tails with a big hat. He used to be so drunk when we came in in the morning. He'd sit, and we'd make him up. Then we'd have to guide him to the stage. We couldn't stick with him because we had other work to do—other people to work on. So we had to aim him at the stage door, which was like two stages up the street. On the left was the corner of another stage, and he would usually bump into that corner, and somebody would have to pick him up and help him. We'd watch this each day.

Munchkin Jerry Maren says that most of the unsavory stories about the little people have ballooned over the years.

"Are you kidding?" Maren says. "It was a lot of hard work, six days a week, going into the

Sisters Mitzi and Emma Koestner in 1938 during production of *Oz*. (Courtesy of Jean Nelson)

Betty Tanner and Ann Rice Leslie pose for a snapshot on the roof of the Adams Hotel in Culver City. In the background is the stately Selznick International Studios. (Courtesy of Betty Tanner)

studio at six in the morning and not getting home until around seven or eight. There wasn't a lot of time for wild parties and that sort of crap. We were wound up, but we were tired, too." Or maybe Maren just wasn't invited to the parties.

Munchkin Fern Formica commented in 1991 about the rumors of wild sexual escapades: "I'm getting so tired of that orgy story," she said. "It's so ridiculous. People can't seem to understand that little people are the same as big people, different only in size. They seem to expect strange behavior of us, so they imagine they see it.

"And anyway, as far as I'm concerned," Formica said, "if you get any group of 124 people together, you're bound to have one or two with a loose screw. But most of us were just working people."

Formica (who went by the name Jeanette

At an outing on the boardwalk in Venice, California, are Munchkins Henry Boers, Ruth Smith, Teddy Boers, Gladys Allison, and Margaret Williams.

Fern at the time) said she was excited by the whole moviemaking process, but was absolutely spellbound at the mere sight of such a unique gathering of humans. "It was literally the first time in my life that I saw so many other people who were in the same boat I was," she said. "It was the first time I could talk to people who knew how hard it was to move big furniture around, who knew what it felt like to be constantly looking up to the big people in the world—even if they were younger than you.

"So the experience made me feel like maybe I wasn't so bad after all. . . . Maybe I was as good as anyone else."

The Munchkins all recall making the most of their trip to California and retain diverse accounts of off-hour activities because they did not all travel the same path. Any group that size will have a variety of obstacles and pleasures.

During weekends, some preferred to hit the city's nightlife. "A group of us girls used to go to a club called the 90-90 Club," remembers Ruth Robinson Duccini. "We loved to go dancing."

This was Hollywood's golden era—the glitz, the stars, and motion-picture palaces such as the Egyptian and Grauman's Chinese. There was no television. The hills and roadways were void of mass-transit freeways, and the whole town existed for one purpose: making movies. The big studios were flourishing, cranking out musicals with bigger-than-life stars. In a time when theaters and nightclub activity were booming, the little people crashed the most exclusive night spots in Los Angeles. Munchkin Murray Wood remembered the midgets dressing to the nines, splashing on cologne, packing into a car, and going out to clubs,

Some of the Harvey Williams Midget Troupe and Kramer's Midgets in front of the house where the Williams group resided during the making of *Oz*. Today, the residence (3816 Motor Avenue, Culver City) is a 7-11 convenience store and parking lot.

where the doormen's eyes would bulge as a horde of midgets hopped out. Even for Hollywood, this was a sight.

On the weekends, the Munchkins took to sightseeing and other activities to rest from the grueling hours under the soundstage's intense arc lights. Margaret Pellegrini tells of taking a quick Sunday trip to Tijuana with her roommate Jessie Kelley and reporting to work the next day completely exhausted—but brimming with great memories to write home.

And so it seems, the legendary stories of the midgets of *Oz* were perhaps relegated to a rambunctious few. Time has not necessarily been kind in repairing the verbal affronts. The survivors shrug it off. . . . They were there, we were not.

Charlotte Sullivan splurged and bought a fur with her *Oz* earnings in Hollywood, 1938.

Little Did He Know

For a time, anyway, the name Singer was synonymous with midgets. Not because these little people sang, but because they were under the management of Baron Leopold Von fon Singer, a balding man with a pot belly who became the respected manager, custodian, and sometimes surrogate father to a conglomeration of European midgets.

Leo Singer was born in Vienna, Austria, on May 3, 1877. He was the grandson of Max Steiner, who introduced Johann Strauss to the music world and who was largely responsible for his European success. The Singer family was prominent in Vienna, and Leo's grandfather was the founder and publisher of the *Vienna Surblatt,* one of the world's first tabloid newspapers.

Although most reports indicate—and to the best memory of many of his midget clientele—Singer was Jewish, his surviving family members maintain that he and his wife, the former Walberga Bernstein, were married in St. Stephen's Cathedral, the church where Singer was baptized, and Singer's children were raised as Catholics.

As legend has it, around 1912 or 1913, Leo Singer's young daughter, Gertrude ("Trudy"), was convalescing from polio or a similar form of infantile paralysis, depending on which article you rely. In order to distract her from the illness, Leo and his wife, "Wally," devoted much time to devising amusements for their little girl.

On a bright spring day, when Singer took his daughter on a stroll along Vienna's famous *Prater* (a massive fairground in Vienna that dates back to the mid-1800s), he stumbled upon a traveling group of performing midgets. The child's eyes lit up with excitement, and she insisted that her father move her closer to the stage where these little people romped.

The fairy-tale imagery these wee folk created was therapeutic to Trudy; soon the elder Singers were accompanying their daughter to regular performances, caught up in the child's curiosity and excitement. In the audience were other children, equally fascinated by the routines of these midgets. It was on one of these visits that Leo Singer and his wife conceived the idea to form a midget troupe.

Despite history books that have popularly credited Leo Singer as sole engineer, Mrs. Singer was heavily involved in the concept from the beginning. A former musical comedy performer herself, she had put the entertainment business behind her when she and Leo married and began a family. With the midgets she saw an opportunity to rejuvenate her interest in the theater life and show business.

Papa Singer, they called him. (Courtesy of Margaret Pellegrini)

A few of the little performers pose with Leo Singer's personal chauffeur, Oscar Long, and the Singer limousine.

Leo Singer and his secretary/mistress, Frances Schmeisser, with Nita Krebs, Christie Buresh, and Jakob Hofbauer at San Francisco's Treasure Island World's Fair in 1939. (From the Nita Krebs collection)

Baron Leopold Von fon Singer had a "commanding" presence, according to those who knew him. (From the Nita Krebs collection)

Soon after, a large space at the *Venice-in-Vienna* amusement center was leased, and ground was broken for the construction of a Midget City. Joseph Urban, who later worked with the great Florenz Ziegfeld, was hired to lay out and decorate the toy town. The attraction would become a midget metropolis, constructed in great detail and complete with gift shops, retail stores, restaurants, outdoor cafe, post office, barber shop, mini-government, and housing for the midgets. Finally, the little community was populated with minute men and women, and the complex was christened *Liliputstaadt*. It was a wondrous showplace in the old Austrian capital.

Authors Bodin and Hershey described *Liliputstaadt* in their 1934 chronicle, *It's A Small World:*

> It was a spontaneous success. *Liliputstaadt* delighted gay, sophisticated prewar Vienna. It was smart. It was different. Adults and children alike crowded its little streets. . . . Such popularity could not be held to parochial bounds. *Liliputstaadt* went into a Vienna theater, and its fame crossed national boundary lines. Berlin producers wanted it, and the Singers finally consented to go abroad. A Berlin success was followed by a tour of southern Germany, so prosperous that it was determined to venture farther abroad. Singer by this time had absorbed his wife's enthusiasm and was definitely cast as a midget entrepreneur. He took the act to London.

By 1914 Singer had to cancel plans for a Continental tour because World War I had erupted; a tour of war-plowed Europe was out of the question. With his family, his troupe of nearly fifty midgets, trunks of wardrobe, and various trained animals, he and the entire act sailed to America.

Outside of two brief return trips to Europe for performing and recruiting, the Singer Midgets remained in the United States and became a celebrated attraction in countless vaudeville houses around the country.

Americans were seduced—and sometimes stupefied—by the unprecedented sight of such a group of entertaining midgets. Singer's troupe became world renowned. The little people were honored guests of President Harding at the White House and even accepted Charlie Chaplin's invitation to visit his set while filming the silent motion picture *Shoulder Arms* in 1918. Singer's Midgets played every theater on the Orpheum and Keith circuits, entertaining audiences of children and adults alike.

One reporter noted, "The Singer Midgets were, and are, the personification of the fascinating inhabitants of Swift's Land of Lilliput." Thus, they were occasionally tagged "Lilliputians."

As the years and miles added up, Singer's role transcended that of employer and exhibitor. To these people he became a confidant, interpreter, teacher, advisor, and foster parent.

Rarely addressed as "Wally," it was Mrs. Singer who was a mediator, when needed, for disagreements between the men and the women. Both Mr. and Mrs. Singer elicited respect and in turn demonstrated social graces. So adamant was Singer that his little people conduct themselves in the proper manner, the women were reflexed to curtsy when in the presence of Mrs. Singer. The most rewarding, and probably the most sincere, gift the Singers provided was dignity. One writer in the early 1930s observed, "[The Singers] have done more than anyone else in history to lift midgets out of the freak class and establish them as men and women with a dignified purpose in life. They have developed their talents, pointed their ambitions, made their lives livable . . . they have taken midgets out of the never-never-land and the books of mythology and revealed them as living, breathing, purposeful men and women."

In the mid-1930s, many of the veterans from the troupe left to return to the homeland, vanishing into the Transylvanian hills whence they came. Until the erection of Midget Village at the Chicago World's Fair Century of Progress in 1933 and 1934, practically all midgets on public "exhibition" in the United States were of European extraction. Gradually, midgets from within the United States began embarking on similar careers in show business, and numerous midget troupes were formed in imitation of Singer's. But none matched them in popularity and prestige. Surprisingly, there were many American-born midgets. (Contenders for the top-troupe position included Graham and Eagle's Midgets, Rose's Midgets, and Hermine's Midgets, to name but a few.)

Singer's flock had dwindled, but those who remained in the troupe were still performing and traveling at the time of *The Wizard of Oz* in 1939. Directly following what became the pinnacle of his career as monarch of the midgets, Singer received devastating news while out on the road: His daughter, Trudy, had committed suicide.

Singer continued to manage midgets through the Second World War, booking the waning group to appear in a few additional motion pictures, at World's Fair expositions, and events such as the Golden Gate Exposition in San Francisco in 1940 and 1941. By the mid-1940s, the steam ran out, and his troupe had completely dissolved. The midgets all went their separate ways, some joining less renowned midget troupes, others retiring from a life of performing altogether.

Leo Singer retired to an apartment in New York City with

Mrs. "Wally" Singer was like a mother to many of the little people. Clockwise from left: Betty Tanner, Hilda Lange, Christie Buresh, Fini Balluch, and (seated) Nita Krebs.

In the Singer living room, some of the little people relax in conversation with Mrs. Singer (far right).

Singer's men, all in a row, around 1924.

his secretary and mistress, Frances Schmeisser, and kept in scant contact with his little clients. His estranged wife, Wally, remained in Hollywood and lived into her eighties. Singer's surviving daughter, Gloria, married and had nine children.

Singer died on March 5, 1951, "a pauper," added a veteran of his troupe. He was buried in Westchester, New York. His daughter, Gloria Singer Nicholson, died in 1995, with only the grandchildren and great-grandchildren of Leo Singer surviving.

Gloria Singer's son, Tim Nicholson, never got the opportunity to sit on his famous grandfather's knee, but he grew up looking for his grandfather's name on the credit roll of *The Wizard of Oz* each year on television.

"From what my mother and friends of hers have told me, he had a tremendous amount of influence on people and my mother," Nicholson says. "He had absolute command of himself and his environment. I think there was something about him—an aura. You either absolutely hated him or absolutely loved and respected him."

Singer's grandson adds, "I would have truly loved to have met him."

His grandfather not only left an imprint on the lasting legacy of *Oz*, but he contributed a landmark for the ages: *Liliputstaadt*. The original village built by Singer still stands today. A spokesperson at the American Embassy in Vienna describes the structure as a children's attraction in an amusement park area of the *Prater* where kiddies can board a miniature train that transports them into the fantasy tiny town.

This gem shows nearly half the Munchkin actors gathered for a special portrait on Stage 27 with Victor Fleming and Leo Singer.

THERE'S NO PLACE LIKE HOLLYWOOD

The first few weeks the Munchkins were at MGM, their time was devoted to rehearsals, costume fittings, and more rehearsals. Choreographer Bobby Connolly put groups of actors in lines and showed them a dance step. By their repeat performance, he could gauge which of them were more inclined to dance well and which would simply bob up and down in the background. At this point, the Lullabye League and the Lollipop Guild were chosen. For the Lullabye toe dancers in pink tutus, Nita Krebs, Olga Nardone, and Yvonne Moray were selected. The three little tough guys with an oversized lollipop between them were Jacob "Jackie" Gerlich, Gerard Marenghi (aka Jerry Maren), and Kurt Schneider (aka Harry Doll).

Other parts for the sequence—including the mayor, coroner, barrister, city fathers, three trumpeters, town crier, five Sleepy Heads, twenty-five soldiers, a carriage driver and footman, and five fiddlers—were also cast.

"It was indeed an honor to be chosen out of all of the little people," said Nita Krebs, the "tall" Lullabye Leaguer on the left. Krebs also played one of the four who approach Dorothy near the end of the scene, directing her to "Follow the Yellow Brick Road."

In the rehearsal hall, there were folding chairs set up, a piano, and a large staircase similar to bleachers in a gymnasium. Here, the Munchkins were each given two mimeographed pages of the scene's songs. They

A studio pass issued by casting director Fred Datig to Munchkin Mickey Carroll.

One of the most elaborate sets built for a motion picture at that time, Munchkinland has earned a permanent place in our memory. (Courtesy of National Screen Service, Inc.)

Producer Mervyn LeRoy and director Victor Fleming pose on the yellow brick road with a group of the Munchkins. LeRoy has his arm around Harry Doll, and sidled next to Victor Fleming is Frank Cucksey.

A wardrobe test for the Lollipop Guild. (L-R): Harry Doll, Gerard Marenghi (aka Jerry Maren), and Jackie Gerlich. (Courtesy of Academy of Motion Picture Arts and Sciences)

The dainty Lullabye League. (L–R): Nita Krebs, Olga Nardone, and Yvonne Moray.
(Copyright © 1939 Loew's, Inc., renewed © 1966 by MGM)

rehearsed the songs until they knew them fairly well. They were not required to memorize the songs perfectly because the actual Munchkin vocals would be dubbed in later. In the same open area, the "Munchkin skip" was taught. This is the same behind-the-foot skip that Dorothy made famous on her trek down the Yellow Brick Road. Most of the Munchkins can still perform it.

The staircase was in place so the actors playing Munchkins could get accustomed to running up and down it. In the shot after the Munchkins arise, a group of little people quickly scale the steps and wave into the camera as the Sleepy Heads awake from little green eggshells in a huge nest. ("Wake up, you sleepy head / Rub your eyes / Get out of bed / Wake up, the Wicked Witch is dead. . . .")

The MGM wardrobe department was under tremendous pressure as the deadline for the actual filming drew near. Outside of the endless amounts of green fabric dye used in preparing the Emerald-City garments, hundreds upon hundreds of yards of multicolored felt were being stitched into oversized—yet tiny—vests, jackets, slippers, bonnets, bows, and dresses for the Munchkins. Every pair of Munchkin shoes, slippers, soldier's boots, and footwear (even Dorothy's ruby slippers) was constructed with a felt bottom to buffer the sound of walking and dancing on the stage.

Designer Gilbert Adrian put his personal

The Lollipop Guild were also known as the "little tough guys" in the script. Soon after they present Dorothy with a welcoming sweet, the oversized sucker disappears. (Courtesy of Jerry Maren) Inset, L–R: Jackie Gerlich, one of the Lollipop Guild; handsome little Jerry Maren was chosen to hand Dorothy the Lollipop; Harry Doll in a portrait made by the famous photographer Clarence Sinclair Bull. (Courtesy of Tiny Doll)

The little people heading to the studio on a chilly December morning.
(Courtesy of Mary Ellen St. Aubin)

Judy Garland poses in a rare wardrobe test photo
with Munchkins Nona Cooper, Karl Kosiczky, and Nita
Krebs.

An uncommon photograph of some of the enlisted Munchkins.

A rare uninhabited view of the Munchkinland set. (Courtesy of Eric Daily)

touch on each and every costume by sketching the rainbow-colored outfits and selecting the material with which they would be stitched. For the designs, there were no restrictions, no research, and no formulas—simply pure imagination. One of Hollywood's most ingenious costume designers, Adrian (who was married to actress Janet Gaynor) created for the Munchkins a range of oversized buttons, bows, and accessories to accent their tiny stature.

Today, some of the actual costumes remain prized pieces in private collections. Some wardrobe was sold at the MGM auction in 1970. Other garments were reportedly stolen from the wardrobe department. MGM attempted to maintain a tight hold on all wardrobe items through the years, but some items filtered out of the studio and into the private sector.

The mystery of the ruby slippers—several pairs of which "walked out" of the wardrobe department—is still a topic of conversation among the movie's fans. Today, there are three legitimate pairs of the red-sequined pumps on display in different areas of the country, including the Smithsonian Institution, which also proudly displays Ray Bolger's original Scarecrow costume.

Jack Dawn, credited with designing the indi-

To Oz?

Director Victor Fleming, who later left *The Wizard of Oz* production to direct *Gone With the Wind*, was a competent professional, to say the least. Those who worked with him agreed he was a director who knew what he wanted. Directing the midgets was a job for which he realized he needed assistance. He had crew members such as assistant director Al Shoenberg, dance director Bobby Connolly (and his assistants Arthur "Cowboy" Appell and Dona Massin), and production manager Keith Weeks aid in staging the Munchkins and maintaining their adherence to schedules. With more than one hundred extras, problems were bound to arise.

"One time the director yelled at Billie Burke," remembered Munchkin Gus Wayne. "He really let her have it. She couldn't get over some word or something and, man, he jumped all over her. That had no class. It was right in front of everybody."

Karl Slover recalls a dress rehearsal when the three trumpeters leading the mayor's procession functioned more like the Three Stooges. "We were about the shortest of the bunch. Little Kayo [Erickson], me, and Major Mite. Every time the director gave the cue for Kayo to come out, he'd stand there like he was asleep. Major Mite and I used to say, 'Come on, Kayo, let's go!' We'd give Kayo a shove, and he'd get madder than heck.

"The director had us do it two or three times, and Kayo missed it every time. Finally the director came over to us and said, 'Okay, we can't have this.' So I told him that I could

Short-Tempered: It appears as if director Victor Fleming is restraining Jack Glicken during a slight altercation with Charlie Becker during production. Just behind Judy Garland is makeup man Charles Schram. (Courtesy of Jerry Maren.)

come out on cue, and he said that would be fine. So on film, first comes me, then little Kayo, and Major Mite."

Munchkin Karl Slover had another job, too. Slover, who was affectionately called "Karchy," was one of Leo Singer's favorites, the tiniest of the men, with an equally charming high-pitched voice. After hearing Karchy sing "We're Off to See the Wizard" a few times, it became a ritual for Fleming to pull Karchy aside and have him perform a solo rendition for visiting dignitaries or celebrity guests on the set.

The filming went relatively uninterrupted for the Munchkins' sequences. Fleming knew exactly how to regroup the little people so every shot created the illusion of a sea of Munchkins behind the action. Study of the sequences reveals the way he strategically placed certain Munchkins, mainly the smaller ones such as Jeane LaBarbera. Noticeably, LaBarbera pops up all over, regardless of continuity. One second you spot her in a group near the thatch houses; then, in the blink of an eye, she is next to Dorothy. Although the Munchkin shifting was creatively accomplished, Fleming probably assumed that with the Munchkins' basically matched sizes and rainbow-colored costumes, no one would notice. And he wasn't planning on the invention of the VCR for instant replay.

During breaks in filming, when Judy Garland wasn't busy with her schooling, she cleared herself a little spot near the Munchkinland City Hall, sat down, and chatted with the Munchkins. She was as curious about their lives as they were about hers. "We didn't get much chance to talk with Billie Burke or Margaret Hamilton on the set," says Meinhardt

Producer Mervyn LeRoy (in the dark suit) and director Victor Fleming (holding Toto) congratulate Judy Garland and the little people on a scene well done during one of the last days of production in December 1938. (Copyright © 1939 Loew's, Inc., renewed © 1966 by MGM.)

Raabe, "but Judy was just great to us. A very pleasant young girl."

While some of the Munchkins gathered around Garland, sharing a few giggles and some small talk, others were busy playing host to visitors on the set.

"Many of the stars at MGM would drop by the set and say hello to us Munchkins," remembers Margaret Pellegrini. "We had Mickey Rooney stop by several times, and Eleanor Powell, Myrna Loy, Walter Pidgeon, and Victor McLaglen all stopped by.

"Norma Shearer's kids came with her to the set one day, and we took the kids up the stairs and by the Sleepy Head eggs," says Pellegrini. "They thought that was neat."

Pellegrini eyed another famous star at the studio, this one close to her own height. "I'm not sure what he was doing at MGM, but I saw little Alfalfa from the Little Rascals on a tram at the studio one morning," she says. "These trams were right outside the soundstage to take us to other parts of the lot, like to the bathrooms."

By the time lunch hour rolled around, the Munchkins were hungry little people. Sometimes they were brought box lunches on the set. Sometimes, still in costume, they ate in the studio commissary—but not often. The commissary was not adequately equipped for the Munchkins, and the tables and chairs proved too large. So a mini-commissary with a private caterer was set up for them near the soundstage, complete with with lowered tables and benches.

The Munchkins also went across the lot to Marie's Restaurant, where they usually ate breakfast and dinner. "If you didn't get there quickly, you'd have to wait in a line that went clear out the door," remembers Margaret Pellegrini.

When not needed for filming, the stars retreated to their dressing rooms when the break was called. The lights shut down, and cool shadows fell on the Yellow Brick Road. Billie Burke had her nicely decorated tent with its pink-and-blue interior right alongside the Kansas farmhouse that fell on the witch. Margaret Hamilton had, as she described it, a nook in the corner with a table and a lamp, but she didn't complain. Judy Garland had a tent of sorts, until one day when the stu-dio surprised her—with all the Munchkins watching.

"Near Christmastime, MGM presented her with her own private dressing room on wheels," remembers Margaret Pellegrini. "They had a big red ribbon and bow tied over the door, and when she came to work a few days before Christmas, she cut the ribbon. She let us all go inside and look at it."

The holidays for the Munchkins don't seem to have been noteworthy. Only a handful recall exactly what they did that Christmas. They had already missed being with their families on Thanksgiving, and now the most important holiday of the year was approaching, and they were stranded on a Yellow Brick Road waiting for Santa.

Munchkin Ruth Duccini still keeps in her scrapbook the telegram she received from home during the holiday season. It was her first Christmas away from her family.

"There was a church that had invited a group of us over to help trim their tree," remembered Alta Stevens Barnes. "A bunch of us went with Grace and Harvey Williams over to the church and we all had hot chocolate and sang songs."

Judy Garland wanted to do something very special for the Munchkins. She ordered a huge box of candy to be delivered to the set one day. Garland gathered all the little people around, and with a big smile she opened the box, inviting all of them to enjoy the expensive confections.

"It must have been a twenty-five- or thirty-pound box of chocolates, 'cause it was enormous," says Margaret Pellegrini. "That was her Christmas present to us."

It was at this same gathering that Garland went into her dressing room, got her blue fountain pen and a huge stack of photographs, and inscribed 8 x 10 portraits of herself for those requesting a memento.

These are the treasured few items and memories that remain like relics in the collections and hearts of the little people. The autographed photos are yellowed now, and the memories are dimmed, but cherished thoughts always accompany them whenever the Munchkins glance at the autographed portrait of the beautiful girl who gave them candy one Christmas long ago.

vidual character makeup for all the *Oz* actors, hired nearly twenty extra makeup artists to assist in the preparation of Munchkins every morning.

"Makeup was a pain in the ass," says Jerry Maren. "It was cold—freezin'—and you weren't used to getting up that early. It was around five A.M. When we got to the studio, we had to go downstairs in a basement underneath one of the stages. They had about twenty makeup chairs with makeup people ready for us."

"That was in a basement of a building where Fred Astaire and Gene Kelly used to practice," recalled veteran MGM makeup man Jack Young. "We would get all that tapping and conking below."

Young recalled the early mornings with the Munchkins in an interview with this author in 1989. "We'd start around six in the morning, and it took almost three hours to get the whole thing set up," he said. "We had a regular assembly line. We trained makeup men and hired a few nonmakeup men to go around with trays of noses and cheeks. We had taken stills of them first to go by. It was quite a lengthy preparation.

"The women didn't use the appliances," Young added, "but we stylized each one, almost overexaggerated, like for the stage."

The little actors went through the assembly line for their specially fitted noses, bald-head skin, and assorted hairpieces. One by one, they popped from chair to chair, getting facial appliances and the rubber headpieces glued on, then

Munchkin Billy Curtis in the foreground: "And oh, what happened then was rich!" (Courtesy of Margaret Pellegrini)

A rare out-take image of the Munchkins. (L–R): Fern Formica (partially obscured), Daisy Doll, Hazel Resmondo, Christie Buresh, Jeane LaBarbera, Dolly Kramer, Tiny Doll, and Mickey Carroll. (Courtesy of Mickey Carroll)

a base coat of makeup, then added details to the makeup. Finally their hairpieces were attached.

"They would put that skullcap on first," remembered Munchkin Nels Nelson, "then the hairpiece and the rest. When it got hot in the studio, you'd sweat underneath it, and the makeup would run down your face."

Undoing the makeup was a drudgery remembered by a few of the Munchkins. "When we'd take the stuff off, it'd practically rip our skin," says Lewis Croft. The spirit gum used in those days was not as kind to the skin as the glue formulas used in special-effects makeup today.

MGM makeup artist Louis LaCava remembered the long hours involved on *Oz*. "I had to go to work around one in the morning with another man, Holly Bane, to make two hundred rubber caps to glue on the Munchkins' heads, the monkeys' masks, and such," he said. "We were constantly busy preparing appliances for the next day's shooting, because once they used it and tore if off, it couldn't be used again."

In creating the dreamland known as Munchkin City, the talents at MGM couldn't accomplish the feat without "reaching out into the infinite," as a Wizard might say. Cedric

"We welcome you most regally": Many of the Munchkin actors recall Judy Garland being as curious about them as they were about her.

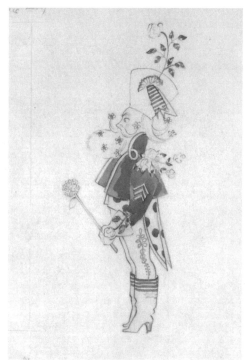

Gilbert Adrian's original costume design sketches for the whimsical Munchkins of Oz. His use of ornamental flowers, polka dots, tassels, winged stand-up collars, and unfathomable headgear were exotic for the time. Any of these might be considered street fashion on Hollywood Boulevard these days. (Tod Machin collection)

A wardrobe test photo of fiddler Freddie Retter. (Courtesy of Academy of Motion Picture Arts and Sciences)

"With its thatched cottages and cobbled streets, the Munchkin City is a vaguely Elizabethan village. Female residents romp around in full skirts with laced bodices; male residents are dressed up either as late medieval burghers—with their pointed shoes and multicolored hose—or early nineteenth-century soldiers from Central Europe (known in Hollywood as Ruritania). In general, the merry Munchkins seem to be refugees from one of Bruegel's paintings of peasant life in sixteenth-century Northern Europe."

—Paul Nathanson, author
Over the Rainbow: The Wizard of Oz as a Secular Myth of America

Karl Florian (right) taught fellow Austrian midget Freddie Retter how to play the violin in the late 1920s when they both appeared with Singer's Midgets. Appropriately, Retter became one of the five fiddlers who escort Dorothy safely to the border of Munchkinland. (Tod Machin collection)

Johnny Winters was the Munchkin commander of the navy. (Courtesy of Academy of Motion Picture Arts and Sciences)

Karl Kosiczky was the first Munchkin trumpeter. (Courtesy of Academy of Motion Picture Arts and Sciences)

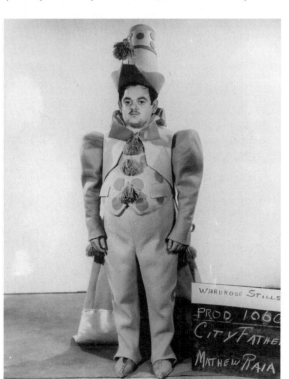

Mathew Raia portrayed one of the City Fathers. (Courtesy of Academy of Motion Picture Arts and Sciences)

Two of the twenty-five Munchkin soldiers, Jakob Hofbauer (left) and Willi Koestner. (Courtesy of Academy of Motion Picture Arts and Sciences)

Gibbons, the film's art director, explained some of the preliminary concepts to *Photoplay* magazine in 1939:

> So they gave us a script in which a little girl from Kansas lives a great adventure in a country of her own imagination. But in neither the script nor the original book was there any description to indicate along what lines her imagination might build such a country! Which left us, first of all, to do some imagining ourselves.
>
> Take one scene of the fifty, for instance, the country the book calls "Munchkinland," to be inhabited by very tiny people called Munchkins. To fashion a Munchkinland which a little girl from Kansas might have dreamed, we began with a premise that the smallest things she had ever seen were probably ants. And how do ants live? Under grass and tree roots. So with toadstools and anthills as our architectural pattern, we made proportionately larger grass and flowers, such as, for instance, hollyhocks twenty-feet-tall.

When the Munchkins were in costume, made up, and ready to shoot, they were escorted to Sound Stage 27. The beauty and elegance of the immense Munchkin City set was the single foremost feature on which every surviving Munchkin readily commented during interviews for this book. According to an MGM press release from 1939, the milieu of panoramic majesty stood ninety feet high.

The Munchkins, nor anyone else at MGM, had never witnessed such unveiled extravagance built on a soundstage—this the largest soundstage on the lot. It was *the* spectacle to see, not to mention the little inhabitants in bright costumes and bizarre makeup wandering around it. Many of the Munchkins recall that Clark Gable couldn't stay away from the place.

Munchkin maidens. (L–R): Olga Nardone, Hildred Olson, and Ruth Robinson. (Courtesy of Ruth Robinson Duccini)

A wardrobe test photo of Munchkin townsmen. (L–R): Lajos "Leo" Matina, Joseph Koziel, and Tommy Cottonaro. Cottonaro ultimately wore different wardrobe in the film. (Courtesy of Academy of Motion Picture Arts and Sciences)

Frank Cucksey

"MUNCHKIN MUSICAL SEQUENCE"

Good Witch: Come out, come out wherever you are
And meet the young lady who fell from a star.
She fell from the sky...she fell very far.
And Kansas she says is the name of the star..
Kansas she says is the name of the star.
She brings you good news or haven't you heard?
When she fell out of Kansas a miracle occured.

Dorothy: It really was no miracle, What happened was just this
The wind began to switch, the house to pitch
And suddenly the hinges started to unhitch
Just then the witch to satisfy a itch
Went flying on her broomstick thumbing for a hitch

Munchkin: And Oh,.. what happen'd then was rich.

Several
Munchkins: The house began to pitch the kitchen took a slitch
It landed on the wicked witch in the middle of a ditch
Which...was not a healthy seat---u-a-tion for a wicked witch.

All Munchkins: The house began to pitch, the kitchen took a slitch,
It landed on the wicked witch in the middle of a ditch
Which...was not a healthy sit---u-a-tion
For a wicked witch who began to twitch
And was reduced to just a stitch of what was once the wicked witch.

Munchkin #1: We thank you very sweetly for doing it so neatly,

Munchkin #2: You killed her so complitely that we thank you very sweetly

Good Witch: Let the joyous news be spread, the wicked old witch at last is dead.

All Munchkins: Ding Dong the witch is dead
Which old witch, the wicked witch
Ding Dong the wicked witch is dead....
Wake up you sleepy head, Rub your eyes, get out of bed..
Wake up the wicked witch is dead.
She's gone where the Goblins go below...
Below below yo ho,...Let's open up and sing...
And ring the bells out Ding Dong! The merry Oh...
Sing it high - sing it low
Let them know the wicked witch is dead.

Mayor: As Mayor of the Munchkin City
In the county of the land of Oz...
I welcome you must regally...

Barrister: But we've got to verify it legally to see if she is
Morally ethic'ly

Father No. 1: Spiritually, physically,

Father No. 2: Positively, absolutely,

All Fathers: Undeniably and reliably dead....

Coroner: As Coroner I must aver I thoroughly examined her
And she's not only merely dead,
She's really most sincerely dead.

Mayor: Today is a day of independence
For all the Munchkins and their decendents

Barrister: If any.

Everybody: Ding Dong the witch is dead
Which old witch, the wicked witch
Ding Dong the wicked witch is dead!
Wake up you sleepy head, Rub your eyes, get out of bed
Wake up the wicked witch is dead.
She's gone where the Goblins go below below below yo ho
Let's open up and sing...And ring the bells out
Ding Dong! The merry oh...Sing it high, sing it low
Let them know the wicked witch is dead.

(CONTINUED)

Each Munchkin was provided with this two-page mimeographed script. This one belonged to
Frank Cucksey who was "Munchkin #2." (Courtesy of Tod Machin)

MUNCHKIN MUSICAL SEQUENCE (Cont'd)

Three Tots: We represent the lullaby league, the lullaby league,
                The lullaby league, and in the name of the lullaby league
                We wish to welcome you to Munchkin Land.

Three Tough
    Kids: We represent the Lolly-pop guild, the Lolly-pop guild,
                The lolly-pop guild, and in the name of the Lolly-pop guild,
                We wish to welcome you to Munchkin Land.

    All
Munchkins: We welcome you to Munchkin Land
                Tra-la-la-la-la-la, Tra-la-la, Tra-la-la, Tra-la-la-la-la-la-la
                From now on you'll be history,
                You'll be hist, you'll be hist, you'll be history
                And we will glorify your name
                You'll be a bust, be a bust, be a bust
                In the Hall of Fame.....
                Tra-la-la-la-la Tra-la-la Tra-la-la Tra-la-la-la-la-la.

(Left) Frank Cucksey in a costume test photo. The wardrobe personnel decided to
forgo Cucksey's stovepipe hat in the film. (Right) Frank Cucksey a few years post-*Oz*.

"Come out, come out . . ." Little Jeanette Fern curiously peeks out from the shrub. Years later, Fern became one of the more visible Munchkins at *Oz* festivals around the country, sometimes dressed in a replica of her Munchkin costume. (Courtesy of Fern Formica)

Thanking Dorothy very sweetly are Munchkins Frank Cucksey and Leon Polinksy.

Meinhardt Raabe, who was in awe like the rest of the Munchkins, tried to elaborate: "Well, to put it mildly, it blew your mind," he says. "The set was the size of a coliseum. And as a farm boy coming from Wisconsin, to see all this color and magnificence was . . . well, it was out of this world. None of us could believe what we were looking at."

Raabe also recalled the peaceful lily pond in the middle of the town square with blue, rippling water running under the bridge. Besides the fact that the pond occasionally leaked, and puddles had to be mopped off the yellow brick road area, the water caused another dilemma.

"Naturally, a pond only shows blue if it can reflect the sky," Raabe pointed out. "So they kept pouring bottles of bluing in the water, and when they did, the little ducklings they had in there began turning blue. So they removed the ducklings, emptied the water, and painted the bottom of the pond blue, and that worked. Off to the side there was someone off camera creating ripples in the water with a paddle."

Lighting the vast Munchkinland set was a difficulty in and of itself, and repeated color tests had to be made before each shot. The Technicolor process of filming, still embryonic, took considerable research to perfect the tones used in every scene of *The Wizard of Oz.* (For instance, color photography made Judy Garland's dimples apparent, while the black-and-white did not reveal them.) Every evening the cameras were tested, the color filters were changed, the lenses were polished, and the whole mechanism was adjusted. By morning the camera was ready for shooting the next day's scenes.

Oz was one of the earliest successful Technicolor motion pictures, and the rows of arc lights on the set were necessary for two reasons: to create the illusion of being outdoors and to aid in the film's volatile color development. As described in a 1939 issue of *Movies* magazine, "Each morning, the huge soundstages were chilled to 52 degrees. As soon as

Filming certain characters and objects presented lighting problems. Glinda's brilliant jewel-encrusted crown posed lighting complications; technicians lit actress Billie Burke from strategic angles, deflecting the projection of points of light that otherwise would have shot directly into the camera. The ruby slippers required similar care.

the lights were turned on, temperatures rose to 70 degrees where, by pumping in air of 52 degrees, a level was maintained." Up until that time it had been said that *The Wizard of Oz* used more light than any other film. On the Munchkin set, 250 huge arc lights burned to achieve the look necessary.

The hanging arc lights became stifling at times, according to several Munchkins. Rising temperatures combined with itchy, cumbersome felt costumes, added up to uncomfortable hours. Many of the male Munchkins wore undershirts, regular shirts with ruffles, vests, and jackets, as well as several coats of makeup, plus hats. "We were almost sweltering," says

Meinhardt Raabe, who, as the coroner, donned a long, royal-blue, layered robe that went down to his feet.

Technicians adjusted the light with the use of a "ju-ju"—a Technicolor light meter calibrated in footcandles that operated like the conventional light meters for black-and-white film. Someone would roam the set and test the light at the spot where the camera would be focused and make sure there weren't "hot spots," or intense burns of direct, blinding light reflecting into the camera lens.

According to John Arnold, A.S.C., then the camera chief at MGM, the limitations of color photography on *The Wizard of Oz* called for some ingenuity. In a 1939 article Arnold wrote for *Minicam* magazine, he described the one difficulty encountered specifically on the Munchkinland set:

> The set for the scene in the land of Munchkins had great cellophane hollyhocks which caused halation when light was reflected into the camera. The studio photographer was kept busy watching for "hot spots" while lights and sometimes the hollyhocks themselves were tilted or adjusted. Each camera set-up saw the same process gone through.

But once the Munchkins were on their toes, and the elements of lighting and photography were in place, the action began. For four weeks, Stage 27 came alive as Munchkins sang and danced and Judy Garland graced their company with her innocent, gleaming eyes and her delicate yet powerful voice. And of course, as with most film production, there was an ample amount of down time, just waiting around.

Munchkins can be seen in some behind-the-scenes photos sitting on the ledge around the pond waiting for the next shot to be set up. That's when Judy Garland would sit on the Munchkin steps and visit with the little people.

"How About a Little Fire, Scarecrow?"

————————————————✳————————————————

Billie Burke sprained her ankle on the set, and MGM made a big fuss over her. When I was torched, MGM didn't send me home in an ambulance. MGM never even mentioned my accident in the newspapers!

—Margaret Hamilton

There was a three-alarm in Munchkinland one afternoon, and it involved an accident that could have cost the life of one of the film's stars. Indeed, the wicked witch might've been dead long before her time.

Some film productions—especially those involving great preparation for technically intricate special effects—can be plagued by accidents. For instance, a fire, injured cast members, and other assorted mishaps held up the filming of *The Exorcist* for many weeks. *The Wizard of Oz* was a similar case. Calamities began when actor Buddy Ebsen, originally cast as the Tin Man, was poisoned by the silver makeup.

Tall, lanky, and a beautifully creative eccentric dancer in his own right, Ebsen (who later found fame as TV's Jed Clampett on *The Beverly Hillbillies*) was the original Tin Man, and he held the role well into the third week of filming. But he fell severely ill and was hospitalized for ingesting the silver makeup (pure aluminum dust), which then coated his lungs. Ebsen was replaced by Jack Haley, a competent and acceptable alternate, without a doubt. While Ebsen lay in a hospital bed under an oxygen tent, MGM's makeup department produced a new silver *paste* to apply on Haley's face to avoid a similar disaster.

But like his predecessor, Haley still detested the makeup and costume. "Like hell it was fun," he later said in a bittersweet tone.

An MGM memo of January 5, 1939, records the date of December 28, 1938, as the day a fiery accident occurred in Munchkinland involving Margaret Hamilton, although there are conflicting dates.

The scene we ultimately see in the film was one of the first takes: The Munchkins' celebration of the death of the Wicked Witch of the East is interrupted by the startling intrusion of her sister, the Wicked Witch of the West. ("She's worse than the other one.")

The stunt involved Hamilton's stunt-double, Betty Danko, coming up through the floor (on an elevator or small "catapult," as Danko and Hamilton both described it in interviews).

Danko's back was turned. Then the shot was stopped, and Danko was replaced by the wickedly convincing Hamilton. Her appearance is heralded by a burst of fire and billowy red smoke.

Hamilton screeched her lines and departed through the same hole in the floor, but her exit had to be done precisely, without a film cut or a stand-in. Her broomstick, in hand, had to be held up perfectly. So Hamilton practiced the tricky shot going down the chute.

Hamilton explained later, "I had to back away from Judy and Billie Burke and land on this little piece of flooring on top of the platform just right. It was a very complicated shot," she said. "I had to be in the exact place, and my skirt had to be down around me. It was an enormous skirt. I had to be careful not to trip on the long cape while I was walking backward . . . there were two men below, at the bottom of the platform, in case I should fall off the pedestal going down."

The enormous blast of orangy flame in the middle of Munchkinland was felt by all those within yards of it. Hamilton laughed later when she recalled that Billie Burke, in her precious pink Glinda gown, complained about standing near the hot bursts every time the scene was reshot. Hamilton said, "She was forty feet away, and I'm going to be right in the *middle* of it!"

After a few takes, lunch was called. When everyone returned, director Victor Fleming wanted a few more takes for insurance; it was the last of these that proved detrimental to Hamilton's health. It all happened so fast.

This time, before Hamilton sunk on the little elevator, the fire and smoke were triggered prematurely; flames engulfed her face, hair, and hands. Her costume and broom ignited, but she didn't realize the emergency until she was grabbed by technicians rushing to her aid.

"Somebody yelled, 'Get somebody, she's burning!'" remembers Munchkin Jerry Maren. "Members of the crew and others were running up to the floor area."

Another Munchkin has a different memory: "Something the public doesn't realize is that just out of the camera range was a fireman with a soaking wet blanket," says Meinhardt Raabe, Munchkin coroner. "The only damage she sustained was singed eyebrows and melted makeup. She was back on the set the next day and had no serious injuries."

Actually, Hamilton was driven home and did not return to the production for nearly six weeks. Because that particular shot was her last for the scene, none of the Munchkins saw her after that nearly catastrophic day. Her injuries were worse than anyone envisioned.

"When I looked down at my right hand, I thought I was going to faint. That's when the pain really took hold,"

Margaret Hamilton flaunts a heartwarming smile in this 1954 portrait. Now, does this look like a mean witch to you?

Margaret Hamilton signs autographs at the Yellow Brick Road Gift Shop in Chesterton, Indiana, December 1980. (Courtesy of Jean Nelson)

Hamilton said later. "The fire had singed my eyebrows off and burned my cheeks and chin. At first, I had just felt some warmth on my face, and I didn't realize what had happened."

Hamilton credits her makeup man, Jack Young, for reacting quickly to prevent infection. Young wiped off the toxic, copper-laden green makeup so it would stop seeping farther into her skin. Young used alcohol as an antiseptic and wiped the makeup off while Hamilton was being smeared with salve and bandaged. The cleaning process was more than a mere moment of excruciating pain. Hamilton remembered it for the rest of her life.

Because of the raw skin, which left her hands quite fragile and fleshy, Hamilton wore slick green gloves in a few shots. In a candid interview with Gregory J. M. Catsos later printed in *Filmfax* magazine, Hamilton recalled her return to the studio:

When I came back, Victor Fleming asked me how my hand was. I said, "It's coming along," and I removed the glove covering it. He said, "Let me see it," and suddenly grabbed my hand. The pain was so unbearable that I almost passed out. "It looks fine!" he said. But I begged him to please leave my hand alone. Fleming apologized and said, "Well, we have that shot, and it was great!"

When Catsos asked Hamilton if she considered suing the studio for negligence, she replied, "I couldn't do that. I felt that if I sued them, I would never work again in any other studio. They had the power to do that. And I wanted to work again."

Most of the Munchkins vaguely remember the accident. One of them, however, described a valiant rescue he performed, saving Hamilton's life by scooping pond water with his Munchkin hat and dousing her. Hamilton said in an interview with this author that she did not recall any Munchkins coming to her aid.

Ironically, days before the accident dance director Bobby Connolly and director Victor Fleming had made repeated announcements asking all the little people not to step on the witch's trapdoor and to carefully watch their movements around the area.

Munchkins Nita Krebs, Garland Slatten, and a few others recall that one day, just minutes after Connolly made the daily announcement, he himself stumbled into the hole and landed on the shoulders of stand-in Betty Danko. Later Danko recalled the mishap, also mentioning back problems she suffered from Connolly's unexpected plunge.

"We laughed when he fell," said Slatten. "He had just told *us* to watch it!"

Margaret Hamilton was a petite, gentle woman who taught elementary school before she entered show business. She said in 1957, "I've frightened more children than practically anyone else. It always seems so funny to me, too, because I love children so much." Hamilton lived a nice long life and adored her *Oz* fans as much as they adored her; this wispy little woman died peacefully at the age of eighty-two in a Connecticut nursing home in 1985.

(Left) Munchkins Jerry Maren and Billy Curtis pose with fellow *Oz* alumni Ray Bolger and Margaret Hamilton in May 1983. (Courtesy of Jerry Maren) (Below left) Margaret Hamilton autographed this portrait for Munchkin Gus Wayne on the set of *Oz*. Hamilton often signed *Oz* photos "W.W.W." for Wicked Witch of the West. (Below right) Rehearsal: Broomstick in hand, Margaret Hamilton rehearses with her script when she recreated her role as the Wicked Witch of the West at the famous outdoor St. Louis Municipal Opera in 1975. Her live performance, while still commanding, was far less menacing, with a dash of tongue-in-cheek humor. The Tin Man, Scarecrow and Lion were played by the Hudson Brothers.

Hearing Little Voices

✳

For pure fantasy, there may be no more memorable musical moments on film than when the inhabitants of Munchkinland open up to sing. For years, until sufficient documentation from MGM's vaults had been rescued, controversy arose over whose voices we are actually hearing.

"That is the biggest misconception everybody has," says Munchkin coroner Meinhardt Raabe. "Whenever I wasn't in the action, I was behind the camera watching what was goin' on. All our voices were recorded, and they went through an oscilloscope. For the girls, they eliminated the low notes when they rerecorded it so their voices were high. For the boys, they did the opposite. What you hear is actually my voice, but it has been manipulated. There was no dubbing for any part."

According to Raabe, all the Munchkins' voices (or vocal dialogue) were recorded during the filming by one boom microphone mounted on the huge camera crane. However, this is unlikely for several reasons.

For the voices to have been recorded during the actual shooting of the scene, several unsolvable problems would have had to be overcome. For instance, Charlie Becker, who played the mayor of Munchkinland, spoke in a thick German accent. The film's mayor speaks perfect English.

In addition, had the Munchkins' voices been recorded during filming, the huge dance sequences would have been a disaster because the mikes would have picked up the constant rustle and sweep of body movement. Moreover, there would have been no way to recondition the high and low pitches in a recording of men and women singing together. Men and women would have had to record separate tracks, then the pitches could have been adjusted and the sound remixed. This process could not have been achieved by the relatively primitive audio equipment available in 1938.

It seems obvious the Munchkins' voices were dubbed in after the photography was completed. In fact, if you observe closely, you can see the worst of the dubbing during the Lollipop Guild's little ditty. Unfortunately, the song and lip movement hardly match.

Who then, sang "Ding Dong! The Witch Is Dead"? One of the film's arrangers, Ken Darby, stated emphatically that none of the midgets recorded any of the songs. In the same interview he added, "None of them could carry a tune."

This broad statement is ludicrous, of course, because many of the midgets successfully sang on Broadway, in other films, and in nightclubs and stage shows for years. Some even made careers out of warbling. Furthermore, an MGM daily music report dated December 15, 1938, mentions "an orchestra and three midgets recording scene 2070/Bars 249-265," which seems to indicate that at least three little people were involved in dubbing.

Only one of the surviving Munchkins interviewed by this author maintained involvement in the dubbing of *Oz* vocals: Mickey Carroll. As a talented nightclub and stage entertainer, Carroll sang and tap-danced in musicals on the giant outdoor stage of St. Louis's Municipal Opera with performers such as Alan Jones, a young Donald O'Connor, and Jack Haley—years before production of *The Wizard of Oz*.

Many answers about *The Wizard of Oz* were finally provided in the mid-1990s with the release of two state-of-the-art audio and visual gems: the ultimate *Oz* laser disc boxed set (MGM/UA Home Video) and the deluxe edition of the original motion picture soundtrack compact disc set (Rhino Movie Music).

Both extravagant packages feature rare audio recordings discovered and retrieved from MGM's vaults. The laser disc contains some visual treats such as outtakes and home movies, and it also includes original audio tracks and outtakes from the recording sessions of the Munchkin voice-actors before and after the tracks were altered for the finished soundtrack. Finally we hear the Munchkins minus the helium.

The double-CD package is a formidable gold-mine of *Oz* on audio, and significant for a variety of reasons: For the first time, original full-length recordings of the Academy Award–winning score by Herbert Stothart became available, as well as rare selected outtakes from the vocal recording sessions.

Most unusual, however, is an eerie version of "Over the Rainbow" deleted from the film. Only this audio track survives. It's a brief, tense moment in the witch's castle when a teary-eyed Dorothy peers into the crystal ball and begs to return home. Judy Garland struggles to sing a snippet while sobbing ("I'm frightened, Auntie Em"). This soundbite illustrates the extraordinary acting talent of the teenage Garland as you hear her simply turn off the waterworks for the director at the end of the take. This particular audio track is more haunting than the brutal swooping monkeys.

There are other treats on the compact discs: Buddy Ebsen's unused version of "If I Only Had a Heart," as well as recorded takes of the cast's rehearsals with just piano accompaniment. Interestingly, the CD features a never-before-released recording of the Lollipop Guild's song performed by three midgets, although this track was scrapped when Ken Darby opted for a dub of regular studio vocalists with a sped-up track.

Here, finally—and factually—is the identification of the

Munchkin vocals. After all the trial and error, prerecordings, and postdubbing alterations of vocals, what remains in the film is this: Only two lines in the whole Munchkin sequence of the film survive unaltered from the mouths of the actual midget performers who deliver the lines on-screen. They are those of two Munchkins who approach Dorothy in a carriage. Leon Polinksy, dressed in a brilliant blue costume, bows and says, "We thank you very sweetly, for doing it so neatly." Frank Cucksey, in a tan costume, presents Dorothy with a bouquet of flowers and adds, "You killed her so completely, that we thank you, very sweetly."

It is known that two performing groups provided the Munchkins' vocals: The King's Men Octet and The Debutantes. The names of the singers include: Lois Clements, Zari Elmassian, Nick Angelo, Robert Bradford, Abe Dinovitch, and Virgil Johansen.

"As Mayor of Munchkin City"—the sequence with the Munchkin City officials—is performed by Billy Bletcher, Vance "Pinto" Colvig, and J. D. Jewkes. The coroner is performed by Harry Stanton; the Lullabye League are the voices of Lorraine Bridges, Betty Rome, and Carol Tevis; the Lollipop Guild is performed by Bletcher, Colvig, and Stanton.

Pinto Colvig, a radio actor, was one of Walt Disney's favorite vocal performers. Disney used Colvig's pipes for the voice of one of the pigs in *Three Little Pigs,* as the original voice of Goofy, and in dual roles as Sleepy and Grumpy in *Snow White and the Seven Dwarfs.* Colvig was seventy-five when he died in Los Angeles on October 3, 1967.

Billy Bletcher was also a cartoon veteran and a noted character actor who worked in a handful of early Laurel and Hardy films. William Bletcher was the voice of the Big Bad Wolf in Walt Disney's *Three Little Pigs,* and a clown in *Dumbo.* Bletcher was also a voice of the *Lone Ranger* on radio. He died in 1979 at the age of eighty-five.

It is interesting to note that the process utilized to throw the voices into a high-pitched "Munchkin octave" is not just the simple increasing of the tape speed. It involves recording the voice at a slower speed and playing it back at normal rpm. (The actor's delivery into the mike is also a bit more thorough and drawn out than normal.)

This audio process was used in Disney's *Three Little Pigs,* and years later Ross Bagdasarian employed the technique for his original Chipmunks voices. Famed voice characterizationist Mel Blanc had technicians alter his voice in the same manner while performing the particular cartoon voices of Daffy Duck, Speedy Gonzales, Tweety Bird, and the Goophy Gophers.

Pinto Colvig and Adriana Caselotti, both of whom supplied voices in *Snow White and the Seven Dwarfs* and *The Wizard of Oz.* Caselotti, the voice of Snow White, lent her sweet vocals for a single line in the Tin Man's solo: "Wherefore art thou, Romeo?" (Courtesy of Adriana Caselotti)

All in Good Time

One thing Dona Massin could claim: She was probably the first woman to sing "Over the Rainbow"—beating Judy Garland by mere minutes. The year was 1938, and the place was MGM Studios.

"I remember being on the rehearsal set, and Arthur Freed came over with Yip Harburg," said Massin proudly. "They played this tune on the piano and asked me if I'd mind just singing it. So I sang it with them. They had just finished writing it.

"I remember it was a little hard to sing because it has quite a scale, but I thought it was a beautiful song," she said.

Massin was the assistant choreographer on *The Wizard of Oz,* the girl Friday to Bobby Connolly. She and another dancer, Arthur Appell, known to everyone as "Cowboy," spent six weeks with the Munchkins "setting" the dance steps, rehearsing, and assisting with the filming. Not only did she teach the little people the famous bouncy "skip," of Yellow Brick Road fame, but Massin also had to put in extra time to instruct the Cowardly Lion, Bert Lahr.

"He was horribly insecure," she revealed. "He had to have me as his audience all the time. When I taught him the skip, I realized he didn't know his left foot from his right. Poor little Bert. He was so clumsy, and I loved him for it."

This was the first time Massin had worked with Lahr, but she later danced in an Eleanor Powell film, *Ship Ahoy* (1942), which also starred Lahr. In *Broadway Melody of 1940* she danced alongside Eleanor Powell again, and worked again with the wizard, Frank Morgan. Her *Oz* alliances even date back to her childhood. "Judy [Garland] I knew when she was eight years old as Baby Gumm," Massin said. "We went through singing and dancing lessons. Her mother taught, or coached me, rather, to sing. I was very close to Judy's older sister, Mary Jane, who later committed suicide in Las Vegas."

Consequently, Massin felt very much at ease on this production and fit in perfectly at MGM during the studio's sparkling era. Starting her career in films at Warner Bros., she had moved over to MGM with Bobby Connolly, whom she called her "mentor." It was at the beginning of her work in films that she simplified her name from Lucianna Thomassin to Dona Massin.

When Connolly—a balding man usually topped with a hat and holding a cigar between his fingers—was chosen to direct all the dance sequences in *The Wizard of Oz,* Massin was assigned also. During her career, she has appeared in more than a dozen musicals while under contract to MGM, but *Oz* is what will endure most.

"The first day I went to work on the picture was with Buddy Ebsen and Bobby Connolly," Massin recalled. "We were trying to work out the bit where you put something in your shoes and lean far to one side. Very hard on the legs.

"It may sound funny," she added, "I can remember the cigarettes Buddy would smoke. They were Parliaments, and I was fascinated with the box. After that, I smoked Parliaments for years."

Even though her talents were tapped more for the behind-the-scenes duties, you can spot Dona in *The Wizard of Oz* if you look closely: When the plucky foursome finally reach Emerald City, they are escorted into the Wash & Brush Up Co. for primping for their audience with the Wizard. Dona is one of the tall, leggy brunettes in short green skirts giving the Lion a trim. Dona is the attendant on the very left, with shears in hand, singing "Clip, clip, here, clip, clip, there . . ."

Moreover, Massin said she could never forget her six weeks with the Munchkins, corralling them, rehearsing the numbers, timing the steps, and spending hours on the stage with the little people just chatting. "Now, Jerry Maren I remember vividly. He was so little and cute," she said. "If I remember, he was about eighteen and at the time, I was maybe twenty-one or twenty-two. We used to talk a lot on the set. I think everybody was intrigued by the little people is what it was."

Another Munchkin, Billy Curtis, came to mind as being a "well-dressed" midget, full of charisma. "He was a sharp individual; I liked him a lot," Dona said. "Billy smoked a cigar and was a bit like a leader among many of them. Very well liked, but not as handsome as Jerry Maren was.

"And the little foreign lady right next to Judy on the cover of your book," she said, pointing out Nita Krebs. "She had an accent. We used to talk about little people and their lives and families. I was curious about whether or not they had little parents or children who were little. She was so dainty and polite. I enjoyed that very much."

Massin's duties for this film did not require intricate footwork. She was disappointed when the "Jitterbug" segment was cut because it was a full routine that she and Ray Bolger predominantly "worked out." The rest of the film had minimal movement as far as routines were concerned, and the Munchkins' scene was no exception. "We did not require much dancing from the midgets. Mostly little movements and things," she explained. "Of course there were some who did some dancing. I think for the three ballerinas, Bobby Connolly chose three little ladies who knew a little something about toe dancing. They were graceful."

"Clip clip here, clip clip there." Assistant choreographer Dona Massin (far left) appeared briefly in the film as one of the Lion's manicurists. Massin taught the Munchkins their famous "skip" on the Yellow Brick Road. (Inset, left) A publicity photo of Massin, circa 1939. (Inset, right) Massin in the 1990s. Dona Massin died on May 26, 2001, in Los Angeles.

Without being asked, Massin interjected a few words about the ongoing rumors of the midgets's wild activities during *Oz*. Possibly she knew there was no way to sidestep the interrogation because questions had arisen many times before.

"I've heard a lot of stories over the years. To tell you the truth, a lot of that came about as something interesting to talk about. Really.

"I'm sure [the midgets] had parties," she said, "they were only human. But I personally never saw anything distasteful about them in any way at all. They worked well and were very nice to me. What they did at night or who they slept with is none of my business, and I don't know about anything."

Once Massin visited entertainer Mitzi Gaynor in Vancouver, and the two dancers giggled and reminisced in Gaynor's dressing room after the show. "The first thing she asked me was, 'Dona, did they really fall in the toilet?'

"I told her, 'Well, I wasn't really *there,* but the rumor was that one did.'

"See how those stories circulate?" Massin mused.

Winged Monkey Business

✳

For children, the goblinlike Flying Monkeys, squealing servants of the Wicked Witch of the West, are the stuff of nightmares. For the most part, the monkeys were *not* played by the same small actors as the Munchkins. Only a few of the more athletic midgets were asked to don the monkey makeup and costumes fitted with battery-powered wings. The wings were motorized so they would flap while the monkeys were airborne.

Veteran Hollywood midget stuntman Harry Monty was one of the actors who played a Munchkin *and* a Winged Monkey. "Those who played the dozen brown flying chimps were too tall to portray Munchkins," Monty said. "They were short like jockeys.

"They had a harness around us and strung us up on wires, and we'd swoop down," he recalled. According to Munchkin Hazel Resmondo, it was midget Walter Miller (a Munchkin also) who was the monkey that dropped down in the murky forest, grabbed little Toto, mugged for the camera, and ascended.

Ray Bolger told a story of how the stuntmen were to be paid twenty-five dollars every time they performed their "swoop" at Dorothy and her companions in the forest. Director Victor Fleming assumed payment was twenty-five dollars for the day. "He kept saying, 'Take 'em up again!' for a retake, and they knew they wouldn't get paid each time," Bolger said. "So they struck the picture. Stopped it cold for a while."

There they were. More than a dozen Winged Monkeys sitting on chairs with their arms folded and legs crossed, arguing with Fleming over money. Finally, the financial arrangement was settled, and back in the air they went, buckled to harnesses that were attached to black cables.

The rest of the illusion was created by dangling little rubber, painted monkeys about eight inches in length. These molded figurines—complete with foamlike wings and a pipe cleaner for a tail—were suspended on wires, much as the actor/monkeys were, and flown along at the same time to create a whole army of evil beasts. (Interestingly, in 1996 one of the decaying, now rock-hard rubber monkey props used in the film was auctioned off, fetching $3,000 from a hardcore *Oz* collector in Los Angeles.)

The only other Winged Monkeys noted in MGM docu-

A wardrobe test photo of a Winged Monkey. The wire leading from his back side was attached to experimental motorized wings which were ultimately abandoned in favor of battery-powered wings.

ments are Sid Dawson, in a wardrobe photograph dated December 13, 1938, and Pat Walshe, a Hollywood midget stunt double who played Nikko—the hissing head monkey in the witch's castle. Harry Monty remembered the name of only one other little stuntman, Buster Brody, as playing a monkey.

After more than sixty years, the slim steel tracks that were built and installed in the reinforced rafters of MGM Sound Stage 29 are still there, high above the floor as a haunting reminder of *Oz*'s monkeyshines.

M·G·M· lot
Sunland·Calif
3-19-37

Karl Kosiczky and Nita Krebs, two of Leo Singer's most talented midget performers.

AN INTERVIEW WITH THE LAST OF THE SINGER MIDGETS

When he arrived in America at the leap of the Depression, this tiny Hungarian fellow was severely disadvantaged—but not in the common monetary sense.

He was separated from his family and displaced in a world where he was forced to contend with a foreign language before mastering his own, and at the tender age of ten he could barely reach a doorknob. The simplest things, like crawling into bed, were painstaking, but he adjusted.

Now, nearing eighty, this little man has the advantage: the final say. Because Karl Kosiczky—"Karchy" to his Munchkin contemporaries—long outlived Leo Singer, the man who "purchased" him in 1927. (The word "rescued" might be more appropriate.) Karl has lasted the decades, surviving every member of the renowned troupe of midgets to which he belonged. (The supplementary little people appearing in *The Wizard of Oz* were not members of Leo Singer's nucleus.)

Since the 1940s he's gone by the name of Karl Slover, a name adopted from a family who provided him employment and a home life. All in all, Karl has had an eccentric, if you will, existence. And not merely because his perspective on life was physically askew. There are some who would have seriously considered trading places with him simply because he worked in the most magical film of all time, *The Wizard of Oz*. For the first time in print Karl reflects with candor about his lifetime, a reality of Kafkaesque quality—the ultimate trip along the yellow-bricked pathway of life.

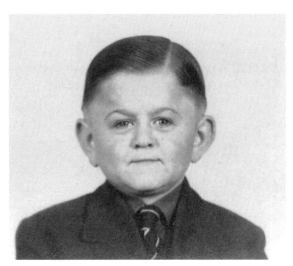

Karl Kosiczky in 1940.

Karl Slover is a man of simple tastes, still entangling his English a bit, having never been formally educated in the American school system. Notwithstanding, he made the best of his life, a quiet spirit to be reckoned with in the face of human adversities. How he remained a warm and utterly likeable individual through it all is a mystery in itself. Even today he has no use for a misanthropic attitude, indicative of his gentle nature.

He was born on September 21, 1918, in Prakendorf Deutch, an area of Hungary prior to German usurpation. He was a typical child until age four, when he simply stopped growing. For many years following he was mistaken for a toddler because of his cute, angelic face.

Quite contentedly, he scratches an itch to tell his story, for he'll be hist-, he'll be hist-, he'll be history.

I heard that your father attempted some unconventional means of making you grow when you were very young. Are those stories true? Did he really put you on a rack?

My father didn't really care for me because I stayed so small. He tried everything to make me grow. He took me to Budapest, Hungary, and there were about six or eight doctors,

Leo Singer and a group of little people are among the passengers aboard the S.S. *Roosevelt* sailing from Europe to the United States in 1928.

besides the doctor who brought me to life. They put me on a stretching machine, and they kept pulling me until one of my bones made a loud noise and they thought they'd broke a bone in my body. It did hurt me.

The doctor who brought me to life, he said, "You're gonna kill that little boy!" He told that to my dad. He really chewed him out in front of all the doctors.

What were you doing while this was happening?

I was laying there like I was hypnotized. After my bone made that noise and I screamed, they stopped. Then two doctors tried to stretch me by hand. One doctor would pull my legs, the other would pull my arms.

My dad did something else I didn't like, and neither did my mother. She was going to go hysterical. At home, he had the bright idea to get a big wooden barrel, and take coconut

Dr. Ales Hrdlicka, famous for his work as curator of physical anthropology of the Smithsonian Institute, interviewed some of Singer's midget troupe in 1928 in Washington, D.C. The little people are (L–R): Lida Buresh, Karl Kosiczky, Hattie Angerer, Stella Royale, and Christie Buresh.

leaves, boil them in hot water and put me in the dern thing. Supposed to make me grow. When they took me out, my mother was about to have a fit. I couldn't hardly move. I guess I was terrified with all the stuff going on. I remember that.

How did you first meet Leo Singer?

When I joined the midget show I was only nine years old. There was a midget show playing in Germany somewhere. Singer had twelve agents looking for midgets. He had some in the United States and some in Europe. One of the agents notified Singer about me, and Singer sent the agent over to the house where I lived with my

Out for beer and pretzels with one of Singer's managers in 1929. (Nita Krebs collection)

parents. He talked with me and my dad, and then he went back to Germany, and he told Singer he thought I'd be alright for the show. Then my dad went with me to Germany and stayed one week with me, and then he went back home.

Was that the last time you saw your father?

Yes. My parents both spoke to me about going with the midget show and asked if I wanted to go. I thought maybe I would be better off. My dad had made a remark on the day we were getting ready to get on the train. He told the agent he was glad to get rid of me because I was small. He tried to act like he was kidding, but the agent didn't take it like that, and neither did I.

Where did you meet Singer with your father?

When we got to Berlin, we went over to the hotel where the midgets were living. It was the Rusischer Hoff. Singer was pacing the lobby floor waitin' for us to get in because it was about midnight.

Did you cry when your father left after that week?

No. In a way I didn't even know I would feel bad because he made that remark, and that really hurt me. He told me I would be alright, and Singer told him I would be fine with them. Singer was supposed to send money to him ever' so often, but he never did, I found out.

I missed my mother. She told me that anytime I don't feel that I want to go along with them anymore, you come on home. She said, "You be sure to write," and me, well, you know how kids are. They don't like to write.

How did you react when you saw all the other midgets?

In Berlin, Singer took my father and I in to meet his wife and some of the other little people. I thought I was the only little one there. I met Karl Florian, the one who became my regular roommate, first. He taught me a lot of stuff, you know. He was probably at least fifteen years older than me.

When you went to America in 1928, who went along?

There was probably about twenty-eight or thirty midgets, maybe more. Besides me, there were some who were coming to America for the first time, like Nita Krebs; Freddie Retter; Fini and Mike Balluch; Christi, Lida and Eddie Buresh; Jakob Hofbauer; and a lot of the older midgets.

Karl Kosiczky looking sharp in 1945.

When you arrived in America, did you think you would be staying here the rest of your life?

I didn't know. Originally Singer told us we'd be in America for as long as we had bookings. It would all depend.

How did you learn the language?

After we got into New York, and after traveling, Singer had a stagehand, a carpenter, two electricians, and a handyman that traveled with the show all the time, and a stableman for the animals, too. Every day, the stagehands and all of them would talk to me and ask me questions. When I didn't know what they said, I'd turn to Florian and he'd tell me what to say.

The older midgets that had been in America before, they knew the language. The ten of us that were new in the troupe had to learn, and I learned it faster than the other midgets did, I guess because I was so young. In Germany we talked German, but after we got to the United States, Mr. Singer wanted us to speak English all the time.

What was your first experience onstage with the show?

During the first few weeks with the midget show, Mr. Singer had me sit in the audience to watch. I enjoyed performing on the stage once I got the chance. My first job was a policeman in this bit with two of the midgets as wrestlers. I'd be dressed as a policeman and arrest the one that won the fight. Then the next scene I had was in the last number; I was dressed like a cardinal, and I would marry a couple. Later on I sang and played the ukulele.

Did you work with any of the animals?

One time I had to ride a turkey. His wings were right over the top of my legs. I rode a donkey

on stage, and we had a midget camel and a pony in the show. On Billy Rose's Jumbo Show at the old Hippodrome Theater I rode an elephant.

Was Singer protective of you because of your age and height?

He favored me a little bit, I think. He was afraid to let me walk along the street alone because I was so small. In a way, it made me happy that there was somebody to look out for me.

We had this assistant electrician who had a habit of being funny, and he pulled my cap down over my eyes all the time. Singer was in the audience one night and spotted him doing it, just as I was about to come out on the stage. Mr. Singer came back and raised holy cain.

Mr. Singer or Mrs. Singer made sure that no one even joked about locking any of us in a trunk. That was forbidden.

Did Singer always treat the midgets as adults?

Oh yeah. He never wanted anybody to treat us like children. If people were staring, he would go up and say, "Is something the matter?"

But you were a child at the time.

Before we came to the United States Singer had the papers fixed to make it look like I was sixteen years old. He told me to tell people I was sixteen. If I told people how old I was they would've never allowed him to take me to the United States.

Just how tiny were you then?

When I joined Singer I wasn't quite two feet tall. I couldn't reach the doorknob unless I stood on my toes, and then I had to stretch.

In 1929, when I first met John Ringling North, he wanted to buy me out. Singer said

"No way." Ringling wanted to trade Major Mite for me. He was working with the circus.

How else did your height affect your everyday life?

My roommate, Karl Florian, would hold me on the toilet seat anytime I had to go. Or one of the other midgets, like Vincent or Fritz Tarabula.

Did that embarrass you?

No, because I had to do it. Thank God I never fell in. Later on, I learned how to get on the seat myself.

At the hotels, when I went to bed, I had to put a chair in front, a suitcase on top of the chair, and a large suitcase down below to use as steps so I could get up on the bed. When I wanted to take a bath, I had to do the same thing in front of the sink. I could take a bath in the sink. That's how small I was.

What about your clothing?

They had a hard time getting underwear for me. When we went into big cities, the manager, Mr. Latendorf, would go into a big department store. They took some of them off mannequins, and still the boxer shorts and undershirts were too big. Mr. Singer would have a tailor make suits for us. Mrs. Singer would usually have costumes made for our show and make sure they were done right. And some of the little ladies would sew.

Where would the Singer Midgets perform?

We traveled all the big cities around the country. We played the Roxy Theatre in New York and the Hippodrome. We were booked for three years steady on the RKO circuit and kept going. One week here, one week there, and so on. Mr. Singer would stay in New York for a while and book the midget show. He wasn't with us every day. Once

As a publicity stunt for a 1929 Singer's Midgets appearance in Montreal, Canada, little Karl Kosiczky assisted in traffic direction—a sight which no doubt made the newspapers.

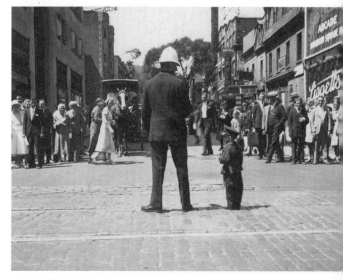

After *Oz*, many of the little people maintained friendships, like these folks: Jackie Gerlich, Karl Kosiczky, Jessie Kelley Becker, Charlie Becker, Margaret Williams, and Mike Balluch, circa 1940.

in a while he'd come out and visit, sit in the audience, and watch a show. Mrs. Singer was with us all the time.

We were in Hawaii for almost three years, traveling on all the islands. I think we left for Hawaii the latter part of 1936, after the San Diego World's Fair, and we came back in 1938 just before *The Terror of Tiny Town* was made. In Hawaii they called us menehune [pronounced "mini-hoony"], which means "little people" in Hawaiian. I liked Hawaii a lot. The only thing I didn't like was the time they had an earthquake. That really scared the wits out of me.

How were holidays celebrated when you were with the midget show?

Most of the time during holidays we worked in the theater. I remember we were booked in Buffalo at Christmas, and we had five shows, and man, that was a lot. The place was sold out, and the owner of the theater came back and asked Mr. Singer if we couldn't put on another show because people were waitin' to get in. And one time I remember we had a big

Christmas party at the hotel in Mr. Singer's room. He had an extra-large room where they'd put a Christmas tree and all that, and we had a party in there.

Before The Wizard of Oz, *didn't many of the veteran midgets return to Europe?*

That's right. There's a story about that. What happened was, in 1934 most of the midgets had gone back to Europe, for good. I found out later that all the older midgets that worked for Mr. Singer, they weren't American citizens. They only had permanent residents cards good for seven years. I stayed, but it was not my idea to stay, it was Mr. Singer's. At the time, Mr. Singer didn't have doodley-squat for me to do, and eventually, a few months later, I got a job working for Billy Rose and his Jumbo Show in New York. The only midgets who were still in the United States were me and Charlie Becker, who was working some elephants in the park somewhere.

One day I was at the hotel, and a man named Julius May calls me up and says, "Karl, you are a friend of mine. Do me a favor, don't come to the theater." I asked him why, what happened, and he said, "Don't you know?"

I says, "No."

He says, "There were ten of you on the bond, and since all the other midgets went to Europe and you didn't, there's a man here looking for you at the theater. If you come over here, they're gonna find you and send you to Europe, and you'll never be able to come back to the States."

Where was Singer?

Singer must've been at his apartment somewhere. Anyway, I didn't come. About an hour later, here comes Singer to the hotel. He says to me, "What are you doin' here? You're supposed to be at work."

I says, "Oh yeah? I supposed you don't know they're lookin' for me because you didn't renew my bond."

He said, "Oh, my God, that's right, I didn't. You did the right thing." And I found out the FBI, or whoever, they checked the hotels and different places, so Mr. Singer came and told me, "I'm gonna have to move you from this hotel." I heard they came there but I was already gone. They kept lookin' for me.

Did he renew your bond?

In the meantime he moved me to Doc Steiner's place. I stayed with Doc Steiner for a week in New York, then Mr. Singer finally came one day and says, "I got just the place where they'll never find you." So he took me to Newark, New Jersey, where a lady lived that used to cook for the midget show—a big lady—and her husband, who used to drive Singer. I stayed with them for almost a year. Their name was Mr. and Mrs. Futerer, and they had four daughters.

You stayed in hiding for a year?

About that, yes.

What did you do during that period?

I remember it was during a wintertime, and I'd listen to the radio and kibitz around. We went sleigh riding and all of that.

Did you keep in touch with the family?

Oh yeah. There are only two of the daughters living now. The oldest one just died not long ago.

When did you rejoin Singer?

Well, finally one day Mr. Singer came over, and he says, "I got a lawyer woman, and I'm going

Karl and Hardy: Little Karl Kosiczky appeared briefly in a scene with Oliver Hardy in *Block-Heads* (1938), one of Stan and Ollie's most popular feature films. Karl's only line was, "Out please," which was dubbed by the bass voice of Billy Bletcher, who also dubbed Munchkin vocals in *The Wizard of Oz*. (Courtesy of Bob Satterfield)

to take you to New York. You're gonna have to dress like a child and she's gonna take you to Canada, and you're gonna act as though you're her child and you don't speak. Don't talk to anybody. Let her do all the talking."

You didn't have to dress like a baby with a bonnet and all, did you?

No, no. Just like a little boy, like five or six years old, in children's clothes. We went to Canada, and I got my permanent resident card. She arranged it for me.

Did you go by her name?

Yes, just for a little while, and then I switched back to my name. I don't remember what her name was. I never saw her again. Later on, in 1936, Singer got the midgets back from Europe; his secretary, Frances Schmeisser, who was German, she was going to take me to the courthouse, and we were both gonna see about getting our permanent papers, but Mr. Singer told us we were going out of town for work, so that ruined that.

I got my citizenship around 1943 in Tampa after I began working for the Slovers.

Anyway, after that Mr. Singer got the midgets back from Europe, and we started traveling again.

Did the midgets trust Singer?

For the most part. We respected him because he treated the little people nice. He was a strict

Karl "Karchy" Kosiczky and Margaret Williams were sweethearts in 1940. In 1989, the friends reunited, sharing a hug. (Courtesy of Margaret Pellegrini)

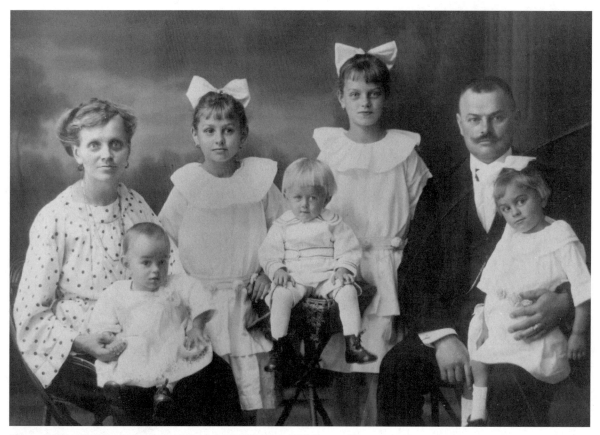

Six-year-old Karl Kosiczky (center) with his family in Hungary, circa 1924. Surrounding him are his parents, Irene and Johann Kosiczky, and sisters Helen, Irene, Eleanora, and Maria. (Courtesy of Karl Slover)

man, and very businesslike. He always paid us, but he pulled some funny stuff. One time, in New York, he was short of money, and he didn't pay the hotel, and they threw us out of the hotel. They kept our suitcases.

When was the last time you saw Singer?

When we got into Florida after we got through with the Royal American Show, he got us a job in St. Petersburg at Thanksgiving. Some of the midgets had already left. It was around 1943. He didn't have any more jobs for us. From what I heard, he lived in New York and died from cancer.

Did you ever wish you were taller, Karl?

When I was really small I used to think, Gosh, I wish I was taller, and at least I wouldn't have to depend on some of these other fellas helpin' me with this and that. Even goin' to the bathroom and all. I'll tell you, in a way it was a little painful.

I know this may be a difficult question, but looking back on the years, do you think you've had a full life?

Oh yes. When I became an American citizen, I was very proud. I think so. I really think so. I've

Karl Slover, in his eighties, the last surviving member of the famous Singer's Midgets.

learned a lot since I was a kid. I enjoyed it being on the midget show. I've been to just about every state, most of the big cities. When we worked, we traveled by train, and Mr. Singer or our advance agent would arrange for us to see the sights and tour like Yellowstone Park or Niagara Falls. I don't have any regrets in my life.

In a noisy train station in 1963 Karl wiped tears from his eyes when he reunited with his mother during his only return trip to Europe. It was maybe the "happiest moment" in his life, he says. His father had long passed away, and his sisters couldn't wait to lay eyes on him.

Today Karl stands just over four feet tall. He's comfortably retired and lives in Florida. During the past eight years he has attended many Munchkin gatherings and *Oz* fests around the country, savoring every moment he is afforded to spend with his family of little people. It's "just like a homecoming."

That's what pleases him most.

POSTSCRIPT: 2002

Karl returned to Germany once again, just shy of four decades later. During his six hour night-flight to Germany, memories rushed through his mind and he couldn't help but wonder what his sisters looked like now and how the cities would appear. He visited his sisters, paid respect at his mother's gravesite, and traveled through some of the countryside; it was a much more relaxed German society than he had known. He realized it would probably be his last time to visit the country where he was from, the last time he'd walk the ground there. His sisters and their children did not know Karl from *The Wizard of Oz*—it was something they were unfamiliar with, and that was okay with him. He was just their little brother. Karl returned to Florida filled with warm memories of all of his relatives and a sense of satisfaction about their lives and his.

"It's Going to Be So Hard to Say Good-bye"

———————————————✳———————————————

It was the close of 1938. Christmas was over, and with the approach of a new year came pleasant visions of returning home. For many of the Munchkins, it wouldn't be soon enough to finally see the movie in which they'd performed

The Munchkins were dismissed from their duties on the evening of December 28. Some of them were already packed, with their train tickets resting on their readied suitcases.

But before the last day was up, MGM's front office sent urgent word to the studio that none of the Munchkins would be cleared to leave the city until a matter with Leo Singer was resolved. Production staffers were in a mild frenzy over Singer and his sudden refusal to cooperate with the studio's final shooting schedule.

Keith Weeks, the film's production manager, had informed Singer the day before that the studio would require twenty of the little people to stay an extra day or so for retakes, photographs, and any other last-minute details. Singer refused, claiming he knew nothing about such requirements.

The MGM legal department quickly reviewed Singer's contract and highlighted the clause that referred to holding the whole group in Culver City. Singer was informed that unless it was honored, the Munchkins' final paychecks would be held.

When Singer signed his contract with Loew's Incorporated, part of the agreement clearly included detaining the entire group in the city for two weeks after completion of filming in case the studio required retakes. But Singer didn't think MGM would enforce this clause, and curiously, he refused the services of any of the midgets.

Weeks immediately contacted the legal department and was hurriedly instructed on how to handle the situation before the ensemble had wrapped for the day. Late in the afternoon on the final day of shooting, Weeks quietly entered the sound stage, staring at the anxious midgets in costume and makeup. As the final "Cut!" was heard from Fleming's perch on the camera boom, Weeks gathered the Munchkins around him and thanked them for their performance.

"At this time and in Singer's presence, I recalled to the set to work the following day approximately twenty midgets," Weeks later typed in a memo. "I stated also that all the other midgets were definitely closed on the picture, but that [Singer] would be paid for the twenty midgets pro rata for whatever time I would need them."

Weeks purposely mentioned the financial addendum aloud so the remaining twenty little people would not be alarmed about compensation. Singer had obviously not told any of them about an extended stay; however, he finally agreed, although he adamantly complained about Weeks delivering the announcement rather than himself. Apparently Singer felt uneasy about retaining only twenty and dismissing the rest. Also, he was probably more concerned with securing any additional work for *his* core troupe of midgets.

"I remember staying for those days when the others had left," said Fern Formica. "It was a lot of us smaller ones. We took some still photos, and one of them is the shot where Glinda and Dorothy look into the bushes and Margaret [Pellegrini] and I are peeking out right next to them." Others chosen for that portrait session included: Frank Cucksey, Matthew Raia, Nita Krebs, the Lollipop Guild (Jerry Maren, Jackie Gerlich, and Harry Doll) Jeane LaBarbera, Betty Tanner, Christie Buresh, and Olga Nardone.

Margaret Pellegrini vividly remembers this particular moment for another reason. "Right when we were taking that picture I got a nosebleed," she says. "I guess they were afraid it would get all over my costume an' everything, but Mervyn LeRoy came right up to me and picked me up out of the bushes. I think someone came and helped me, and I went back to work a little later."

During these affixed days (Thursday, December 29, and Friday, December 30) the twenty Munchkins filmed the sequence where they race after Glinda's pink, glistening bubble ascending over Munchkinland. Waving and bouncing, they look upward and yell "Good-bye! Good-bye!" at virtually nothing because the bubble effect was inserted later in post-production.

Across town during the same two days, many of the little people were weaving in and out of crowds trying to get to their track at the massive Los Angeles train station. Just like Dorothy in the movie—excited, yet sad—they were going home, gushing with memories.

At the Culver Hotel, many of the little people said farewell to friends and promised to keep in touch along their travels. The All-American Bus Lines driver screeched the door closed while his group sat readied in their upright seats. The bus drove through snow and more serious wintry conditions this time, returning the little people to their hometowns along the way.

Other midgets were going back to work with their vaudeville troupes. Still others loaded their cars and headed home, anxious to tell their families about working in something new—a Technicolor motion picture.

They were movie stars.

Judy Garland autographed portraits for all of the Munchkins on the set of *Oz*.

Here, on one of the final days of shooting, some of the little people pose for a final photograph together before they depart for their many destinations. (Courtesy of Beverly Smith)

The Hollywood Premiere
✳

It was the evening of August 15, 1939—almost a year after filming of *The Wizard of Oz* had commenced. The formal affair attracted ten thousand fans and a glittering constellation of movie stars to Grauman's Chinese Theater in Hollywood.

Throngs of movie fans were restrained behind the roped-off sidelines while a limited number of people had the opportunity to experience the premiere from grandstand bleacher seats specially constructed for the event. Yelling fans stretched from the windows of the Hollywood Roosevelt Hotel across the street. Hundreds of police were stationed to handle the crowds trying to catch a glimpse of the stars entering the theater and maybe even obtain an autograph or photograph. Just like any Hollywood portrayal of a premiere, this one really had the massive klieg lights shining brightly into the night air, crisscrossing each other in the sky.

Judy Garland did not attend the California premiere, as she and fellow box-office draw Mickey Rooney were in New York for the East Coast festivities and publicity campaign. In addition to most of the film's cast in attendance, a swarm of top Hollywood celebrities who cheered on the film included: Harold Lloyd, Eleanor Powell, Eddie Cantor, Chico Marx, Ann Rutherford, Darryl Zanuck, Ernst Lubitsch, Wallace Beery, Allan Jones, Orson Welles, Virginia Bruce, Douglas Fairbanks Jr., Edgar Bergen, Stuart Erwin, Preston Foster, and Fred Stone—the original Scarecrow from the successful 1902 stage musical.

Harrison Carroll, critic for the *Los Angeles Evening Herald and Express,* described the gala event in the following day's edition:

> At the Grauman's Chinese Theater, scene of so many important events in its history, Hollywood conquered another frontier last night when MGM's *The Wizard of Oz* picturization of L. Frank Baum's fairy tale scored a lustrous triumph in the almost unexplored realm of fantasy.
>
> The grim realism of a world beset by strife and fears was forgotten for a few hours as a dazzling parade of celebrities converged upon the Hollywood Boulevard showhouse where thousands of fans, in bleachers and at every other vantage point, waited to cheer their arrival.
>
> For the evening, the famous forecourt was almost as fantastic as a scene from *Oz* itself. Ticket holders walked up a replica of the Yellow Brick Road leading to the Emerald City. Around them rose the stalks of a cornfield.

HOLLYWOOD SEES 'WIZARD OF OZ'

Celebrities are shown attending the gala premiere of "The Wizard of Oz," M-G-M fantasy which opened amid lights and fanfare last night at Grauman's Chinese Theater. Left to right, Paula Stone, Mrs. Frank L. Baum, widow of the story's author; Ray Bolger, who portrays the role of the scarecrow in the film, and Fred Stone, who appeared as the wizard in the 1902 stage production.

Billie Burke, widow of the late Florenz Ziegfeld, and Dalies Frantz, concert pianist, are shown stopping to talk with midgets who performed as Munchkins in the movie. The little people were on hand to lend color to the premiere.

It was a worthy setting for Hollywood's most daring venture into the world of imagination.

Most notable was the presence of Maud Gage Baum, the widow of the Royal Historian of *Oz* himself, L. Frank Baum. (The house they shared was literally just blocks from the theater on North Cherokee Avenue. "Ozcot," as the residence was called, was not the location where *The Wonderful Wizard of Oz* was penned; however, it was the site of L. Frank Baum's death on May 6, 1919. Today the site is an empty lot.)

Years later, Baum's granddaughter, Ozma Baum Mantele, described in *The Baum Bugle* her experience at the premiere. Mantele was just a child in 1939, but at least one aspect of the evening remained vividly dissatisfying in her mind:

Typical of my grandmother, she became engulfed in that magical world at this time, and as a consequence, she forgot about her family, and we were not invited to the movie premiere. So the family bought tickets and took all the grandchildren to the movie. I remember being lined up at the curb in front of Grauman's Chinese Theater, and when Grandmother Baum was on the podium being interviewed by the press, we all filed by her and waved. She never batted an eyelash. This incident was never discussed by my grandmother or my parents, and things went on as usual afterward.

At the premiere of the film on Tuesday evening, August 15, 1939, several of the midget actors still residing in California were asked by MGM to don some assorted Munchkin wardrobe once again as a promotion at Grauman's Chinese Theater in Hollywood. (L–R): Nona Cooper, Victor Wetter, Tommy Cottonaro, Billy Curtis, and Jerry Maren as the Mayor.

The Pasadena Tournament of Roses Parade in January 1939 featured an *Oz* float—many months prior to the film's release. Most spectators probably wondered what in the world this crazy crysanthemum and pom-pom monstrosity was all about. Several Munchkins, including Charlie Becker (the mayor), Karl Slover (trumpeter), and Freddie Retter (fiddler), were aboard. (Courtesy of Academy of Motion Picture Arts and Sciences)

Premiere Night: In the mayor's costume, midget Jerry Maren greets Chico Marx at Grauman's Chinese Theater. Maren had recently finished a role in the Marx Brothers film *At the Circus*. (Courtesy of Academy of Motion Picture Arts and Sciences)

Mickey Rooney presented Judy Garland a special miniature "Oscar" as the outstanding screen juvenile of 1939 at the Academy Awards banquet held February 29, 1940. The statuette, which Garland nicknamed her "Munchkin Award," became the only Academy Award she received in her career.

Munchkins Alta Stevens and Christie Buresh pose proudly in front of a *Wizard of Oz* theater display in August 1939.

A group of Munchkins (and spouses) reunite with their *Oz* dance director, Dona Massin, at a 1993 Chesterton, Indiana, *Oz* Fest.

6

MEET THE MUNCHKINS

THE WOMEN

Gladys W. Allison
Josefine Balluch
Freda Betsky
Christie Buresh
Lida Buresh
Nona Cooper
Elizabeth Coulter
Ethel W. Denis
Hazel I. Derthick (Resmondo)
Jeanette Fern (aka Johnnie Fern, Fern Formica)
Addie Eva Frank
Thaisa L. Gardner
Carolyn E. Granger
Helen M. Hoy
Marguerite A. Hoy
Jessie E. Kelley (Becker)
Emma Koestner
Mitzi Koestner
Dolly Kramer
Nita Krebs
Jeane LaBarbera (aka "Little Jeane")
Hilda Lange
Ann Rice Leslie
Yvonne Moray (Bistany)

Olga C. Nardone
Margaret C. H. Nickloy
Hildred C. Olson
Leona M. Parks
Lillian Porter
Margaret "Margie" Raia
Gertrude H. Rice
Hazel Rice
Ruth L. Robinson (Duccini)
Helen J. Royale (Wojnarski)
Stella A. Royale (Wojnarski)
Elly A. Schneider (aka Tiny Doll)
Frieda Schneider (aka Gracie Doll)
Hilda E. Schneider (aka Daisy Doll)
Elsie R. Schultz
Ruth E. Smith
Alta M. Stevens (Barnes)
Charlotte V. Sullivan
Betty D. Toczylowski (aka Betty Tanner)
Grace G. Williams
Margaret Williams (Pellegrini)
Marie Winters (Maroldo)
Gladys V. Wolff

THE MEN

John Ballas
Franz "Mike" Balluch
John T. Bambury
Charles "Charlie" Becker
Henry Boers
Theodore "Teddy" Boers
Eddie Buresh
Colonel Casper
Thomas J. Cottonaro
Lewis Croft (aka "Idaho" Lewis)
Frank H. Cucksey
Billy Curtis
Eugene S. David Jr.
Eulie H. David
Prince Denis
James D. Doyle (aka "Major Doyle")
Carl M. "Kayo" Erickson
Michael Finocchiaro (aka Mickey Carroll)
Jakob "Jackie" Gerlich
William A. Giblin
Jack Glicken
Joseph Herbst
Jakob Hofbauer
Clarence Chesterfield Howerton
    (aka "Major Mite")
James R. Hulse
Robert Kanter (aka "Lord Roberts")
Charles E. Kelley
Frank Kikel
Bernhard "Harry" Klima
Willi Koestner
Karl Kosiczky (Slover)
Adam Edwin Kozicki (aka Eddie Adams)
Joseph J. Koziel
Emil Kranzler
Johnny Leal
Charles Ludwig (aka "Prince Ludwig")
Dominick Magro

Carlos Manzo
Howard Marco
Gerard Marenghi (aka Jerry Maren)
Bela Matina (aka Mike Rogers)
Matjus Matina (aka Ike Rogers)
Lajos Matina (aka Leo Matina)
Walter Miller
George Ministeri
Harry Monty
Nels P. Nelson
Franklin H. O'Baugh
William H. "W. H." O'Docharty
Frank Packard
Nicholas "Nicky" Page
Johnny Pizo
Leon Polinsky (aka "Prince Leon")
Meinhardt Raabe
Matthew Raia
Billy Rhodes (aka "Little Billy")
Fredreich "Freddie" Retter
Sandor Roka
Jimmie Rosen
Charles F. Royale (Wojnarski)
Albert Ruddinger
Kurt Schneider (aka Harry Earles, Harry Doll)
Charles Silvern
Garland "Earl" Slatten
Elmer Spangler
Pernell Elmer St. Aubin
Carl Stephan
George Suchsie
August Clarence Swensen
Arnold Vierling
Gus Wayne
Victor Wetter
Harvey B. Williams
Johnny Winters
Murray Wood

It may have seemed like a cast of a thousand. However, it was a mere 124 or so. That is the number Leo Singer was contracted to supply MGM. Of the consistently reported 124 Munchkins, only twenty-nine surviving little people and three of the children could be located for interviews when I began this endeavor in late 1987.

Based on the dockets that have turned up in private *Oz* collections (such as an incomplete daily sign-in sheet, which Munchkin Margaret Pellegrini saved), plus MGM legal records and extensive research, I have compiled a list of the names of 122 of the midgets.

In the film there were forty-seven little ladies and seventy-five little men who portrayed Munchkins. It is doubtful that any more than one or two additional midgets were in the cast. Nearly a dozen children are reported to have played Munchkins, so the total number of individuals to have actually worked in the film as Munchkins seems to have been about 134 (midgets plus children). Therefore, this is probably the first and only definitive Munchkin cast list.

After half a century it is natural that the Munchkins' whereabouts were hard to trace; I have gone to great lengths to include only those who actually participated in the motion picture. (Several little people and individuals of average height approached me during my research claiming to be ex-Munchkins when in fact they were not.) Several more women have claimed to be child Munchkins (unsubstantiated at this point): Theresa Hawes, Eleanor Keaton, Donna Stewart-Hardway (formerly Donna Jean Johnson), Eva Lee Quiney, and Patsy May.

This *is* the most complete answer to the often asked question: "Whatever happened to the Munchkins?" As you will see, most of the little people have led an "Oz-some" past.

JERRY MAREN was just eighteen when he got a telegram from Loew's Incorporated request-

Little Gerard Marenghi, a.k.a. Jerry Maren, in 1938. (Courtesy of Jerry Maren)

ing his presence in *Oz*. It guaranteed six weeks' employment, transportation, food— "the works," he says.

Born on January 24, 1920, in Boston, Massachusetts, Maren was originally named Gerard Marenghi, the youngest of eleven children. He took dancing lessons when he was young and aspired to be an entertainer, appearing locally in an act called "Three Steps and One Half." In November 1938, standing just three feet four, he met up with the *Oz*-bound group of little people in New York City and traveled by bus to California. "I don't remember much about the bus trip, except that it was long. There was a bus full of us and we all became friends. It was an experience because I'd never been around other little people before, so I learned a lot. We'd stay in different cities and they'd stuff several of us little ones in a

Jerry Maren and Billy Curtis are a couple of tiny gangsters in this publicity shot with Humphrey Bogart and Alan Ladd at a Friar's Club event. (Courtesy of Jerry Maren)

Liza Minelli and Jerry Maren share a warm moment together backstage at one of the singer's concerts in Los Angeles, 1995.

Jerry Maren doubles for ventriloquist dummy Charlie McCarthy in the RKO film *Here We Go Again* (1942).

Billy Curtis (center) and Jerry Maren (right) were simians in *Battle for the Planet of the Apes* in 1973. (Buddy Douglas is the ape on the left.)

Munchkins Billy Curtis, Jerry Maren, and Johnny Bambury (and non-*Oz* midget Tony Boris) portrayed Mole Men creatures in 1951.

"That's my dog Tige, he lives in a shoe . . . I'm Buster Brown, look for me in there too." In the late 1950s, Jerry Maren was Buster Brown on radio and in television commercials.

Jerry and Elizabeth Maren on their wedding day.

As "Professor Atom," Jerry Maren confounds the Marx Brothers inside his miniature dwelling in *At the Circus* (1939).

Jerry Maren is tiny pickpocket "Light-Fingered Lester," squaring off with Gordon "Porky" Lee in the Our Gang short *Tiny Troubles* (1939).

room together and we'd leave again early the next morning and the driver would travel as much as possible," he says. There, at MGM, because of his dancing abilities perhaps, he was chosen to be the middle "tough guy" of the Lollipop Guild who hands Dorothy the over-sized sucker. It became his most memorable role to date.

"I remember they had a monstrous crew on the set," Jerry says. "A man who wore tall boots would go into the pond and fix the lilies and then walk out, and the other crew members would mop up the water. When we had time, we used to sneak off and try to watch the other movies being made. We ran into everybody. I snuck over to watch *Lady of the Tropics* with Hedy Lamarr."

The Wizard of Oz was the first of many movies Jerry made. After *Oz* he went directly into a few Our Gang comedies and a featured role in *At the Circus* (1939), starring the Marx Brothers. (It's the one where Groucho sings "Lydia the Tattooed Lady"!) Jerry was permanently transplanted to southern California from that moment on.

Maren has worked steadily in films ever since, on camera and behind the scenes as a stunt double or as a costumed character. In the

1950s he became one of the four Little Oscar chefs for the Oscar Mayer company, mainly working the West Coast in television spots and personal appearances. For more than ten years he toured supermarkets, shopping centers, and appeared in parades, popping out of the hatch of the famous Wienermobile and throwing the little weeny-whistles to the eager kids. It was a tough job on Maren, and even he admits the jumpy, screaming kids used to rattle his nerves at times. "I used to get sick every weekend," he recalls. "Every kid was my size and I'd meet them and interact with them and say, 'Hi ya, pal' and they'd breathe on me or cough. Every third kid had a runny nose or a cold. And then the Wienermobile would break down on weekends while we were out of town somewhere and that was a pain in the ass believe me."

Eventually, in the 1950s, after he had left the Oscar Mayer company, Jerry was persuaded to undergo some brief hormonal treatments to increase his height. He worked with endocrinologists at California's Scripps Clinic who tested out some new growth hormone injections. "I started dreaming how great sports and things would be for me if I were taller," he says. But he grew only a few inches, and after waking up in the morning with aching limbs, he decided to discontinue the injections. The treatment thrust Maren directly into puberty, which was a life-altering metamorphosis at his age, but his height was not drastically modified. So Jerry remained a little person (four feet three), and he is now quite satisfied with his stature, and proud to be a little person. Although he's rarely given credit for it, in the 1950s, with his pal actor Billy Barty, he helped co-found and organize the Little People of America organization.

Commercials on television proved quite lucrative for Maren when he played Buster Brown on radio and television in the 1950s and 1960s and performed in McDonald's televisions commercials under the hefty costume of Mayor McCheese and the Hamburglar for a decade. He is constantly recognized as the little guy in the black tuxedo who scattered confetti at the end of each episode of TV's *The Gong Show*. His list of film and television appearances is as long as that of any major Hollywood star. Jerry became one of the most prolific—as well as one of the wealthiest—of all of the midgets who remained in show business after working in *The Wizard of Oz*.

Among Jerry's film work: *Maisie Was a Lady* (1941), *Beyond the Blue Horizon* (1942), *Fingers at the Window* (1942), *Here We Go Again* (1942), *Flesh and Fantasy* (1943), *Johnny Doesn't Live Here Anymore* (1944), *Show Business* (1944), *The Great John L.* (1945), *Duffy's Tavern* (1945), *When My Baby Smiles at Me* (1948), *Three Wise Fools* (1946), *Samson and Delilah* (1949), *Superman and the Mole Men* (1951), *The Planet of the Apes* (1968), *Little Cigars* (1973), *The Battle for the Planet of the Apes* (1973), *The Bad News Bears Go to Japan* (1978), *Where the Buffalo Roam* (1980), *Under the Rainbow* (1981), *Tron* (1982), *Something Wicked This Way Comes* (1983), *The Being* (1983), *It Came upon a Midnight Clear* (TV movie, 1984), *Hot Moves* (1985), *House* (1986), *Spaceballs* (1987), *The Great Outdoors* (1988), and *Dreamer of Oz* (1990). Additional television credits include: *Smilin' Ed's Gang* (aka *Andy's Gang*), *The Andy Williams Show*, *The Beverly Hillbillies*, *Bewitched*, *Star Trek*, *The Lucy Show*, *Laugh-In*, *The Wild Wild West*, *The Flip Wilson Show*, *Get Smart*, *The Sonny and Cher Comedy Hour*, *Daniel Boone*, *The Odd Couple*, *Switch*, *No Soap, Radio*, *Julia*, *The Tonight Show*, *Truth or Consequences*, *Lidsville*, *Mary Hartman, Mary Hartman*, *Logan's Run*, *The Twilight Zone*, *Wizards and Warriors*, *Geraldo*, *Maury Povich*, *To Tell the Truth*, *Night Court*, *The Daily Show*, *The Man Show*, and *Seinfeld*.

Jerry and his wife, Elizabeth (Barrington), an actress and also a little person, live in the Hollywood Hills; their home was completely built to scale with lowered counters and smaller chairs, tables, etc. As he lights an ever-present stogie, which is almost bigger than he is, and leans back glancing outside at his pool, Jerry seems to enjoy his retirement and talking about his most famous role—as the only surviving member of the Lollipop Guild. His golf game is good, he says, and he plays softball during summers on a team known as The Hollywood Shorties. Even in his eighties, he still enjoys running the bases—just not as fast.

During the past ten years Jerry has been one of the most sought-after Munchkins for television interviews, commercials, and *Oz* festival appearances. "I'm a little heavier nowadays," admits Maren. "Some kids come up to me and ask me if I was the Mayor."

In a memorable Converse sports shoe commercial that aired nationally during the 1993 Super Bowl, Jerry was made up as a troll-like Munchkin dressed in a striped referee's uniform. He welcomed basketball superstar Larry Johnson "to three-point land" in an *Oz* lampoon that did well for the company.

"I can mention a long list of credits, movies, TV shows," Jerry says, "and nobody cares about any of it except *Oz*, and that was my first."

After all, everyone remembers the Lollipop Kid, don't they?

For Jerry, *Oz* is perpetuated by the frequent personal appearances he makes, with a large lollipop in tow. As one of the most requested of the Munchkins, Jerry has been interviewed more times than he can count, with usually the same questions about *Oz*. He tries to keep his responses fresh, he says, and inevitably he's plied to sing the song that has become his theme. "I was on *To Tell the Truth*, the new version, just a year ago and stumped a few of the panelists at least. I can tell you how many airplanes I've been on or how many cities I've been to in the last ten years. One of my favorite

For more than ten years, Jerry Maren dressed as a myriad of characters in McDonald's commercials, including Mayor McCheese. (Courtesy of Jerry Maren)

moments was attending the movie with my wife at Grauman's Chinese Theater when they released it again recently. When I walked out into the courtyard where all the footprints are in the cement there were news cameras waiting for me to come out of the show. The place was mobbed and they all clapped. It was amazing, all these years later."

In the opening of the Munchkin scene, when the Munchkins come out, you'll notice a little fellow climb out of a manhole. Don't blink. Just after that, **MICKEY CARROLL** saunters right across the screen holding a bell as the town crier. He's in a deep purple cloak with a yellow flower sticking out from his striped vest. He also plays one of the fiddlers who escorts Dorothy out of the land of Oz (second from left, as you look at the screen). "I did voice-overs for several of the Munchkins," Mickey says.

Now in his eighties, Mickey reflects with much pride on his entertainment career. His pictures of Judy Garland and other celebrities he's worked with or met hang on the wall of his office and in his living room. Mickey started tap-dancing and performing when he was in grade school in St. Louis. He had a one-man act and traveled around to nightclubs and theaters, closely managed by his older brother, Bud.

His fondest memories of being on the road include dancing with a young Donald O'Connor and his sisters and having Ronald Reagan room with him briefly in Hollywood.

But his trip to the MGM studio is not one of Mickey's fondest memories. "Bud and I were on our way out to make *The Wizard of Oz* when we had a big car accident in Albuquerque. A truck hit us head-on. We had to stay there for weeks, and we ended up suing the truck driver's company and won." Mickey arrived late on the set and missed almost all the rehearsals. Luckily, he was a quick study, and dancing was no trick for him to pick up. Director Victor Fleming took a liking to Mickey and put him in several roles: town crier, soldier, and that of one of the fiddlers near the end of the scene.

Mickey's real name is Michael Finnocchiaro; he has a twin sister, Jennie, who stands five feet four. Another sister, Mary, and a brother, Leo, were of average height. Born in St. Louis, Mickey returned to the Gateway to the West after his nearly ten-year excursion on the road entertaining. He has lived in St. Louis ever since.

Recently he retired and sold his business, Standard Monument Company, a family-owned

operation for more than sixty years. "After I got out of show business, I came home and worked in the shop and eventually took that over," he says.

In more recent years, Mickey has given much of his time to promote *The Wizard of Oz* and his role as a Munchkin, while affiliating the appearances with charities. His pet projects are raising money for the Special Olympics and other needy causes. The plaques on his office wall commend him for many hours of fundraising for such causes as the USO, the Muscular Dystrophy Association, the Variety Club, and the Ronald McDonald House.

When asked what he remembers most about *Oz,* Mickey says, "Probably how beautiful Judy was. And her voice. She was fantastic. And how she used to get tired on the set. . . . When we sang the songs on the set, some of us Munchkins

St. Louis's Munchkin, Mickey Carroll, in the vaudeville era. (Courtesy of Mickey Carroll)

Mickey Carroll accepts an autographed poster from President Harry Truman while serving as master of ceremonies for a celebration in Truman's home state of Missouri, October 7, 1945. (Courtesy of Mickey Carroll)

In MGM's parking lot, Mickey Carroll holds his nose at Stella Royale's fur stole, while Lewis Croft does the romancing. (Courtesy of Ruth Duccini)

Mickey Carroll impersonated Mae West in his vaudeville act. (Courtesy of Mickey Carroll)

used to joke and say, 'Ding dong, the witch is dead, which ole witch, the son of a bitch!' I also remember how the pond leaked and we'd slip on the Yellow Brick Road sometimes. They'd have some guy come out and mop it up."

In the past ten years, Mickey has been sought out to make appearances on national television shows and travel the country. With a quick wit and always an eye-popping line for the reporters and radio show hosts, Mickey continues to talk about *Oz* and his show business experiences. At an age when retirement usually means just that, Mickey wants no part of sitting at home and watching television all day. "I love meeting the people," he says. "The kids are great, and the parents, they are my biggest fans. I could talk myself silly telling stories and singing, and the autographs. My god, I don't know how many thousands of autographs I've signed over the years."

On his eightieth birthday, Mickey threw out the first baseball at the Cardinals game at Busch Stadium in his hometown of St. Louis. "Now how many people get to do that?" he asks.

MARGARET (WILLIAMS) PELLEGRINI was also known as "Popcorn" or sometimes "Li'l Alabam" to her friends and colleagues. She was a tiny southern gal who got whisked away from her hometown of Sheffield, Alabama, to a movie set to be a Munchkin. It's the kind of dream come true that movies are made of.

Margaret, who is in her late seventies, was born on September 23, 1923, around the corner from where Helen Keller lived. Margaret's venture down the Yellow Brick Road actually began at a potato chip booth in the Tennessee State Fair. "My sister's husband worked for a potato chip company in Memphis, and they had a booth at the state fair. I was helping them out, and some little people came walking by and spotted me. They introduced themselves as part of Henry Kramer's Midgets and asked me if I wanted to join their show.

"At that time I didn't think I was a midget,"

Margaret Williams celebrates her thirteenth birthday with famous fan dancer Sally Rand in 1936. (Courtesy of Margaret Pellegrini)

says Pellegrini, who then stood about three feet four. She gave the people her address and eventually was contacted by a booking agent who worked with Leo Singer. "I got a letter from Thelma Weiss in Hollywood to come out to make the movie."

If you look closely, you can spot Margaret in several corners of Munchkinland—even as one of the Sleepy Heads who wipe their eyes and "get out of bed." The director used her in more than one place, no doubt, because she was so small, perfect for the setting. And she still knows the entire scene by heart. It was a fantasy to make the movie, and she has never regretted it, remembering almost every detail as though it were yesterday.

"For us girls, our dresses were so big, and we had such big petticoats, that we had some ladies who were there to help us go to the bathroom," Margaret remembers shyly. "We'd go to sit on the commode, and we couldn't lift 'em up enough. The ladies had to help us lift 'em. It seemed odd havin' someone help you go potty at our age."

With a bit of a raspy voice Margaret looks back on *Oz* as a "fantastic experience." Afterward, she traveled with some midget troupes and later married an average-sized man, ex-fighter Willie Pellegrini. They had two children, Margaret Jo and William Joseph Jr. (who refers to himself as "a son-of-a-Munchkin"). Margaret is even a great-grand-Munchkin, she says. After her marriage in 1943, she devoted her life to raising her children and steered clear of show business, except for a brief appearance in the unusual Dalton

Margaret Pellegrini and Ruth Duccini visit the massive Sound Stage 27 at MGM (now Sony Studios) where they filmed *Oz* fifty-five years earlier. Oddly, on the day of their visit, the fantasy film *Indian in the Cupboard* (directed by Frank Oz) was wrapping production.

At Christmastime, Margaret Pellegrini occasionally doubles as one of Santa's helpers.

Trumbo film *Johnny Got His Gun* (1971).

"There were many years where I didn't even tell people I was in *The Wizard of Oz*," Margaret says. "Unless the topic came up. I thought people would think I was lookin' for attention. And then it started showing on television, and as time went by, people started asking me questions. It's all very exciting, even now."

Of all the midgets from the film, perhaps Margaret was the one who stored the memories with the most accuracy over time. In vivid detail she has been able to recall nearly every aspect of her *Oz* experience. She happily remembers the first time she saw herself in the film at a theater in 1939.

"I was at Treasure Island World's Fair working with Singer's Midgets," she says. "The movie came out on August 15th and Mr. Singer picked out a couple of us little ones. His chauffeur took us over to San Francisco to a large theater, like one of the vaudeville houses, maybe the Fox Theater, and it was premiering there that afternoon. A lot of people came to the movie. I believe Singer had Nita Krebs, me, and a little man . . . I think it was Karchy [Karl Kosiczky Slover], and we were at a card table in the lobby and we autographed some programs or photos as they went in and when they came out.

"When the show started, they let us stand in the back by the railing that blocks off the seats from the aisle and we stood there and watched the movie," she remembers. "I saw myself and I started jumping up and down and I was saying 'That's me! That's me!' I got all excited and everybody turned around and looked. They thought something had happened. I just put my hand to my face and said, 'oh, I'm sorry.'"

What Margaret can't recount is how many times she's watched the movie since that day in 1939. "Too many to count," she laughs.

Today Margaret is widowed and makes Glendale, Arizona, her home. She has become one of the most visible of all the little people who appeared in the movie, usually donning a replica costume at personal appearances. To follow her travel route over the past ten years would be to master the Etch-A-Sketch game. During the anniversary year she turned up on countless television shows, including *Good Morning America*, *Larry King Live* on CNN, *Geraldo*, *The Marsha Warfield Show*, *Maury Povich*, and *The Jm J and Tammy Faye Show*. She has greeted crowds at *Oz* festivals and waved in parades (including the Indianapolis 500 parade) all over the country and maintains a hectic schedule. Luckily, her memory for names, places, dates, and times is fantastic. She saved much from her show business and traveling days and is planning to remodel and devote one room in her house to her treasured *Oz* collectibles. "Right now," she says, "it's

More Than a Handful: Spencer Tracy holds Karl Kosiczky and Nita Krebs during a break in filming the circus sequences for *They Gave Him a Gun* (1937).

crammed so full I can barely walk into it. I get so much stuff every time I go to these festivals. I love it!"

KARL SLOVER says he was the tiniest of the Singer Midgets who portrayed Munchkins. He's grown now, from three feet tall when he played a trumpeter in *The Wizard of Oz* to four feet four. His father was six feet six. "Mr. Singer told me I would grow," Karl says. "He seemed to know who would and who wouldn't grow later in life."

Originally, Karl's last name was Kosiczky. Born in Hungary, he changed his name to Slover when he became a U.S. citizen in 1943. His odd nickname, "Karchy," originated when he was working with Singer's Midgets and there were too many midgets named Karl to keep them straight. Karchy, which is Hungarian for

Karl, was pinned on him for years, although he seldom answers to it now.

Karl played the first of three trumpeters who lead the mayor's procession. Besides *Oz*, he appeared briefly in the film *Block-Heads* (1938) with Laurel and Hardy, and *They Gave Him a Gun* (1937) with Spencer Tracy. He was the town barber and a saloon bass player in *The Terror of Tiny Town* (1938), and you can also spot him in the baby carriage in *The Lost Weekend*, a 1945 blockbuster starring Ray Milland.

Karl, who still speaks with a slight accent, said, "We knew English when we did *The Wizard of Oz*. I've read in places that all the Munchkins were German, and they didn't know how to speak English. We learned way before that."

Karl remembers the first day on the set of *Oz*: "They took us through the studio. Here they had these fruit trees," he says. "Well, at this time, I didn't know they were rubber. They looked very real. I saw the trees move, and I said, 'What the heck?' My roommate thought I was nuts, and we kept walking around, and then he saw it, too. About that time, the prop man said, 'Oh, there's a man in those trees.' That tickled me."

Karl is now the last of Singer's midget troupe, and has earned a sort of "royalty" status in the Munchkin world, commonly meeting celebrities who seek him out and wish to meet him. In 1995 when David Copperfield toured the country and stopped in Tampa with his extravagant show, the magician requested a meeting with Karl, who happily obliged.

Today Karl, who is now in his eighties, remains retired from full-time work and lives with a family he has known for many years in Tampa, Florida. For the past fifteen years he trained poodles and performed them at various functions, but lost his little dogs a few years ago and decided to call it quits. His time is spent corresponding with friends and relatives and gearing up for the frequent *Oz* festivals he attends each year. In 2001 Karl was honored at a banquet given by the Sons of the Desert organization (the longtime Laurel and Hardy fan base) in Los Angeles, where he was even congratulated by Ray Bradbury.

MEINHARDT RAABE (pronounced "mine-heart robby") was probably the most formally educated of the small actors. This may have been why he was given the role of the Munchkin coroner who pronounced the Wicked Witch dead, unraveling an oversized certificate of death in honor of the occasion.

Born on September 2, 1915, in Watertown, Wisconsin (his parents were German), he stands four feet eight now. He's grown six inches since he was twenty years old.

To fund his own college education Meinhardt worked at world's fairs, performing in expositions such as the Chicago World's Fair in 1934, the San Diego Exposition in 1935, the Texas Centennial, and Cleveland Great Lakes World's Fair in 1936. Meinhardt earned his bachelor of arts degree in accounting from the University of Wisconsin and his master of arts in business administration from Northwestern University, all the while juggling a career—of sorts—in show business. "Years ago, the public conception was small body, small mind," he says. "The door was slammed shut in my face as far as an accounting career.

"There was a well-established midget grapevine around the country," Meinhardt says. "So I went to California when I heard MGM needed little people for the movie. The casting director picked me as a result of my public-speaking experience, I assume. I probably had a little bit better diction and enunciation than maybe some who were foreign-born.

"I went around and got autographs of all the people associated with the picture," he says. Judy Garland inscribed a beaut to him: "She wrote, 'To Meinhardt, a perfect coroner and a

"She's really most sincerely dead." The Munchkin City Fathers entourage (L–R) in view are: Jack Glicken, Johnny Winters, Meinhardt Raabe (the coroner holding the death certificate), Little Billy Rhodes (the barrister; shaking his fist), Charlie Becker (the mayor), Matthew Raia (holding his hat), and soldier Jakob

Hofbauer. It is interesting to note that the date inscribed on the prop death certificate for the demise of the Wicked Witch of the East was actually the death date of L. Frank Baum—May 6th. (Copyright © 1939 Loew's Inc., renewed © 1966 by MGM)

perfect person too. Love from Judy' on a picture I still have in my scrapbook. I also have Jack Dawn, the makeup man, and Mr. Brown, the chief electrician, along with Margaret Hamilton and Billie Burke, Ray Bolger, Jack Haley, and Bert Lahr. It was fun."

Before and after *Oz*, Meinhardt worked for the Oscar Mayer company as their mascot and goodwill ambassador. Known as "Little Oscar, World's Smallest Chef," he toured in promotions for the company's meat line. He was right there traveling in the first Weinermobile produced in 1936. After the market widened, he took on three protégés as Oscar Jrs. The employment with the Oscar Mayer company was something Raabe relished for thirty years. It was during this time that he met his wife, the former Marie Hartline, also a little person.

Marie had performed with Rose's Royal Midgets in the early 1930s, but declined a job as a Munchkin in the movie.

During the 1980s, Meinhardt worked in the public school system in Pennsylvania as a special education teacher, also instructing in horticulture. He and his wife Marie moved down south to Jacksonville, Florida in 1986 where they lived in a retirement community, owned by the J. C. Penney Company, and continued to frequent many *Oz* functions around the country each year. Dressed in a long blue robe, reminiscent of his costume and hat from the film, Meinhardt says he never tires of spouting his famous coroner's spiel . . . only having to write it out for autograph collectors, which he rarely does. He has been most proud to sign the array of Munchkin character merchandise which has hit the market in years past: Coroner Munchkin statues, dolls, trinkets, and Christmas ornaments by Hallmark, to name just a few.

In 1997, the Raabes were involved in a tragic automobile accident and Marie Raabe died from injuries on October 22, 1997. Meinhardt's life changed suddenly and he gradually recovered from a broken ankle and other injuries. Now nearing ninety, he lives in an assisted-living residence within the retirement community and still answers fan mail and travels as much as his health will allow. "I don't move around as swiftly as I used to," Meinhardt said recently, "but I still try to meet the fans at various functions when I'm able. What's the word on the grapevine? Any *Oz* conventions coming up out your way?"

Meinhardt Raabe, the famed Munchkin coroner. (Courtesy of Jean Nelson)

RUTH (ROBINSON) DUCCINI met her husband, Fred, also a little person, in the restaurant where the Munchkins regularly dined during production of *The Wizard of Oz*. Fred was just another face among the little people at the eatery, but he had a good job at a nearby hotel and chose not to abandon it to work in the movie. "We used to call the restaurant Ptomaine Marie's," Ruth laughs. She has very fond memories of *Oz*.

For Ruth, being a Munchkin introduced her not only to her husband, but also to one of her closest friends, Alta Stevens, who was a Munchkin villager as well. In 1937, shortly after she graduated from high school, Ruth worked as a telephone operator and later joined the Harvey Williams Midget Troupe, performing in stage shows and carnivals around the country. She and the rest of the troupe drove from Minneapolis to Culver City to apply for jobs as Munchkins. (The ten in the group included Grace and Harvey Williams, Emil Kranzler, James Hulse, Lewis Croft, Carolyn Granger, Hildred Olson, Alta Stevens, Kayo Erickson, and Ruth Robinson.) "It was the first time I had seen so many little people in one place," she says.

Oz was her first movie, and oddly enough, her last film appearance was *Under the Rainbow*, where again she was a Munchkin. (Duccini and Jerry Maren were the only two original Munchkins from *The Wizard of Oz* to appear in the parody film. "I really didn't like how they portrayed us," Ruth admits. "I thought Chevy Chase was crude and vulgar and I regret doing [the movie], but it was a good paycheck and that movie paid for a beautiful Alaskan cruise Fred and I took, so I guess it wasn't so bad. Don't believe anything you see in that movie. It was all for laughs.")

After making *The Wizard of Oz* in 1938 she returned to Minnesota briefly; following Pearl Harbor Day in 1941 she headed back to California, where she worked for Douglas Aircraft in Santa Monica for two years. During those years she reunited with her old boyfriend, Fred, and in 1943 they were married. The couple lived in the Los Angeles area for many years, had a son and a daughter (Fred Jr. and Margaret), both of average height. Eventually Fred and Ruth retired to Bullhead City, Arizona, where they enjoyed life in the budding city along the Colorado River. Although Fred's health began to fail, the couple was able to celebrate their golden wedding anniversary in 1993 with a big party. Fred passed away a year later, and Ruth decided to relocate to central Arizona.

Ruth Robinson in 1938.

Munchkins Grace Williams, Ruth Robinson, and Alta Stevens at MGM in 1938. The three remained close friends long after the production of *Oz*. (Courtesy of Ruth R. Duccini)

She and Fred enjoyed *Oz* festivals and reuniting with many of their friends from yesteryear.

In a 2001 *Washington Post* article, writer Megan Rosenfeld described Ruth: "She's the breeziest Munchkin, commonly known as a 'sweetheart.' A widow, she looks like a tiny version of everybody's grandmother, with soft gray-blond hair, glasses, and practical no-wrinkle clothes. She won't wear a costume, which perturbs her friend Margaret Pellegrini mightily."

Even today, as a great-grandmother, she jumps at the chance to travel and enthusiastically recalls her work in the famous MGM film. Ruth and fellow Munchkin Margaret Pellegrini have made numerous personal appearances at the Emerald City Gift Shop in Las Vegas's MGM Grand Hotel casino and complex. "I don't think it would be for me to wear a replica costume," she says. "It's just not me. I was a Munchkin in *The Wizard of Oz* and I don't have to wear a costume to prove it.

"The MGM Grand treated us beautifully," she says. "We had a nice room, and we could go anywhere for meals. They'd send a limo to the airport to pick us up. Pretty good for an old lady, huh?"

Her eyesight has deteriorated a bit over the

years, so she has limited her appearances at *Oz* festivals. She attests that *Oz* surprised her late in life with many new friends and adventures which she never imagined. "I always wanted to go to New York City, and I finally did," she says. "The Munchkins had a reunion on *The Maury Povich Show* and that was very nice, but too brief a stay. I barely got a look at the city, go out to eat, and we were gone. Later on I made an appearance in New York again and had a great time and looked around. I can't complain. I've had a full life."

Most remarkable about Ruth is her generous outlook on life and friendships, and she has always maintained that beautiful, warm laugh. When she smiles, it's a rare, intimate smile with brightness, as her eyes smile right along. "There's something I'm most proud of, though," she points out. "I worked as a riveter on the inner wing of the C-54 transports used in the war. I could get in spots where others couldn't. I feel I made my contribution to the country during the war that way and that makes me feel good. A lot of us little ones did that or worked in other war plants and that's something that should be noted."

Munchkin Ruth Robinson Duccini and her husband, Fred, in 1989. (Courtesy of Jean Nelson)

The four **DOLL** siblings are special not only because of their involvement in *The Wizard of Oz*—all as Munchkins—but also because of the unusual phenomenon of four midget children born to their parents, Emma (Preusche) and Gustav Schneider.

"There were seven kids total," says Tiny Doll, born in the town of Stolpen, Germany. Tiny is the only survivor of the four who played Munchkins. "I have one brother and two sisters of normal height who still live in Germany."

All of the midget siblings were about two pounds at birth and grew until they were about four years old when the growth gradually stopped. Gracie, Harry and Tiny all remained about the same height, just under three feet tall. Daisy Doll surpassed the others in height by almost a foot, but this was later in her life.

The Schneiders, Kurt, Frieda, Hilda, and Elly—all doll-sized—were born in Germany to parents who both stood about five feet five. "We were in the Eastern Zone," says Tiny, still with a strong residual accent after all these years.

Kurt and Frieda came to America with their friend, Bert W. Earles, in 1914, began performing, and even took his last name. They were in America to tour with the Buffalo Bill Show. (To complicate things even further, for a brief period during their early years performing in Europe, Kurt and Frieda were known professionally as Hans and Gretel.) In 1922 Hilda emigrated to America, and in 1926 the last to follow, Elly, joined her sisters and brother in the United States. They all lived in Pasadena, California, with the Earles family, all adopting the name as well.

"After Mr. Earles died, we wanted to be on our own," Tiny explained, "so we changed our name to Doll because they said we looked like dolls. Kurt is Harry Doll. My name is Elly, but I became Tiny. Frieda became Gracie, and Hilda was Daisy." It was not long after that the family of little people joined the Ringling family traveling with their reknowned circus.

A very early portrait of Daisy, Grace, and Harry when they went by their given surname, Schneider. (Courtesy of Tiny Doll)

Harry Doll, the most prolific of the bunch, costarred in the 1925 silent film *The Unholy Three* with the legendary Lon Chaney. Harry was Tweedledee, the pseudo-baby gangster in a bonnet. (Harry later reprised his role opposite Chaney in the talkie remake of the same title in 1930. It was to be Lon Chaney's final film role.) Harry and his sister Daisy also costarred in the controversial 1932 MGM horror film *Freaks,* now a popular cult favorite for which they are perhaps best remembered.

Directed by the man who created several horror film classics, Tod Browning (*London After Midnight, Dracula,* et al), *Freaks* is a bizarre circus drama which starred some of the most famous sideshow attractions of the day: Siamese twins Violet and Daisy Hilton, Prince Randian (human torso), Johnny Eck (half man), Frances O'Connor (armless girl), and Peter Robinson (human skeleton) among them. This story

involves a traveling sideshow and a cruel trapeze star, Cleo (Olga Baclanova), who seduces the midget (Hans, played by Harry Earles) and playfully steals him from his fiancée (Frieda, played by Harry's real-life sister, Daisy Earles). The evil seductress attempts to poison the little man to get to his wealth, but it is his circus compatriots who take revenge on Cleo in the end.

When the film was released in 1932, it was called many things: daring, pathetic, repellant, grotesque, ghastly, unkind, and brutal. It ultimately became a box office flop. *Freaks* was pulled from many theatres around the country and banned in England altogether. And today, seventy years later, it is a cult classic embraced by film enthusiasts around the world for its

By the mid 1930s, the famous family adopted the last name of Doll.

All Dolled Up: The four siblings, circa 1929.

Siblings Grace, Daisy, and Harry around 1924. (Courtesy of Tiny Doll)

Harry and Daisy in a scene from the horror film *Freaks*. In the movie they portray love interests, yet in reality they were brother and sister.

Daisy striking a pose for publicity for the film *Freaks*. (Courtesy of Tiny Doll)

utter uniqueness. Film historians recognize Tod Browning as one of the most original and fascinating of the motion picture pioneers.

Tiny (aka Elly), the youngest of the family, was present on the set during the filming of *Freaks*. She recalls the pinheads (microcephalics), especially the most famous one, Schlitzie, quite clearly. "You had to be careful around them," she says, "because they were unruly. Every once in a while they would pitch a fit and become ferocious and start yelling and hitting."

Harry Earles/Doll (and occasionally his sister Daisy) appeared in a handful of films, including *That's My Baby* (1926), *Baby Clothes* (1926), *Baby Brother* (1927), *Three Ring Marriage* (1927), and *Good News* (1930). Outside of *The Wizard of Oz*, Tiny Doll appeared in only one other film, an early Eddie Cantor silent film called *Special Delivery* (1927).

The Dolls were a close-knit family who always lived, ate, and worked together—with the exception of Daisy's brief marriage in 1942 to an average-sized man, Louis E. Runyan, which ended in divorce less than a year later. The family settled in Sarasota, Florida, in the mid-1930s and adopted the last name Doll during this time; they all became naturalized United States citizens. In 1938, while working for the Ringling Brothers and Barnum & Bailey Circus, the family of four midgets drove from Sarasota to California to appear in *The Wizard of Oz*. (Actually, the Dolls owned the new automobile, but were driven by their friend "Pee Wee," a taller man who worked as an usher with the Ringling circus. Eventually the auto was customized with special lifts. Daisy, the tallest of the family, undertook all the driving duties from then on.)

En route to Culver City, they stopped along the way in Albany, Georgia, and picked up their friend Thaisa Gardner, another little lady who was hired to work in the film as well.

Harry is first seen in Munchkinland as the lit-

Legendary horror-film director Tod Browning poses with Daisy, Tiny, and Harry Earles during the production of his early talkie, a bizarre and fascinating film called *Freaks*, released in 1932.

tle guy in a blue shirt and a corncob pipe in his mouth who pops out of a Munchkin manhole. Later in the scene he is one of the tough little Lollipop Guild members (on the right), while the Doll women were cute Munchkin villagers.

"We had a nice time in the movie," Tiny, the youngest of the family, remembers. "We all liked Judy Garland. She talked to us a lot. And they had such a beautiful set. That's what I remember."

Tiny Doll (aka Elly Schneider) was actually thirteen years old when she appeared with Eddie Cantor, playing an infant in the silent film *Special Delivery* in 1927.

The Doll Family poses with the world's largest incandescent lamp: 50,000 watts, made by General Electric in 1937.

Tiny visits with her brother, Harry, and sister Daisy on the set of *Freaks*.

Harry Earles revived his role in a "talking" remake of the 1925 silent film *The Unholy Three,* starring Lon Chaney (at right, holding cake). Here, on April 14, 1930, the cast celebrates Lon Chaney's forty-seventh birthday on the first day of production. The film turned out to be Chaney's last. The legendary actor died of bronchial cancer just months later in August 1930. (Courtesy of Tiny Doll)

Tiny was twenty-four years old when she was a Munchkin. She says that Harry was the shortest of the family ("not quite three and a half feet").

After *The Wizard of Oz,* the foursome headed back to Florida, where they worked for the circus; the four were featured in the opening parade and sang and danced in a sideshow act before and after the circus performance. For the Dolls, this was a profitable way for them to earn a living, by exhibiting themselves on a sideshow stage, and they were never ashamed as millions strode past them and whispered and marveled at how small they were: "just like dolls." The family of petite adults just waved and greeted crowds, signed postcards and sold memorabilia while all of humanity passed their station. During those years their friends were the circus folk and the

Silent film star Harold Lloyd smiles for the camera with the Earles family.

Tiny Doll, the youngest of the famous four.

Tiny, the only surviving member of the famous Doll family midgets, autographing a photo at her Florida home in the mid-1990s. In 2001, Tiny turned eighty-seven and became the oldest surviving Munchkin.

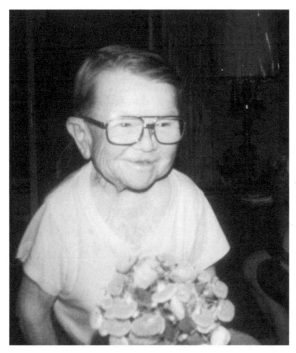

Lollipop Guild Munchkin Harry Doll one month before his death in 1984. (Courtesy of Anna Mitchell)

Grace, Tiny, and Harry on tour in 1942.

The Dolls on exhibit with the Ringling Brothers circus in the 1950s. (Courtesy of Tiny Doll)

The Dolls fit snugly in their "sleeper" while aboard a Ringling Brothers touring train the 1950s. (Courtesy of Tiny Doll)

sideshow acts such as Jo-Jo the Dog-Faced Boy, giants Jack Earl and Al Tomaini, Jeanie the half-woman, as well as Priscilla the Monkey Woman and her husband the alligator-skinned man. Freak shows continued as a source of carnival and circus entertainment into the 1970s, until it basically vanished.

The Dolls became a famous attraction while traveling by train with the Ringling show until 1956, when the circus temporarily halted. Briefly the family went on the road by trailer for two years with the Cristiani show, then returned to Sarasota where they jointly retired. The four continued to live together in a large home they had purchased in Sarasota, leading relatively private and moderate lifestyles, rarely traveling out of Florida again.

Grace Doll was the first of the four to pass away on November 8, 1970, at the age of seventy-one, and as in life, she was exhibited in death. Although she was cremated, three-feet-tall Gracie was laid out in a child-size casket for a funeral at the Wilson Funeral Home which was attended by many of her circus friends including Mrs. Emmett Kelly, the widow of the famous clown, and other little people who worked as Munchkins in *The Wizard of Oz*. Her friend and fellow Munchkin, Frank Cucksey, not only paid his respects, but also described Gracie and the Dolls to a reporter: "Tell them Gracie Doll has gone to the Big Lot. That's what we circus people call heaven. The midget acts are gone now. But in their day, the Doll family was the greatest and they played the biggest circuses in the state.

"You see, Gracie Doll was magic," Cucksey continued. "Gracie could stand in front of millions of big people and when they saw her, something happened. They saw this tiny person in front of them, dancing, singing, laughing. And she turned the big people into little people. She made them children once again. She was a very special person. I will miss her."

Gracie's ashes were scattered around the rose bushes she planted in the yard of their Sarasota home on Bee Ridge Road. Daisy died on March 15, 1980, at age seventy-two; Harry died at the age of eighty-four on May 4, 1985. Tiny Doll, now in her nineties, still resides in the home she and Harry shared for several years. Although her health is good and she's quite fond of *The Wizard of Oz*, in recent years she has declined all invitations to attend *Oz* festivals around the country and her failing eyesight prevents her from handling fan mail anymore.

"My traveling days are over," she says, contentedly. "I'm stayin' put."

LEWIS CROFT, also known as "Idaho" Lewis, came from—you guessed it—and still resides there. Lewis, born on May 2, 1919, in Shelley, Idaho, was the smallest of six brothers and two sisters. He stood three feet eight when he played a soldier in *Oz*, but he has grown to

"Idaho" Lewis Croft holds the original Munchkin soldier's vest he wore in *Oz*. A fan from Kansas owns the tiny stitched piece of history, which Lewis admits wouldn't fit anymore.

An unidentified friend poses with a group from the Harvey Williams midget troupe, circa 1934. (L–R): Alta Stevens, Grace Williams, Carolyn Granger, Lewis Croft, and Hildred Olson.

about four feet nine—almost out of the range to be considered a little person.

Touring with the Harvey Williams group back in the 1930s, Idaho Lewis just a teenager and was never without his guitar. He joined the troupe while at the Cleveland Exposition in 1936. "A Christmas show that winter was the start of my career in show business."

After *Oz,* he worked in a machine shop in Idaho and later worked for the parks department in his city and the R. T. French Company until his retirement. He was married in 1948 to another little person, Delores Del Rio, and had two sons. He was widowed in 1978 and remarried in 1984 to his wife, Eva, who accompanied him to many *Oz* events in the 1990s. Lewis,

now a widower in his eighties, is fully retired and living in an assisted-living residence where everyone is aware they are in the presence of a Munchkin. He's still quite a mild-mannered gentleman, despite all of the attention.

As for his stint as a Munchkin, Lewis says, "Meeting all the stars and being with Judy Garland was the most incredible thing. There in California I stayed at the Culver Hotel and roomed with Emil Kranzler. It was a job, and I never in any way thought it would become this big."

AUGUST CLARENCE SWENSEN was born on December 29, 1917, in Austin, Texas. He was the smallest of five brothers and one sister. Four-feet-six-inch Clarence (nicknamed "Shorty") began a career in show business when he appeared at the Dallas Texas Centennial of 1936.

"In 1937 I was supposed to be in Stanley R. Graham's All-Midget Circus in San Antonio working with Christy Ball's elephants, as well as playing the saxophone and drums with a band," he says of the indefinite engagement. "After nearly eight weeks of rehearsals, we opened for a day and a half, when we were shut down because of monsoon rains."

Not long after, he hopped a train and headed to Hollywood to appear in *The Terror of Tiny Town;* a few months later he landed the role of a Munchkin soldier in *The Wizard of Oz.* Directly following, he worked in an ape costume in the film *Tarzan Finds a Son!* (1939) with Johnny Weissmuller, whom he describes as a "very nice gentleman—not the star type at all." During this period Clarence says his height was around four feet one.

When World War II broke out he went to Kelly Field Air Force Base in San Antonio, Texas, where he worked for four years as a radio technician. From 1945 through 1973 he worked at the University of Texas Research Center as an electronic technician.

Clarence married his sweetheart, Myrna Myrle Clifton, in 1945. Myrna is a most extraordinary little person in that she is the off-spring of midget parents—quite a rarity in the annals of recorded medical science. "Doctors and researchers keep saying that midgetism is not inherited," Myrna explained.

Considering this type of dwarfism is a medical condition caused by a malfunctioning pituitary gland, somehow the condition was not only transmitted from Myrna's family, but also passed on to her and Clarence's children and grandchildren. Clarence and Myrna had three daughters, two of whom are small in stature. They admit that when they became grandparents, they were curious as to what the future would hold for their grandkids. "One of our grandchildren—we think—would have been small," says Myrna. "He showed all the signs, but his parents took him in for hormone treatments, and he grew."

Medical science should be grateful that Clarence and Myrna are the patient, thoughtful type, genuinely concerned about the human race and those presented with this type of challenge in life. Several years ago the couple submitted themselves to an extensive battery of tests administered at the respected Johns Hopkins Hospital. "We were like guinea pigs," says Myrna, laughing, "and they still don't know why it is passed through our family."

The Swensens reside today in Texas just outside of Austin, disproving the old adage about dimensions and Texas, you might say. They attest, however, to the tune that Texans are deep in heart.

It wasn't until 1989, Oz's golden anniversary, that Clarence—the authentic Munchkin of the family—was reunited, after all those years, with some of the other little folks with whom he worked in the movie. It was the start of a whole new chapter in his life, something out of left field, he admits. In the ensuing years Clarence and his wife have traveled the country and attended many Oz festivals, and he has appeared on television programs such as The Maury Povich Show as well as in a variety of

A group of Munchkin men board a studio tram at MGM in December 1938. Clarence Swensen (squatting on right) remembers those early morning calls all too well.

television documentaries about the making of Oz. You can spot him in his tailored Munchkin soldier costume, which perfectly replicates the original wardrobe he wore in the film, right down to the striped fez-like hat with a fuzzy plume atop. "It's the fans who have made us stars," Clarence points out, "and we Munchkins are grateful for that."

Munchkin Clarence Swensen and his wife, Myrna, at Chesterton, Indiana's, *Oz* Fest in 1995. (Photo by Dan Thome)

Many of the male Munchkins found work immediately after *Oz* as apes in the film *Tarzan Finds a Son!* starring Johnny Weissmuller. (Courtesy of Clarence Swensen)

"PEOPLE COME AND GO SO QUICKLY HERE"

Sadly, my search for the Munchkins led me to many of the ensemble who had passed away, and this chapter inevitably expands. It would be virtually impossible to locate and list complete biographical information, whereabouts, and death dates on every single Munchkin actor who worked in the film. (A more comprehensive grid can be found at the back of the book.) Herein are some biographical sketches and appended interviews with Munchkin actors I was fortunate enough to contact in 1988, but who have died since the original edition of this book was published. I am happy to share the following unpublished materials and research data regarding additional Munchkin actors as well.

GUS WAYNE said he didn't grow much taller after *Oz,* "just wider," he said. At the height of four feet four, this Munchkin soldier was a lad of eighteen when he left New Jersey with his pal Leon Polinksy to make *The Wizard of Oz.* "I was very young at the time and the money sounded good. So I was gone. I had a ball."

Gus resembled a miniature Jackie Gleason, with a suave style to match. He and his wife of more than thirty years, Olive Brasno, also a little actress, lived in Florida for more than twenty years. Gus and Olive argued with the bite and humor of Ralph and Alice Kramden in *The Honeymooners.*

Olive, who wasn't quite as tall as Gus, said she and her two brothers, who were also midgets, were offered roles in *The Wizard of Oz* as well, but declined. "They offered seventy-five dollars a week, and in vaudeville we were

In the early 1960s, Gus Wayne was "Mr. Lucky," a wandering mascot in the Las Vegas casino.

During the 1940s, Gus Wayne dressed as the Philip Morris bellboy and cried out the famous line, "Call for Philip Morris!" on radio and for promotional tours around the country.

Company in their elaborate display at World's Fair exhibits, and also boxed at the Steel Pier alongside other acts like Abbott and Costello and the Three Stooges.

For seven years he put on a bellhop uniform, cupped his mouth, and shouted "Caaaallll for Philip Morrrrrisssss!" This line became a national catchphrase in the 1940s and '50s. (The original Philip Morris midget was Johnny Roventini, and it was he who performed in most of the national television commercials and opened the *I Love Lucy* episodes each week with the catchphrase.) As one of the little bellhops delivering the line on radio and television and in personal appearances, Gus was one of only a half dozen little guys to officially promote Philip Morris cigarettes on tour.

Gus then moved on to Piper Aircraft, where he was a small-parts mechanic until he retired in the 1970s in Florida with Olive. They had no children. Before Gus's health prevented him from traveling, he and Olive made a few rare appearances at *Oz* festivals. Once, Gus and a few fellow Munchkins were in the studios of KMOX radio in St. Louis for an interview that was to promote an appearance. During the drilling, the host asked, "How much did you all get paid for making *Oz*?"

Never sharper, Gus quipped, "We got paid about as much as we're gettin' right now."

Gus added, "When we were making the movie, I thought for sure it was gonna be a hit. Especially the songs; they were out of this world. Truthfully," he said in 1988, "would you believe I haven't seen the whole picture?"

Gus spent the last three years of his life in a Florida nursing home, the victim of a stroke that affected his memory and his mind, but not his mobility. It was distressing to the family and mostly to Olive, as Gus rarely recognized anyone. Olive tried to keep a positive attitude, but inevitably she grew depressed over Gus's deterioration and wanted to give up, she said. Being separated was devastating to them. Gus died of

making a hundred and fifty." Olive, part of a renowned vaudeville act called Buster Shaver, Olive & George, also worked in films. She and her little brother George appeared in such films as *The Mighty Barnum* (1934) and *Charlie Chan at the Circus* (1936). In the latter film, she and her brother played a married couple. You can also spot Olive appearing with Shirley Temple in *Little Miss Broadway* (1938) and in memorable scenes opposite Spanky McFarland in the Our Gang short *Shrimps for a Day* (1934). Olive danced with Donald O'Connor at the Sahara Hotel in Las Vegas during the 1950s and 1960s. O'Connor said of Olive: "She was one of the finest dancers I ever worked with. Working with her on the stage I forgot she was a little person. She suddenly became six feet tall."

For Gus, *Oz* was just a portion of a career in the entertainment industry. He worked as a costumed "baker" for the Sunshine Biscuit

Gus Wayne feasting on a Dunkin' "Munchkin" Donut.

Munchkin Gus Wayne and his wife, Olive Brasno, in their Florida home in 1988. Brasno turned down the role of a Munchkin because she was making more money on the road with her act.

heart failure on January 23, 1998. Olive was frail and in ill health at the time and was not made aware of Gus's passing; just two days later, she died of heart failure in a Florida hospital. Maybe she knew after all.

HARRY MONTY was still doing pushups at age ninety. Yes, it was true. He maintained a healthy diet most of his life and remained very trim, well built, and he exercised regularly. Harry stopped lifting weights years ago, but in his younger years a larger person would have thought twice before tangling with him.

Born Hymie Lichenstein in Poland ("but it belonged to Russia," he says), Harry came to America with his parents and four brothers (all average-sized) when he was about five years old; the family settled in Dallas, Texas, where Harry grew up. After some schooling he became interested in acrobatics. In the 1920s he and his vaudeville partner had an acrobatic act called Monty and Carmo, playing vaudeville theaters for nearly a decade. The team gained notoriety and worked many theaters in Chicago and New York before their comedy and balancing act was featured in the "Music Box Revue" in Hollywood, which starred Morton Downey Sr. Eventually, Monty and Carmo were signed with the famous Franchon and Marco circuit and toured all across the country for approximately three years. "We broke up around the Depression," said Harry.

For most of his life, Harry stood four feet five, three inches taller than he did when he played a Munchkin villager and a Winged Monkey in *Oz*. "For the Winged Monkeys, they put a harness on us and we swooped down to the ground, one after another," he said. "I remember one of the other monkeys was Buster Brody, but most of the others were a bit taller than me. This scene only took about a day to film."

Despite the story that a few of the actors who played monkeys crashed to the floor when their support cable snapped, he doesn't recall having any fear of being suspended. But after all, he was on his way to becoming one of Hollywood's busiest midget stuntmen.

After *Oz* Harry went directly into another film, doubling for Johnny Sheffield in *Tarzan Finds a Son!* (1939). "I had to fly forty feet in the air swinging on a rope," he said. "Lucky I was an acrobat." Eventually, his career was carved from such abilities. He later landed stunt and doubling jobs for some of Hollywood's finest. "I doubled Margaret O'Brien in several movies," Harry says. "I walked around MGM in a dress and a wig and makeup like a little girl, and I got kidded a lot." Dressed as little O'Brien, Harry says one scene involved his skating on one skate across the room and crashing into a wall.

"In *Bad Bascomb* I was dressed like little Margaret O'Brien again, and they set me on an oxen and let me go into the deep water," Harry said of the 1946 western. "Then they shot me off of the oxen and into the Jackson River, a very fast river in Wyoming.

"I've done all kinds of stunts in my career," he said. "I've fallen down steps fifteen feet high. They used to drag me from horses all over the place. In the movie *Swiss Family Robinson* I had to fall off an elephant, and in another scene they tied a rope around an ostrich and the other end of the rope around me. Then they hit the ostrich, and it ran and pulled me about five hundred feet.

"I had a lot of close calls, but I never had any broken bones," said Harry. "I padded up and figured the stunts out first."

Additional film credits (on camera and as a stuntman) include: *Hellzapoppin'* (1941), *Tarzan's New York Adventure* (1942), *Ride 'Em Cowboy* (1942), *See My Lawyer* (1945), *George White's Scandals* (1945), *Crack-Up* (1946), *Invaders from Mars* (1953), *River of No Return* (1954), *The Court Jester* (1956), *Mysterious Island* (1961), *How the West Was Won* (1962), *Our Man Flint* (1966), *Planet of the Apes* (1968), *Hello Dolly!* (1969), *Papillon* (1973), and *Hometown USA* (1979). His television credits include: *The Adventures of Superpup, Bonanza, Bewitched, Daniel Boone, Lost in Space, H. R. Pufnstuf, Lidsville, Buck Rogers in the 25th Century,* and a string of commercials.

Harry was fully retired and lived a very simple life in a Hollywood apartment for the last fifteen years of his life. He received fan mail from around the world due to his work in *Oz,*

Harry Monty, midget stunt double, fifty-three inches and eighty pounds in 1945. (Courtesy of Harry Monty)

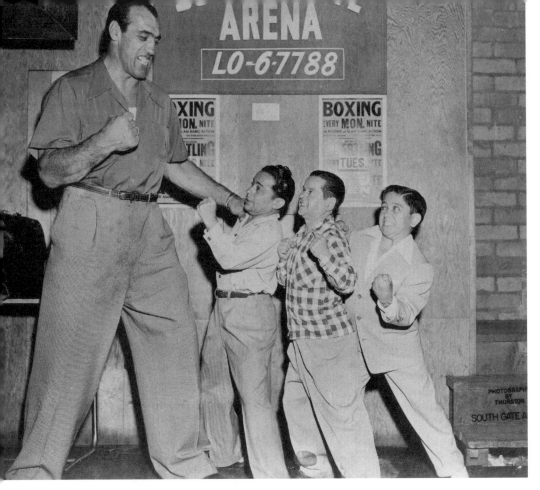

Famous fighter Primo Carnera puts his dukes up for this gag shot with "The Wrestling Midgets," Harry Monty, Billy Curtis, and Jerry Maren.

Tiny Doubles: Munchkin Harry Monty doubled for dwarf actor Jerry Austin in the film *Saratoga Trunk* (1945).

Harry Monty holds a vintage portrait of him and his partner from their vaudeville acrobatic act.

and he accommodated as many autograph requests as he could. Harry came out of retirement and appeared in front of cameras only one time, in 1997, for an interview that took place in his Hollywood apartment. Joined by fellow Munchkins Jerry Maren and Margaret Pellegrini, the three little actors reminisced about *The Wizard of Oz* for a local television news reporter, and it remained Harry's final interview. He died of natural causes on December 28, 1999.

MURRAY WOOD was born on June 12, 1908, in Nova Scotia and started his career in show business by singing with Kate Smith onstage in New York. Since his teens, he had aspired to become an entertainer and went to New York to become a tap dancer and a singer. "I never took a step back in my career," Murray boasted. "I was successful all the way."

For most of his adult life, he stood four feet two (and in later years grew to about four feet six, his height when he married Jean Lanier, also a performer, but of average height). In *Oz*, Murray played one of the city fathers in the mayor's entourage, wearing a long, sky-blue

Harry Monty, at age ninety-two, held his original Munchkin villager wardrobe more than fifty years after he wore it in the film. The rare vest portion of his costume, made of felt, had been framed and preserved.

Munchkin Murray Wood had that certain air of savoir-faire in this unique publicity photo, circa 1940.

Florida, the pair performed together, headlining in hotels in southern Florida. Murray worked behind-the-camera as a stand-in for young actor Clint Howard for two years on the television series *Gentle Ben* (an offshoot from the 1967 motion picture *Gentle Giant*). One episode of *Gentle Ben*, written especially for Murray by Rance Howard (father of actors Ron and Clint), involved Murray in a rare on-camera dramatic performance. Dressed in cowboy togs and sporting white hair and beard like Colonel Sanders, Murray portrayed Matt Marlowe, a tiny, conniving carnival owner bent on purchasing—or stealing—the Florida town's talented bear for a wrestling act.

Murray continued to perform on local radio and television shows, occasionally doing bits with his pal Jackie Gleason, another famous Miami resident. Around several Florida hospitals he was known as "Tiny" the clown, a little visitor who spent time coaxing smiles from bedridden children. For the last twenty years of his life, Murray and Jean were fully retired in Miami, responding to fan mail as much as his

robe. He said he loved working in *Oz*. "It was a fantasy, and I always thought the film would do well from the start. I watch it every year on television."

Murray recalled an incident with Leo Singer upon completion of filming. "On the last day of shooting, I went looking for Leo Singer for my paycheck, and I couldn't find him anywhere. Someone said he was up the street, and I went running after him. He was going away from the studio when I got to him. I'm not sure whether I would've gotten paid if I hadn't run after him."

Murray had been a nightclub and stage singer and a superior master of ceremonies since he was young, playing New York's Irish Village and many other stops around the country. He was also a member of Nate Eagle's Hollywood Midgets Troupe in later years.

During the 1960s when he and his wife, Jean, moved from Philadelphia to Miami,

Little by Little: Munchkin Murray Wood (right) doubled for young Clint Howard during the production of the CBS television series *Gentle Ben* (1967–1969).

Murray Wood portrayed an enthusiastic circus owner who wants to buy the bear in a memorable episode of TV's *Gentle Ben*.

Murray Wood in his late eighties. Murray was blessed with a natural head of dark hair all of his life—a trait inherent in a good percentage of midgets.

health would allow. Murray's failing eyesight, in addition to an excessive weight gain during the last fifteen years of his life, greatly restricted his mobility. Although he was invited to *Oz* functions, he gracefully declined; however, he occasionally received fans at his home and enjoyed telling stories from his career. Murray died in September 1999 after a long illness.

TOMMY COTTONARO was approached by midget actor Billy Curtis on the street one day in Hollywood. He was out of work when Curtis asked him about joining other little people for *The Wizard of Oz.* Tommy heartily agreed, and thus a Munchkin villager was born.

"I almost didn't get to be in the movie," he said. "Leo Singer told me I was too tall and said they wouldn't need me. But later, at the studio, when some man was asking for all of the little people's social security numbers, I gave him mine, too, and they told me I was hired. Weeks later, when Singer realized that I had got in anyway, he just gave me a dirty look."

Tommy remembered one particular incident on the MGM lot: "Back then, I drove a 1934 Pontiac every day. One day we got out early, and it was raining cats and dogs. I had the priv-ilege of parking on the lot. Mickey Rooney, who was on the lot that day visiting Judy, had jacked up the rear end of my car. It was raining so hard that we all jumped into the car. I started it, put it into gear, and of course nothing happened. Mickey Rooney and some others were looking out a window at us laughing."

Back then Tommy was about four feet three, and later in life he stood four feet six. He was born on March 20, 1914, in Castrogiovanni, Italy, and came to the Buffalo, New York, area as an infant. After school, he worked in a number of restaurants and wine cellars before and after his fifteen-year stay in Hollywood, working in films and television. After *Oz,* he went directly into working as an ape in the MGM film *Tarzan Finds a Son!* (1939). Later he and many other little people worked with Danny Kaye in the classic comedy *The Court Jester* (1956). Remember the film's chant? "The pellet with

Pals Billy Curtis and Tommy Cottonaro in the MGM parking lot in 1938.

The original Munchkin wardrobe worn by Tommy Cottonaro in *The Wizard of Oz* went up for auction in 1997.

Munchkin Tommy Cottonaro, of Niagara Falls, New York, proudly held the second edition of this book in 1997. Cottonaro never attended any *Oz* festivals in his later years, but he was pleased nonetheless to have participated in the film. (Photo by Mike Mikicel)

127

At ninety-one, Johnny Leal of Ojai, California, was the oldest surviving Munchkin in 1996. (Photo by Juan Carlo)

was one of thirteen children. Being the only midget in a large family of average-sized children had its problems. As his relations describe, there was one instance when the other kids built a makeshift airplane for Johnny and shoved it off a small cliff. The pilot, little Johnny, emerged from the rubble relatively unscathed, but his mother wasn't too pleased about the aviation attempt.

Johnny began performing around 1921, working in a sideshow on the boardwalk in Long Beach, California. Later he worked briefly in films and portrayed an outlaw in *The Terror of Tiny Town,* and that same year, as a Munchkin villager in *The Wizard of Oz.* He continued to make show business appearances at various Midget Village attractions such as the Texas Centennial and World's Fair events,

the poison's in the vessel with the pestle."

In 1952 he met Elizabeth Billingsley, a little lady about his height, in Hollywood and the two were eventually married in 1955 in Erie, Pennsylvania. The couple moved back to Niagara Falls, New York, where Tommy worked in food and beverage management positions before retiring in 1980.

For some reason, Tommy shied away from attending any *Oz* festivals or functions in the 1990s and routinely sent regrets. He met with very few fans, but those who were fortunate enough to visit Tommy at his Niagara Falls home in his last years reported that he was of good cheer and gladly reminisced. Tommy died in February 2001.

JOHNNY LEAL, born on February 26, 1905,

Things were looking up for Johnny Leal in the 1940s. Leal was a midget rodeo performer from Southern California.

showing off his expertise with a rope, wrangling and performing tricks. He was called "the Tiny Will Rogers" in his act, and his girlfriend, Eleanor Stubitz, dressed as Mae West. The couple made the sideshow rounds until 1936 when Stubitz was killed in a tragic car accident that he witnessed. "He had planned to marry Eleanor," says Johnny's niece, Patty Cooke. "He was devastated when she died. He never did marry." Later Johnny worked for Lockheed Aircraft in the 1950s and retired in the 1960s.

Johnny was forty-one inches tall when he was thirty-two years old. Eventually he grew to just four feet. He lived with his sister, Rose Leal Ferard, for most of his adult life until he moved into a nursing facility in 1978, where he lived until his death at age ninety-five, the oldest surviving Munchkin at that time. Proud relatives nearby visited their Munchkin uncle regularly. He later oddly adopted a new nickname of "Charlie," and that's what most people called him.

Johnny Leal died November 9, 1996, in Ojai, California.

Before she was Fern Formica, she went by Johnnie Fern and Jeanette Fern in films.

FERN FORMICA, who was also known as Johnnie Fern McDill and then renamed Jeannette Fern by Leo Singer, sang à la Mae West as "Diamond Lil" when she was just a tot. "Mae West called me her miniature double," Fern said in a 1988 interview.

Fern joined Singer's Midgets shortly before *The Wizard of Oz* at the request of Singer himself, who spotted her talent for entertaining. She worked as one of his troupe in the Midget Village at the San Diego World's Fair and costarred in *The Terror of Tiny Town* (1938) with forty other midgets. Wearing a shiny black gown in the film, she wiggled her little hips and sang the song, "(Hey Look Out) I'm Gonna Make Love to You."

Fern was born in Oklahoma on January 17, 1925, "at ten-thirty in the morning on a Saturday," she said. MGM didn't realize she was only thirteen years old when she portrayed what she calls a "Munchkin Maid." She was cast as a Munchkin while working with Singer, and she stayed at his home while making the movie. "The film was like a wonderland," she remembered. The role seemed like the beginning of a good career, although that was not how she saw it.

"Career? Who knew what a career was? It was work. We were just trying to live!" Fern said. Looking back on her life, she was quite proud of the movie, and also of her one son and grandchildren, for whom she collected *Oz* mementos.

Fern was straight-shooting, irascible, and sixty-three years young when I interviewed her. Most noticeable was her uncanny resemblance to an older Lucille Ball, only in miniature. Fern

A young Fern Formica (aka Jeanette Fern) and her mother on the set of the film *The Terror of Tiny Town* in 1938.

plications with her lungs. In the last few years of her life emphysema caused her great breathing difficulties. In an issue of *Beyond the Rainbow Collector's Exchange,* Munchkin Margaret Pellegrini shared these memories of her friend, Fern:

The first time I met Johnnie Fern was on the set of *The Wizard of Oz.* Fern and I lost touch as she married and had a family and I did the same. Forty-five years later, in 1985, I met up with Fern again at the Denver airport. We were both going to what would become our first *Oz* get-together in Liberal, Kansas. This was a few years before we began going regularly to Chesterton, Indiana, and other cities for *Oz* festivals. She and another little lady, Hazel Resmondo, were in one of those carts rushing from one gate to another. I heard her

could skillfully balance a cigarette out of the side of her mouth while talking, just like Lucy. Living in Hemet, California, Fern owned and ran a ceramic shop, teaching all aspects of the craft. Her ceramic pieces were certifiably Munchkin-made.

Fern added, "When Judy Garland was on this talk show years later, she said a grievous thing about the Munchkins. She said, 'Oh those freaky little things.' I thought, my God, what has happened to Judy? The little people never harassed her. They didn't let us get that close to her. We were well-mannered and knew not to crowd the star. It was her own physical and mental condition that made her come out with a thing like that. How sad, but a lot of things in life are sad."

Fern Formica saddened many friends on January 23, 1995, when she passed away in a Hemet, California, nursing home just a week after her seventieth birthday. She was a heavy smoker with a deep voice and a history of com-

Munchkin Made: Fern Formica with some of her unique ceramic creations in 1990.

A delicate and talented ballerina since she was a young girl in Czechoslovakia, Nita Krebs was a perfect choice for the Lullabye League. (Courtesy of Anna Mitchell)

Nita Krebs dressed to the nines.

talking when her cart was coming down the terminal. When she came into view, I was standing there waiting. She yelled, "Oh, there's Margaret!" We kissed and hugged.

Fern was still the same gal I knew years ago, only wiser. It was Fern who had the first Munchkin replica costume made to wear at the festivals, and she inspired me to have mine made.

When you stepped inside **NITA KREBS**'s home, you could easily guess which Munchkin she played from the mementos of dancers on her shelves and the large oil painting of a pink-clad ballerina hanging prominently. Nita had dual roles of prominence in *Oz*: She was the member of the Lullabye League on the left, and near the end of the Munchkinland scene she was the woman in a green dress who darts out and says, "Follow the Yellow Brick Road" as Dorothy prepares to leave.

This tiny dancer, who was trained in ballet as

a child, entered the United States with Leo Singer. She was born on October 8, 1905, in Bodenbach, Czechoslovakia, "which was then Sudetenland, and now it is Czechoslovakia again," she explained in 1988 in her high-pitched, tiny voice with a lilt. When she spoke, the hint of her accent only added to her dainty appearance.

Nita was eighty-two years old and a frail forty-five pounds when she was interviewed for this book. She retired to Florida in the 1950s after a long life of performing in vaudeville and stage shows with Singer's Midgets and, later, Nate Eagle's midget troupe. After *Oz* she did not grow any; she has remained three feet eight, a height that did not inhibit her work at all.

In their 1934 book *It's a Small World,* authors Bodin and Hershey described Nita's early days:

Unlike the generality of Central European parents of midgets, Nita's father and mother accepted the fact of her affliction with understanding and sympathy. They lavished love upon her. She was always a delightful child, sprite-like in a golden way. She seemed to have been born to dance. When little more than an infant she pirouetted with elfin grace. At nine, her parents put her in charge of Bodenbach's best dancing teacher. In four years she was an accomplished dancer. The art was an obsession with her; scarcely a waking moment passed that she did not dance. She was the perfection of grace.

Krebs later explained in interviews that the only job she could find "was dancing with the children's chorus in an opera house, and I loved the opera house, but I wanted to do something more with my life." When she was twenty-six she visited Prague and saw a show featuring a troupe of midgets. "There were all those adult people, my size, on that stage," she said in a 1990 interview. "I can't describe what it meant to me to learn that I was not alone." It wasn't long before Nita was brought to the attention of Leo Singer, who signed her immediately, and in 1928 she came to America along with Singer's company. She became one of Singer's best, and he favored her for it.

"She did have one vice," says friend Anna Mitchell. "Breakfast in bed. She became accustomed to this when she was on tour staying at the finer hotels. It became something of a treat throughout her life."

Nita was a consummate professional, mastering many types of dance including the Adagio, Russian, Can-Can, and her specialty, the "toe-strut." Although most of her career was spent touring, she took time out to appear in a few films: *They Gave Him a Gun* (1937), *The Terror of Tiny Town* (1938), *The Wizard of Oz* (1939), and *Three Wise Fools* (1946).

In mid-1938, while completing an extensive tour of the Hawaiian islands, Nita, along with the rest of Singer's troupe, was called back to the mainland to prepare for filming what

Little Billy Rhodes, Nita Krebs, and Billy Curtis on the set of *The Terror of Tiny Town*, May 1938. All three eventually became Munchkins in *Oz*.

Nita Krebs poses for a snapshot at the Ringling Brothers circus museum in 1959.

became two of the most unique motion pictures in history: *The Terror of Tiny Town* and, of course, *Oz*. In *Tiny Town* she was a dance-hall girl and gun moll. In one scene she descends from the saloon stairway in a long gown and sings a solo, "The Wedding of Jack and Jill."

When rehearsals began for *The Wizard of Oz*, Krebs had already been at the studio for days "modeling clothes for the wardrobe ladies," as she said. "I modeled different costumes so they could pick out the ones they wanted the Munchkins to wear."

She recalled vividly one particular moment on the set: "I remember this so well. I'll never forget this. There was this little body of water—a pond. And I was tired, I suppose. I was sitting down, and the costumes we had were long, and my costume dipped right into the water. They were ready to shoot the scene. We always had ladies around to help with the costumes, and one came over. Whatever was wet, she chopped if off. She snipped it right off!"

Nita always had fond thoughts about Judy Garland. "She sat down and talked with the little people," she said. "There was a popular pink crocheted poodle at the time, and I made one for Judy and gave it to her."

As for Leo Singer's money management for the Munchkins, Krebs maintained a supportive view of her former employer. She told a reporter for the *Bradenton Herald* in 1990: "People made a big deal of the fact that Mr. Singer kept part of our pay. They forget that we were under contract to him, and we worked regularly as singers and dancers. Mr. Singer was like a father to us. When a new girl joined the troupe, Mr. Singer had a fur coat waiting for her. During the filming of *The Wizard of Oz* we lived in a fine home Mr. Singer rented for us, and we rode everywhere in chauffeured limousines."

Anna Cucksey Mitchell, a close friend to Nita, noted that the elder trouper retired around 1960, "but could still dance circles around the younger members of the troupe.

Longtime friends Anna Mitchell and Munchkin Nita Krebs en route to an *Oz* appearance in Minnesota in 1989.

She built her Sarasota house in 1949 as her winter home while she traveled with the troupe about eight months of the year. When she retired, it was time for her to start taking it easier. After all, she was fifty-five by then. Nita also took a part-time job in the gift shop at the Ringling Brothers Circus Hall of Fame."

In 1990, nearing the end of her life, Nita attended two *Oz* reunions, accompanied by Anna Mitchell. In Liberal, Kansas, Nita was escorted center stage and introduced to a theater full of fans. As graceful as ever, she tilted her head and poised her hand beautifully in the air; her tiny frame was like a dot in the single spotlight shining on her. "I had a feeling it would be her final bow," says Mitchell with a tear in her eye. "She loved that moment."

Nita Krebs died of a heart attack on January 18, 1991, at her home in Sarasota, Florida. Friends gathered a few days later for a memorial. "It seemed it would rain," says Mitchell, "and later in the day the sky cleared. In the afternoon a rainbow appeared over the sun; we all knew it was our message that God was pleased and Miss Nita was home."

DOLLY KRAMER was once labeled "Queen of

the Midgets" and "America's Tiniest Bombshell of Song," partly due to her strong physical resemblance to famed singer Kate Smith.

Dolly was in her late eighties when this interview was conducted in 1988, although I couldn't have guessed, and she wouldn't divulge; it was irrelevant to her. She lived in a comfortable Miami Beach high-rise apartment, and "loved the climate" there in the southern tip of Florida. She was four feet tall and said she had only grown a few inches since portraying a Munchkin villager.

It happened like this: "Singer contacted our group," Dolly said of the troupe she and her husband, Henry, had. "We went out to California to do the movie. Since Singer had the contract with MGM, we had made a special deal with him."

Of the filming Dolly said, "I remember that it was an especially cold November in California that year. As soon as we had to do a scene, the lights went up. In the morning the lights went up and made us warm. We wanted that in the morning."

Dolly and Henry married when she was sixteen and he was two years older. They were high school sweethearts in Brooklyn. She changed her real name, Henny, to Dolly since "Henny" sounded too much like her husband's name. Henry, an average-sized man, managed a group of performing midgets with Dolly as their lead singer and dancer. They traveled across the United States playing countless nightclubs and show houses during the strong vaudeville era.

Dolly lived independently in the high-rise apartment for many years after Henry died in 1981, and she kept busy with a women's club at the complex. In the late 1980s a minor stroke had slightly affected her speech, limiting the movement of her mouth on one side. "I can't entertain anymore because of my health, but I'm doing okay," she said. When this book was originally published in 1989, Dolly was unable

A group of married Munchkins on the MGM back lot pose for a snapshot. The husbands stand behind their wives. (L–R): Henry and Dolly Kramer, Charles and Jessie Kelley, Johnny and Marie Winters, Prince and Ethel Denis, and Harvey and Grace Williams. (Courtesy of Margaret Pellegrini)

Dolly Kramer, retired in Miami Beach in 1989.

HENRY KRAMER
presents
MIDGET STARLETS
of
1942

9647

Bud Kirkendall - Mary Lou Berryman - Marcella Porter - Eddy Adams — Dolly Kramer — Margaret Williams - Mary Ellen Baker - Kyra Erricson

to attend any *Oz* reunions but was grateful for the invitations. Despite failing health the last few years of her life, she replied to as much fan mail as possible and enjoyed autographing pictures of the Munchkins. She always said *The Wizard of Oz* was a highlight in her life.

Dolly died on July 9, 1995, of pneumonia; she was in her nineties.

Anna Mitchell (née Shoulter), who performed with Kramer's show, said: "Dolly had such a beautiful, powerful voice. She belted it out like Sophie Tucker. She taught me how to knit and sew and how to dress for performances. She was very classy."

HAZEL (DERTHICK) RESMONDO didn't quite make it to see the original edition of this book. It was a shame, since she was such a true disciple of *Oz,* perfectly comprehending how

much the motion picture meant to so many people—including herself. During the last years of her life, Hazel had lost most of her hearing, but none of her zest for life. She loved to write letters to fans from the desk of her little room at the Eastern Star retirement home in Los Angeles. Her stationery had rainbows and yellow brick roads, and her words were just as decorative. She'd conclude each enthusiastic correspondence with "I'm off to see the Wizard. Bye for now." In her room dangled rainbow wind chimes, and her bed linens flashed with rainbow designs. All around her room were autographs from Judy Garland, Billie Burke, and Ray Bolger as well as photographs of herself with *Oz* star Jack Haley. Memorabilia from her days in film and television plastered the walls and filled every corner.

Hazel was in her mid-eighties when inter-

Hazel Derthick Resmondo worked as young Jerry Mathers' stand-in for *Leave it to Beaver* during the 1950s. When Mathers grew and she did not, the studio fitted her with lifts.

Munchkin Hazel Derthick Resmondo met Marilyn Monroe while the star was making the film *Bus Stop*.

viewed, standing a whopping four feet four ("I was one of the bigger ones," she said, recalling her weeks in *Oz*), and she could still proudly do the splits and stretch like an Olympic hopeful. It was a carryover from her days as a young toe dancer.

She loved to talk about *The Wizard of Oz,* and if you asked, she did her "Munchkin laugh," a high-pitched giggle. She never laughed discussing her Munchkin-like salary on the picture: "Singer hardly paid me anything. I only got five dollars a day, and some of the midgets told me to say something, but it didn't get me anywhere. There wasn't any union or guild or anything for us then. When I

complained, he said, 'If you don't like your job, you can go home.' I stayed, but I didn't know how to stand up for myself like I can now."

"I met some of Singer's midgets on a street in Hollywood, and I asked if they knew of any work," Hazel said when asked how she came to join the cast. "And they took my address. In the fall, I got a letter about the movie."

Her father drove her from their Hawthorne, California, home to the MGM studios in Culver City every day during the production. "The set was so beautiful, I started to cry," she said. If you look closely during the Munchkinland scene, you can see Hazel, a lone Munchkin villager who waves frantically as the Munchkins

Billie Burke autographed this portrait for Munchkin Hazel Derthick.

pour out of their village huts. "The director said wave, so I did," she said. "Everyone else stopped, but I guess I didn't."

In the mid-1980s, Hazel and two other Munchkins met in Liberal, Kansas, for what would become the first of many *Oz* festivals there. It was Hazel's only visit back home. She was originally from the Oklahoma panhandle just a few miles from Kansas, from where the fictional Dorothy and Toto were transported by cyclone to Munchkinland.

She told a reporter in 1985, "Oh, I've seen several real twisters. There was one that was equal to the cyclone in *The Wizard of Oz*. My dad, my mother, and I had been uptown to eat at the cafe, and we saw it coming down the long street of our town. We ran home, and we held the door shut, just in time! That cyclone practically lifted our house right off the ground!"

Even with hearing aids conversation was not audible to Hazel, but she could talk plenty. "I'm from Oklahoma. Okies love to talk," she explained. Her eyesight had slipped a bit over the years as well, but she could write, and she kept plugging along with her mounting mail. Her bulging photo albums, which she proudly opened, were chock full of pictures from films she had worked in. "I call it Hazel's museum," she said.

For the most part, she worked as a stand-in for children, as in the case of *The Sound of Music* (1965). She also worked in the films *Pygmy Island* (1959), *Dance with Me Henry* (1956), and *The Bad Seed* (1956). Many pages of her scrapbook were devoted to shots of her and Jerry "The Beaver" Mathers from her nearly five-year stint as his stand-in on TV's *Leave It to Beaver.* Barbara Billingsley, who played June Cleaver, stayed in touch with Hazel over the years. "Hazel was such a loveable ham," says Billingsley, "and we all liked her so much. She stayed with us for years, first just Hazel, then with spike heels, and in the end she stood on an apple box. The Beaver wouldn't stop growing."

Of course, photographs of Hazel's late husband, Joe "Buster" Resmondo, were at her bedside in beautiful frames. Buster was a little person as well, whom she adored.

Hazel appeared on the *CBS Evening News* on January 30, 1989, in a story about the anniversary of *Oz.* A few weeks later she died of a massive stroke on February 13, 1989.

NELS NELSON remembered how he became a Munchkin: "A man called me and insisted on taking me down there to MGM. How he got my number, I'll never know. I lived in the [San Fernando] Valley, here."

Nels Nelson was born on November 24, 1918, in Port Wing, Wisconsin. When he was just a few years old, his family moved to Sweden, where his younger brother Lars was born. The family returned to southern California a few years later, where he remained.

Nels spent his seventeenth birthday in a rehearsal hall singing, "Ding Dong, the Witch Is Dead" with a hundred other midgets. Not a traditional birthday celebration, but he had a great time anyway, he said in a 1988 interview. Sometimes, he recalled, the fun was at the expense of other Munchkins.

"There was this one little guy. He wasn't too bright. He wanted a cigar real bad, so they sent

Hazel Resmondo lived the last years of her life comfortably in the Eastern Star Home in Los Angeles, surrounded by her show business memorabilia. She eagerly corresponded with fans of *The Wizard of Oz.* (Photo by Mark Collins)

him over to a false-fronted cigar store on the back lot. He stood there and stood there. He didn't understand. I think they had to go and get him, but we got a laugh out of it.

"The remarkable thing about those days," Nels recalled, "our meals were thirty-five cents for lunch. Good lunches." Prices may have risen, but oddly enough Nels's height did the contrary. "I was about four feet six then and now I'm about four feet three. I shrunk!" His height didn't affect his golf game at the time, a passion with him. He was in his second marriage, and Nels and his wife, Gloria, had two children.

After *Oz* Nels went into real estate with his brother but still worked in show business. Besides *Oz,* he appeared in the films *Ski Patrol* (1940), *Samson and Delilah* (1949), *The Greatest Show on Earth* (1952), *The Proud Rebel* (1958), and *The Wonderful World of the Brothers Grimm* (1962). He spent twelve seasons as a stand-in and stunt double for children on television's *Lassie* series.

Nels was injured in an episode of *Bonanza* (titled "Hoss and the Leprechauns"). The mishap occurred while hoisting another little person onto his shoulders for a scene. "Just then I felt my hip shift," he said.

That was it for acting, stunts, and show business. He got around slowly and carefully afterward, taking small steps (no pun intended) with the aid of a cane during his last years. He and Gloria (an average-sized woman) attended a handful of *Oz* events during the anniversary season, and both truly loved meeting the fans. He was never known to turn down a fan who wished an autograph. His mild temperament and quick sense of humor were a treat to those who had the pleasure of conversing with him.

On May 2, 1994, Nels died of an apparent heart attack, just hours after returning from Bay St. Louis, Mississippi, where he had participated in *Oz* promotional activities. He was the 115th Munchkin to pass away.

JEANE LaBARBERA was always known as "Little Jeane." She was just over twenty-four inches as a Munchkin villager. When interviewed for this book she was the tiniest of all the little people I met with, standing just under three feet tall with a cute pug face and a voice just as teeny and pleasing. She was, for me, a model of the Munchkins who stepped in front of that camera years ago, hardly growing at all since the movie was made. Her presence was an astounding sight merely because of her doll-like appearance and shy stature.

Handled by the William Morris Agency, Little Jeane "inched her way to the top" as she said, when it came to her theater work. Her appearance included shows at the London Palladium, the Hippodrome in New York, and a Broadway production of *Murder by Appointment.* Her scrapbook of clippings and photographs remained a treasured collection of her days in front of the footlights.

She and her husband, Robert Drake, were known as the Comedy Cut-Ups when they performed one of the most unique husband-and-wife acts together during the 1940s. He was six feet tall and she all of two. The Drakes were married for forty-seven years.

Nels Nelson (left) and Jerry Maren met in *Oz* and remained lifelong pals and golf buddies.

Husband-and-wife team Robert Drake and "Little Jeane" LaBarbera in a publicity still from their heyday.

Robert Drake and "Little Jeane" were married for forty years. Here, they posed in their Florida living room in 1988. Jeane was the tiniest Munchkin I interviewed for this book.

Born in Italy, Jeane received her schooling and grew up on Long Island. She was a concert violinist with her own custom-fitted instrument when she was discovered by an agent. That encounter led to a long and prosperous career on the vaudeville stage prior to *The Wizard of Oz*.

Despite the fact that her husband insisted she was never associated with "midget shows" and performed exclusively as a solo, the truth is that after making *Oz*, Jeane did appear at a few of the Midget Villages at World's Fair attractions, working for Leo Singer. Robert unceasingly distinguished his wife from other little people, referring to her as a "Lilliputian," which of course is a fabled characterization. He obviously liked the sound and novelty of the description much better. And she was extraordinary, because she was so tiny.

Interestingly, Little Jeane played opposite another *Oz* alumnus, Bert Lahr, in a popular burlesque sketch titled "Beach Babies," written by Jeane around 1924. It was so successful that the team toured together for several years. In a letter dated October 14, 1967, Bert Lahr wrote to Jeane requesting a transcript of the old routine and permission for his son, John, to reprint it in a book that was being prepared for publication (*Notes on a Cowardly Lion*). Lahr explained, "Everyone who has been contacted to help with the book has kindly offered their assistance not only out of affection for me, but a respect for the enterprise which tries to show burlesque, vaudeville, and Broadway from the 'inside.' As you know, most books about the theater are superficial and poorly documented. The reason it is important as a document is that it is a type of sketch which has not been preserved, and it would be valuable to see in order to understand the language as well as the 'tone' of the scene."

Jeane and her husband, Robert, retired in the 1950s to a home they had built in Tampa, Florida, leading a quiet life. Their activities were mild—eating early dinners at their favorite cafeteria in a nearby mall and watching the years go by. When I initially contacted them regarding this book, Robert Drake made it known he was reluctant for Jeane to be seen after so many years of retirement. It was an old show business ploy, actually, and his guard was let down once the in-person interview commenced. I think he wanted to make sure Jeane was secured a special place in the book.

In their large living room, filled with trinkets and statues from their travels, Little Jeane sat in a petite, customized easy chair upholstered in a spotted leopard fabric. It was her domain, a mere dot amongst the larger furnishings where she could feel comfortable and entertain without her feet dangling. I must admit, when I first met her, looked down, and shook her hand, I was startled to see such a small lady, obviously in her eighties, with a dash of bright lipstick on her smile. She looked a bit cartoonish, if that's appropriate. She was the size of a three-year-old. Amazing, to say the least.

Jeane stayed in touch with only one other Munchkin, Karl Slover, and together they attended a couple of *Oz* reunions in 1989 and 1990. They felt very comfortable around each other. She died of Alzheimer's disease on August 17, 1993, in a Tampa nursing home. Her husband, Robert, had died a year prior of heart disease.

ALTA STEVENS BARNES was born on August 28, 1913, in Minnesota. She was seventy-five years old, with a trembling voice and failing health when I interviewed her for this book. She chose a "good" day to talk, and she was anxious to help and contribute to the publication despite her illness. Foremost, she said she almost didn't make it in the movie.

"When our group got to Hollywood, they told Grace Williams and I that we were too tall," Alta said. "I was about four feet five at the time." (She grew only an inch after *Oz*.)

Alta Stevens
Barnes in 1989.

Luckily, when the studio realized they would need all the little people they could get—especially the little women—Alta and Grace were hired as Munchkin villagers. All in all, their slightly excessive height didn't matter.

Years later Alta married Roy Barnes (an average-sized man), raised their family, and retired in a nice home in the Los Angeles area. They adopted a daughter, Julie, and were quite proud of their one grandchild when I met them in 1989. Alta had stayed in close contact with Ruth Duccini, another Munchkin, over the years and spoke of her like a sister.

Reflecting on her career with the little people, Alta said she was proud that she worked for the San Francisco World's Fair in 1939 as the mistress of ceremonies in the Midget Village. Her bit parts in other motion pictures included *The Magnificent Ambersons* (1942), directed by Orson Welles, and *Beyond the Blue Horizon* (1942).

Alta still remembered the wonderment of *Oz:* "You'd walk on the set in the morning, and you thought you were dreaming. Everyone at MGM was so nice to us. They were all friendly."

Alta's health permitted her to attend just one Munchkin reunion at MGM studios in August 1989. It was a joyful day for her, all dressed up with her hair done. She was honored to receive the recognition and applause from the studio employees and fans who gathered. Alta died just two weeks later on September 3, 1989.

EMIL KRANZLER, a Munchkin villager, was with the Harvey and Grace Williams group when they crossed the country and headed to California for the film. Emil performed with them for three summers after *Oz,* then returned home to his family's farm in Akaska, South Dakota, where he was born in 1911. (He later lived in Minneapolis.)

When interviewed for this book, Emil was in his second marriage, and chose not to discuss his former marriage much (he was wed to a taller woman, and the couple had a son and daughter of average size). He had been married to his first wife for thirty-five years until her death.

His second wife, Marcella Porter, also a little person, performed with Kramer's Midgets when she was younger. Emil and Marcella were married on March 11, 1985. Happily retired, they lived in Tempe, Arizona. Emil stood four feet six and fancied huge, Texan-sized cowboy hats. In his later years he was a maintenance worker and repaired bicycles part time, but he said he never knew how to ride one. He and Marcella were active members of the Little People of America, attending several national conventions.

When asked what his strongest memory of *Oz* was, he answered, "I really got screwed good when I did *The Wizard of Oz.* I think I only got twenty dollars a week. I was bashful then, and it was the first and only movie I ever played in."

When the anniversary of *Oz* came around, Emil and Marcella became regular guests of the festivals. Although initially surprised at the whole notion that people would want his autograph, Emil loved inscribing photographs and posing for pictures, and he especially looked forward to the traveling during his final years. He was a simple man, kind, with a genuine sense of humor and a wandering eye for pretty ladies.

EMIL KRANZLER
1910 - 1993
I'M OFF TO SEE
THE WIZARD

Munchkin Emil Kranzler's fitting memorial in Scottsdale, Arizona.

Kayo Erickson, Emil Kranzler, Matthew Raia, and Jimmy Hulse smile for a snapshot while in California making *Oz*. (Courtesy of Margaret Pellegrini)

Emil Kranzler loved meeting fans and selling autographed pictures at *Oz* festivals like this one in Liberal, Kansas, in 1991.

He never precisely put it all into perspective, but he alluded to the fact that he had a good time partying during the off-hours of *Oz* and he knew exactly who the other partygoers were, too. When he and Munchkin Gus Wayne reunited in 1989, exactly fifty years after the film, the two looked at each other and just laughed aloud and hugged, nodding and grinning like cats who had caught the canary. They had a secret.

Emil died in his sleep on April 7, 1993, due to congestive heart failure following a bout with pneumonia. He was eighty-two.

When the call came, **GARLAND "EARL" SLATTEN** heartily welcomed the offer to do a movie since he and his roommate, Harry Monty, were living in Chicago and both unemployed. "We were on skid row at the time," he admitted hesitantly. "It was hard for us then because small people sometimes can't find jobs." His height in 1938 was three feet six, but he had risen to four feet ten in the ensuing years, basically out of the classification of midget.

Garland had portions of two fingers missing from his left hand, blown off in an accident involving dynamite caps. "I tell kids that it happened from firecrackers so they won't be so foolish to play with explosives when they're young."

Born in Walters, Oklahoma, in 1917,

Garland—sometimes called "Earl"—was twenty-one when he marched past Dorothy on the yellow bricks as a Munchkin soldier. "Half of 'em were out of step," he laughed, "but not me. One time I moseyed over and talked to Margaret Hamilton. It was just small talk, but I remember it well. She was a very nice lady. Also, it was torture trying to eat with that fish-skin on your face. It makes your face stiff. I didn't like that."

After *Oz,* he joined the Dolly and Henry Kramer group of performing midgets and worked for a few years on the road. When interviewed in 1988, he was retired with his wife, Edna, in Sequim ("it rhymes with swim"), Washington. He enjoyed his status as a Munchkin and could hardly believe so much time had passed since he participated. Aside from an occasional letter or holiday card exchanged with fellow Munchkin Margaret Pellegrini, he had not stayed in touch with any little people from the film.

Garland's wife committed suicide in 1994, and soon after he decided to sell his home and travel in an RV. In the early months of 1995 he visited friends in Arizona and Texas and returned to Washington, where he died on April 30, 1995, of complications from a stroke. Garland was cremated, and his ashes were spread over Deer Park in Washington State.

BETTY TANNER was approached in New York by an agent who requested that she work as a Munchkin in *The Wizard of Oz.* She hailed from Lynn, Massachusetts, of Polish parents Kazimierz and Marcyanne Toczylowski. Betty was the third of four children and the only little person in the family. "I remember when I was in the eighth grade, I was shorter than the kids in the first grade." Her height then was three feet eight, but she had increased to four feet three later in life.

Her real name was Betty Toczylowski, but in vaudeville she shortened her name. In *Beyond*

Garland Slatten in Sequim, Washington, in 1993.

the Rainbow Collector's Exchange she related much of her own background:

I wanted to be a dancer and to be on the stage. I took dancing lessons for eight years. Later I met my partner, and we teamed up as Betty Tanner and Buddy Thomas. We got a contract to perform in Chicago for a two week engagement, and we ended up there for over a year. One day our agent called and asked me to come to his office. Buddy and I went, and there we met Leo Singer. He was looking for little people to be in *The Wizard of Oz.* Of course I was delighted to go, but I insisted that Buddy accompany me, and he did. We had very nice accommodations. We went by Pullman and had separate hotel rooms.

The most memorable thing about *Oz* was "all the little people," said Betty. "I couldn't believe there were so many of us." After the film Betty and Buddy headed back East and on to New York. In August 1939 the two traveled abroad and performed at the London Palladium. "It was frightening being in Europe at that time," she said. "Some friends and people at the American Embassy helped us secure ship tickets home."

After performing on the road for many years, Betty rejoined her family and settled back in Lynn. She took up hairdressing and graduated with a hairstyling degree, working in that profession until she retired in 1980. She never married.

It wasn't until 1989 that Betty was reunited with any of the Munchkins from *Oz*. Accompanied by her sister Anne, Betty began

Betty Tanner in a striking publicity shot, circa 1937.

A little looker and a mighty entertainer, Betty Tanner is shown here on stage doing her act in the 1930s.

attending festivals around the country. Rekindling old friendships and staying in touch with friends and fans from coast to coast was a great joy for her right up until the end. "Toz," as she sometimes signed letters, was a lady of extraordinary humor and delicate beauty.

Betty died from a heart ailment on November 8, 1994, in a Boston, Massachusetts, hospital. She was seventy-eight.

JOSEPH HERBST met many other little people for the first time when he worked in the Chicago World's Fair in 1932. Then in 1938 he traveled from Joliet, Illinois, to Hollywood to play the sheriff in *The Terror of Tiny Town,* and headed back home afterward. He made a repeat trip just months later for a role as a Munchkin villager in *Oz*.

Munchkin Betty Tanner, age seventy-three, proudly displayed a copy of the original edition of this book in 1989. If you look closely, she is shown on the cover just behind the mayor.

After *Oz,* he returned home again and worked in his father's grocery store, but he still kept in touch with a few of the little performers he had met in California.

Just under four feet, Herbst, a quiet and gentle little fellow, remained in Joliet, eventually retired, and in 1988 was confined to his home as a result of a stroke. He died on July 6, 1993, at the age of eighty-five.

VICTOR WETTER was born in Metz in the Alsace-Lorraine region of France, emigrating to America with his parents in 1910. Victor became a citizen of the United States when he married Edna Moffit, also a little person, in 1942. (They met while performing at the 1936 Texas Centennial in Dallas.) Victor was about four feet tall when he played the captain of the marching army in front of the Munchkins' parade who helped Dorothy step into the carriage.

During his career as an entertainer, he worked many of the world's fairs during the 1930s and 1940s, as well as theaters and nightclubs. He and his wife, Edna, also appeared in *Northwest Mounted Police* (1940), directed by

Cecil B. DeMille. Other film credits for Victor include *The Howards of Virginia* (1940), *My Gal Sal* (1942), and *Mrs. Wiggs of the Cabbage Patch* (1942). After *Oz,* Victor and Edna and their little friends Nicky Page and Alyeene Cumming toured in an act called Tiny Troupers of Hollywood.

In 1945, Victor, Edna, and five other little people were employed by Walt Disney Studios to don cartoonish costumes and tour the Midwest for advance publicity of a re-release of *Snow White and the Seven Dwarfs.* In 1950 Victor and Edna opened a toy store in New Jersey, occasionally playing elves during the Christmas season and entertaining the kids on a huge, decorated set. The Wetters retired in the mid-1960s.

In the last several years of his life Victor suffered from Alzheimer's disease. As he was unable to think clearly, Edna was helpful in relating background information. "His memory slips a bit," she said in 1988, "but he still keeps his good appetite. Otherwise, his physical health is fine." The Wetters were living in New Jersey, where they had been for more forty years. They had no children.

Following a long illness Victor Wetter died on December 8, 1990, in a New Brunswick, New Jersey, hospital. He was eighty-eight. He was one of the oldest surviving Munchkins at the time.

BILLY RHODES, known professionally as "Little Billy," was one of the top midget actors in Hollywood during the 1930s and 1940s, with some fifty screen credits to his name. A pudgy fellow forty inches tall, Little Billy was one of the Boston Irish and somehow related to MGM casting director Billy Grady. Nepotism may have gotten this Hollywood midget some jobs in films, but his talent carried him the rest of the way. "He looked like the perfect example of a well dressed little man," remembers Jerry Maren. "He was a respectable guy, people

Victor Wetter and his younger, taller, brother Bernard in 1986. (Courtesy of Edna Wetter)

thought a lot of his talents as an actor." Little Billy became a respected actor in the Hollywood community and his devilish humor made him an unforgettable, longtime member in The Masquers Club. In *The Wizard of Oz,* Little Billy played the Munchkin barrister in a long purple robe who steadfastly proclaimed in the Mayor's face, "But we've got to verify it leeee-gally!"

Born August 15, 1894 in Lynn, Massachusetts, he began his career in vaudeville with Flo Ziegfeld and in George M. Cohan's Revue of 1916 in New York City. His first films were silents, *Oh Baby!* (1926) and *The Sideshow* (1928). He continued working in films: *Swing High* (1930), *The Slippery Pearls* (1931), *Polly of the Circus* (1932), *Rule 'Em and Weep* (1932), *They Never Come Back* (1932), *Make Me a Star* (1932), *Regular Trouper* (1932). He performed in many short subjects (two-reelers) in the early 1930s, including two memorable Three Stooges shorts. His first was the Oscar-nominated short *Men in Black* (1934), where he wore a wig and played a sick little chubby lady in the hospital waiting to be diagnosed by the Stooges. In *You Nazty Spy* (1940), a short that has become a favorite among Stooge fans, Little Billy played a huffy little messenger in this hilarious parody on Hitler and the Nazis. In 1932 he appeared with John Wayne in a twelve-episode serial titled *Shadow of the Eagle,* filmed at Republic Studios. Little Billy starred as the heavy, Bat Haines, in the all-midget western *The Terror of Tiny Town* (1938). His post-*Oz* films include: *Skimpy in the Navy* (1949), *The Court Jester* (1956) *Not Tonight Henry* (1961), and as Grumpy the Dwarf in *The Wonderful World of the Brothers Grimm* (1962). His final film appearance, some have said, was a little taste of life imitating art when he played a drunken man in the film *The Embracers* (1967). His television credits include appearances on several Red Skelton "spectaculars" (later called "TV specials"), the 1950s syndicated program *The Adventures of Wild Bill Hickok,* starring Guy Madison, and a Rip Van Winkle segment of *Shirley Temple's Storybook.*

Little Billy died in his Hollywood apartment from a stroke on July 24, 1967.

A longtime member of Hollywood's famous Masquers Club, a professional actors fraternity formed in 1925, Little Billy entertained at benefits with other Masquers, and was a fixture at club meetings—"mostly at the bar," says former Masquer Kay Kuter.

Kuter, who was a friend of Billy's and a pallbearer at his funeral, recalls an unusual incident at the sendoff: "Billy was buried in Holy Cross Cemetery," Kuter says, "and he was buried in a regular-sized casket. When we carried the casket to the burial site, we had to go up this hill and down again to get to the site. As we carried the casket up the hill, we all heard and felt a 'thump!' as Billy shifted in the casket. And on the way down the hill, we heard the thump again as his head knocked into the other end. We all couldn't help but laugh."

FRANK CUCKSEY had one of the most endearing roles in *Oz.* As Dorothy sat in her carriage, two Munchkins approached her to thank her for disposing of the wicked witch. Munchkin Leon Polinksy praises, "We thank you very sweetly for doing it so neatly." Frank Cucksey, wearing a tan coat, bows and seconds the toast: "You killed her so completely that we thank you very sweetly." Then he hands Dorothy a bouquet of Munchkin brushweed.

"Cookie," as Frank was known, was born in Brooklyn in 1919. He was one of the little people to board the bus in New York City and hit

Billy Rhodes was a veteran performer from the stage and films by the time he landed the role of the Munchkin barrister. (From the Nita Krebs collection)

Just months before *Oz,* "Little Billy" Rhodes made his second appearance with the Three Stooges in a short-subject, *You Nazty Spy.*

Appearing as Ralph Edwards' surprise guests on *This Is Your Life . . . Billy Barty* are Munchkins "Little Billy" Rhodes, Billy Curtis, and Jerry Maren (1960). Also pictured is Ruth Delfino Spiering. (Courtesy of Jerry Maren)

the roadways to California for a role in *Oz*. At that time he stood at three feet, but years later he grew to four feet two. During the 1940s he was a member of Nate Eagle's Midget Troupe, entertaining in clubs around the country. Frank also appeared in the film *It's a Small World* (1950). He eventually settled in Sarasota, Florida, where he worked for many years as a circus entertainer and as a member of the volunteer fire department. He retired from the fire department in 1978, but was still employed by the Circus Hall of Fame and the Ringling Museum of the Circus as a security guard, giving lectures and guided tours.

Frank died in September of 1984.

WILLIAM H. O'DOCHARTY was usually just called "W. H." He could be easily spotted in Munchkinland stationed on the back of the carriage that takes Dorothy to the town square. Look closely, and you'll see Dorothy turn her head and glance at little W. H. He answers with a cute grin between his pudgy cheeks.

Oz was W. H.'s second and final film appearance, directly following *The Terror of Tiny Town*

(1938). He was three feet six then, but had grown to four feet seven. In the late 1980s he was living with his mother, Lillian, who was in her nineties. He had never married.

Born on September 12, 1920, in Texas, he worked with a few of the midget shows and at

An Easter Sunday get-together with a group of little friends in the early 1950s. (L–R): Dottie Williams, Patty Maloney, Nita Krebs, Anna and Frank Cucksey. (Courtesy of Anna Mitchell)

With little W .H. O'Docharty standing at the back of the coach and George Ministeri driving, Dorothy gets whisked to her welcoming at the Munchkin City Hall. (Copyright © 1939 Loew's, Inc., renewed © 1966 by MGM) Inset, left, W. H. O'Docharty in 1988. Inset, right, George Ministeri, age sixty-seven, in 1980.

the Texas Centennial in 1936, then traveled with the Ruben and Cherry Circus before going to Hollywood for his film work.

Unfortunately, W. H. did not live to see the original Munchkin book. He died from double pneumonia on December 20, 1988, in a Corpus Christi, Texas, hospital. He was sixty-eight years old. The obituary for W. H. noted that he was a descendant of the O'Docharty family who "established the town of San Patricio, Texas, in the 1830s under the Empresarios. His great-great-grandfather, William O'Docharty, was the original surveyor of Corpus Christi, Texas."

GEORGE MINISTERI, a very handsome and well-built little person, appeared in a handful of films in the late 1930s: as the blacksmith and villain in *The Terror of Tiny Town*, as the coach driver and a Munchkin villager in *Oz*, and as an ape in *Tarzan Finds a Son!* He stood four feet five when he married his wife, Mary. They had three children and raised them in South Boston, Massachusetts.

Ministeri was born in the North End of Boston, but his family moved back to their native Italy soon after his birth. When he was ten, he and his sister returned to South Boston with their uncle. At age fourteen he learned to tap-dance and eventually joined an acrobatic comedy act.

In a 1980 interview in *Boston Seniority*, he commented about his work in *Oz*: "I'm very proud I was in it," he said. "It's one of the best fairy-tale stories that you can think of today, and it survives because it had a really good story.

"Everyone on the set loved Judy Garland," Ministeri added. "She was a wonderful sweet girl and very easy to work with."

After World War II, during which Ministeri was employed at the Navy Yard as "a burner," because he could fit into tight spaces, Ministeri played "Mr. Zero" for the candy bar company. He would also tour area supermarkets in a novelty sports roadster, handing out free candy bars to kids. Eventually he dropped out of show business and struggled financially for a while before Social Security kicked in, he said.

"I was handicapped because of my size," he explained. "Today the handicapped people are getting breaks, but in my day, show business was one of the only places small people could turn. It's hell going through life being a small person. It's amazing how cruel some people can be without knowing what they're doing."

Ministeri considered his motion picture work a sort of consolation prize later in life. "People look up to you being in show business, and it meant a lot to have people looking up at me."

George Ministeri died of lung cancer on January 29, 1986.

BILLY CURTIS was known as one of Hollywood's most prolific midget actors, one of only a handful of little people who made a comfortable living acting (in roles, and not as a stand-in or costumed character) in the film and television industry.

Born in Springfield, Massachusetts, he was forty-five inches tall when he played one of the city fathers in Munchkinland. (Billy, wearing a tall, pointed hat, jumps out in front of the camera and says, "And ooohhh, what happened then was rich!")

Billy came from a family of six children (his sister Mary was also a little person). He was attending Northwestern University in the early 1930s when he and Mary worked up a dance act together. They toured the country in an act billed The Curtises until Billy discovered a new facet of show business—professional midget wrestling.

Eventually he began working in two-reelers and motion pictures. In a career that spanned almost fifty years, Billy Curtis amassed quite a healthy resume of roles in films and television. In his first film, he starred as Buck Lawson, the hero in the all-midget western *The Terror of Tiny Town* (1938). Billy's film work (on-camera roles and as a stunt double) include: *Tarzan*

Finds a Son! (1939), *Meet John Doe* (1941), *Hellzapoppin* (1941), *Maisie Was a Lady* (1941), *Saboteur* (1942), *Wings for the Eagle* (1942), *My Gal Sal* (1942), *Lucky Legs* (1942), *Tramp, Tramp, Tramp* (1942), *Lady in the Dark* (1944), *Incendiary Blonde* (1945), *Three Wise Fools* (1946), *Wedding Belle* (1947), *April Showers* (1948), *Homicide for Three* (1948), *Pygmy Island* (1950), *Two Tickets to Broadway* (1951), *Superman and the Mole Men* (1951), *Three Ring Circus* (1954), *Princess of the Nile* (1954), *Jungle Moon Men* (1955), *Friendly Persuasion* (1956), *The Conqueror* (1956), *The Court Jester* (1956), *The Incredible Shrinking Man* (1957), *Robin and the 7 Hoods* (1964), *Out of Sight* (1966), *Planet of the Apes* (1968), *Little Cigars* (1973), *High Plains Drifter* (1973), *The Battle for the Planet of the Apes* (1973), *How to Seduce a Woman* (1974), *Loose Shoes* (1980), *Eating Raoul* (1982), *The Night They Saved Christmas* (1984), *It Came Upon a Midnight Clear* (1984), and *Head Office* (1985).

During the 1950s, things got a little slow in the film industry so Curtis, along with midget pals Jerry Maren, George Spotts, and Harry Monty, formed a midget wresting act. "The reason we did it was for survival," Curtis recounted to a reporter in 1978. "There wasn't any work at the time." Curtis went by the name of "Champion" while Maren fought under the names "Baby Face Maren" or "Tiny Terror." ("We had different names so it would look like we were a whole mess of midgets wrestling all over the country," says Maren.) Curtis pointed out, "We didn't do any clowning like the dwarfs. You throw them and they slide out on their fanny. We went out there and wrestled."

If ever Billy Curtis had a standout role in his sizeable film career, it was that of "Mordecai" in the compelling western, *High Plains Drifter* (1973), starring and directed by Clint Eastwood. Curtis plays the smallest citizen in the creepy town of Lago, who shadows Eastwood's character, lighting his cigars, tending to the drifter. Eastwood's nameless character makes friends only with Mordecai and eventually appoints the scorned little man the town sheriff and mayor. "He was a good little actor," said Eastwood in 1992. "I liked him. I always wondered what happened to Billy."

In television, Billy kept busy doubling for children and working in front of the camera in some nice roles on a variety of series such as *The Cisco Kid, Superman* (as "Mr. Zero"), *Batman, Gilligan's Island, The Beverly Hillbillies, The Twilight Zone, Here's Lucy, Get Smart, Bewitched, The Monkees, Truth or Consequences, Laverne and Shirley,* and *Knots Landing.*

Billy was married three times; his second marriage to Lois DeFee, a showgirl nearing six feet four, was heavily publicized in Hollywood. It was annulled after three years in 1938.

In 1970 Billy led a drive to provide midgets and dwarfs full membership and voting privileges in the Screen Actors Guild, which previously only allowed them to work in films under waivers. He told an Associated Press reporter at the time, "We've enjoyed many years of not paying dues, but my pride was hurt. It's like saying because you're not five feet five you can't vote for the president of the United States.

"I say we're not freaks," Billy added. "We're the same as big people. Maybe we can't reach the top shelf, but we can touch the floor faster than they can."

Billy died from a heart ailment on November 9, 1988, at the age of eighty. At the time of his death he was living in Dayton, Nevada, with his wife, Joan. Survivors included three sons, a daughter, and six grandchildren.

In the front row of the Munchkin soldiers you can spot **PERNELL ELMER ST. AUBIN** marching along. Pernell was a rarity in Munchkinland, being an achondroplastic dwarf rather than the populace of pituitary dwarfs (midgets) in the movie.

Born on December 19, 1922, on the southwest side of Chicago, "little Elmer" came from a family of seven children, with a sister and brother who were also dwarfs, and parents of average size. At the age of ten he worked for the Chicago World's Fair in 1933 where he sold the

Granny mistakes midget Billy Curtis for a "little green goomer from Mars," on TV's *The Beverly Hillbillies.*

Munchkins Billy Curtis (left) and Jerry Maren remind Jack Haley in 1979 that they're not getting residuals for *Oz* either. (Courtesy of Jerry Maren)

Midget Village newspaper, tap danced, and played the clarinet.

During his summer vacation from school in 1938, little Elmer read in a newspaper that Leo Singer was searching for little people to work in *The Wizard of Oz*. He was interviewed by Singer in Chicago, and in November he boarded a train for Los Angeles. Pernell was about forty-two inches tall, weighed sixty-two pounds, and was only sixteen, turning seventeen during the production.

Pernell told a reporter in 1979, "Being in the movies was a chance to get out of school, and I didn't want any tutoring on the set, so I lied," he said.

After *Oz*, Pernell did some promotional work for Silvercup Bread Company and the Sherwin Williams paint company and, years later, played Scrubby the Pig on a local children's television show in Chicago.

Pernell became a bartender and opened a lounge, The Midgets Club, which became quite a favored tavern in Chicago. (Nationally syndicated columnist Mike Royko featured the establishment in a column.) At first it was a regular-sized bar with regular-sized bartenders, "and we had to use a ramp system," Pernell explained. "I was jumping around all the time and couldn't take it." After remodeling the bar at a new location, the area behind the bar was built up, and customers sat on shorter bar stools. The Midgets Club handed out half-packs of matches (about a half-inch wide), which customers pocketed as souvenirs or used to light up. In the club there were only a few pieces of *Oz* memorabilia displayed on the walls.

Pernell owned and operated the club from 1946 to 1982. It was at the club that he met his wife, Mary Ellen Burbach, and the two were married in 1948. Mary Ellen, also a little person, had worked with Nate Eagle's Midget Troupe and acted in films such as *Three Wise Fools* (1946). Pernell and Mary Ellen tended

Munchkin Pernell St. Aubin and his wife, Mary Ellen, pose with "Princess Ozma" (Elaine Macejack) at the 1985 Chesterton, Indiana, Oz Fest. (Courtesy of Elaine Willingham)

the bar together and greeted customers. In 1982, they accepted an invitation to visit the Yellow Brick Road Shop in nearby Chesterton, Indiana. For the next three years, the St. Aubins were special guests at the annual Chesterton *Oz* festivals.

Pernell died on December 4, 1987, at the age of sixty-four.

Another dwarf who worked in the *Oz* cast was Munchkin villager **RUTH SMITH**. She was born in Fairbank, Minnesota, on November 24, 1895, and moved to Marshalltown, Iowa, in 1934. Eventually she joined Singer's Midgets in the early 1930s and played the piano and sang in the act.

In 1947 she married Albert Kline, an average-sized man, and eventually the two moved to Seaside, Oregon, where they lived for ten years. Albert Kline died in 1967. They had no children. Ruth lived to the grand old age of ninety; she died on September 5, 1985, in Iowa.

Gladys Allison (left) and Gladys Wolff, both Munchkins from St. Louis who traveled together to the West Coast.

Gladys Wolff in St. Louis, shortly before her death in 1984. (Courtesy of Pat Jordan)

Munchkins Ruth Smith and Freda Betsky in 1940.

Munchkin Ruth Smith celebrates her birthday in November 1984 with friends. (Courtesy of Beverly Smith)

GLADYS WOLFF stepped onto a train at Union Station in St. Louis with another little St. Louisan, Gladys Allison, heading for Culver City. Wolff, who was born in 1911, was four feet three. She married twice and had no children.

During the last few years of her life Gladys lived in a nursing home in St. Louis. Ironically, nurses wheeled her into a TV room to watch *The Wizard of Oz* just weeks before she died. She reportedly smiled, and with a tear rolling down her cheek she watched her scene. Gladys died on May 14, 1984, at the age of seventy-two.

JAMES HULSE was disenchanted with show business after his brief stint as Munchkin villager. It wasn't his line of work, he told relatives, so he returned to the Midwest. Born on March 16, 1915, in Circleville, Ohio, Jimmy was one of eight children, the only midget. (On the reverse of his birth certificate is a handwritten notation suggesting his growth was stunted by whooping cough.) Jimmy was four feet six

when he graduated from high school and did not grow further. In the fall of 1938, while working at the Circleville Pumpkin Show, he was discovered by the Harvey Williams midget troupe which was traveling and performing in the Midwest at the time. Williams kept in touch with Jimmy and soon sent a telegram describing an offer to appear in *The Wizard of Oz* with the rest of the troupe. Jimmy accepted and joined the troupe en route to Los Angeles.

Hulse returned home to minor celebrity in the town, but when *The Wizard of Oz* opened in 1939, he was invited to stand in front of the town theater and greet the crowds. His fame was fleeting and according to relatives, he enjoyed it while it lasted. Hulse later moved to Columbus, Ohio, where he worked a variety of jobs in restaurants and at parking garages. In 1956, he was involved in a terrible accident at work when he lost his balance on a lift at a car dealership and fell twelve feet, breaking his back. From then on, he was confined to a wheelchair. He married Dorothy Pugh in 1964 in Columbus, Ohio, and the couple had one daughter. Jimmy was only in his late 1940s when he became much sicker and was put into a nursing home because he needed constant care; he died in Westerville, Ohio, on December 29, 1964.

The sergeant at arms of Munchkinland was played by **PRINCE DENIS**. A hefty military Munchkin in a bright orange-red uniform, he carried a sword prone and marched in front of the soldiers. You can also spot "Little Denny," as friends called him, in the loft waving his sword above Dorothy as she skips out of Munchkinland.

Prince Denis was named by circus owners in the Pyrenees Mountains of France, where he worked as a young boy. His real name was Denis Bernatets, and he was born on January 26, 1892 (although he commonly supplied 1900 as his birth year). He received his U.S.

Prince and Ethel Denis touring with the Pete Kortes Side Shows in 1958.

Prince Denis in 1982. He was in his early eighties.

A vintage postcard of little people, most of whom became Munchkins, taken around 1930. (L–R): Leona Parks, Johnny and Marie Winters, unidentified, Princess Marguerite, and Prince Denis. (Marie, Marguerite, and Prince Denis were siblings.)

Department of Justice Border-Crossing Card, or "green card," on May 4, 1915. Prince had two sisters who were midgets as well, Marie and Marguerite. (Marie was a Munchkin in *The Wizard of Oz,* and Marguerite was not.)

His wife, Ethel Denis, also a little person, drove with him from San Antonio, Texas, in 1938 to California to work in *The Wizard of Oz.* In the years following *Oz,* Prince and Ethel toured with circuses and sideshows around the country, advertising themselves as the World's Smallest Couple—which was not accurate, but commonly touted by midget performers. Ethel, who was a Munchkin villager, died in 1968 at the age of seventy-four in Phoenix, Arizona. Prince Denis died on June 21, 1984, at the age of ninety-two in Phoenix, Arizona. He had been living at a nursing home the last few years of his life.

Another husband and wife team from Munchkinland was **JOHNNY WINTERS** and **MARIE WINTERS**, who legally went by the last name of Maroldo. Johnny acted as the commander of the navy in Munchkinland. (Marie Winters was Munchkin Prince Denis's sister.)

In 1979 Marie, who was born in France and stood forty-one inches tall, died in San Diego. Johnny passed away in 1985.

ANN RICE LESLIE was a descendant of Sir Francis Drake on her father's side. Ann, a forty-inch fan dancer in the flapper era, was making quite a name for herself on the vaudeville circuit. Born on July 4, 1900 in East Greenwich, Rhode Island, of full-sized folks, Ann also had a midget brother, Herbert Rice, who died the summer before production on *The Wizard of Oz.* Herbert was one of the early Buster Brown midgets who traveled and appeared in a Little Lord Fauntleroy outfit, promoting a line of shoes.

Between 1923 and 1930 Ann worked in vaudeville and with Singer's Midgets, later doing a solo nightclub act in a midget circus in

"Giddyup . . . before I make a dime bank outta ya!" Munchkins Johnny Winters and his wife, Marie.

1936 and 1937. In 1933 her fan dancing routine was a featured attraction at the 1933 Chicago World's Fair Midget Village. Ann married Fremont Leslie, an average-sized man, in 1929; Fremont was a stage manager of the Midget Follies, of which his tiny wife was a featured performer. The couple had a daughter, Jane, who grew to average size.

Today Ann Rice Leslie's daughter, Jane Kondrak, recalls that she was just eight years old when her mother left their home in Minneapolis to appear in *The Wizard of Oz.* "I was a little kid and I remember it was my loneliest Christmas," she says. "Mom left in

Little burlesque fan-dancer Ann Rice Leslie with circus giant John Aasen, circa 1920. (Courtesy of Jane Kondrak)

these giggling fits and they'd have to keep re-shooting," Kondrak remembers. "She told me that Margaret Hamilton was very well liked and down to earth, while Billie Burke, the good witch, sort of scoffed at the little people. Kind of snooty."

Jane's mother, Ann Rice Leslie, died on July 27, 1973 in Minneapolis.

JAMES D. DOYLE, better known as "Major Doyle," was an elder statesman of Munchkinland. Born in 1869 in New York City of Irish-American parents, his rank of major was a self-imposed "honorary" title, as one biography stated.

When he worked in *The Wizard of Oz,* Major Doyle was one of few survivors of the Tom Thumb era who personally knew P. T. Barnum's most famous midget. When General Tom Thumb died in 1883, Major Doyle and several other midgets continued working in a troupe with Tom Thumb's wife, formerly known as Lavinia Warren, and the Barnum show. (Mrs. Tom Thumb died in 1919.)

Doyle was an outspoken little man who stood three feet nine at his tallest and walked with a cane. In 1933, during the Great Depression, a delegation of midgets advised Doyle that the World's Fair Century of Progress attraction in Chicago was preparing to import European midgets for their Midget Village attraction. Doyle actively campaigned to make sure American-born midgets were employed instead of foreign-born or newly naturalized midgets in the United States. Newspapers helped him wage a war against "foreign midgets who would take the jobs of jobless American midgets."

A famous—albeit dubious—story of Doyle supplying the complete midget population to MGM for *The Wizard of Oz* was perpetuated by casting agent Billy Grady in John Lahr's book about his father, among other publications. Tagged "Major Doyle's Revenge," the unseemly

November and was there until February. She sent me a book called *Christmas in California.* I still have that."

Ann Rice Leslie met up with another little lady, Betty Tanner, on the train trip out West. The two fast became friends and were inseparable during the whole *Oz* experience—it was the impetus for a lifelong friendship.

"Mom watched the movie on television each year, and the family all had a big to-do with the grandkids," says Kondrak.

"We all watched, and Mom would point out the people she remembered. She used to tell me about Judy Garland and that she would go into

This crinkled, taped photo was the only memento Arnold Vierling saved from the *Oz* experience. (Courtesy of Patty Smith)

One of the few photographs in existence of little Arnold Vierling, known as "Sonny" to his family. (Courtesy of Patty Smith)

tale involved Doyle and a few busloads of his midgets, en route to Culver City, parking outside Leo Singer's New York apartment and simultaneously mooning Singer through the bus windows. Doyle, however, was never contracted by MGM to provide midgets for the film, and it is doubtful anything even remotely similar to this yarn ever occurred.

Major Doyle died in his sleep on October 11, 1940, aboard the World of Mirth Show's train on the fairgrounds in Spartanburg, South Carolina. He was seventy-one years old.

ARNOLD VIERLING was born on May 24, 1919, in Seymour, Indiana. "Sonny," as his family called him, was cared for by an aunt when he became ill during his preadolescent years. Arnold's only surviving brother, Lynn Vierling, now sixty, recalled his brother's early days in a recent interview.

"Sonny was bedfast for a long time," Vierling says. "His aunt, who was my mother's sister, raised him practically, because he was so sick. She took him in her home and kept him. He

was just sickly in nature, and our aunt had more money to care for him. And I think she enjoyed spoiling him. Everybody liked Sonny."

Sonny's health improved, and he eventually graduated from St. Ambrose Catholic School and attended Shields High School in Seymour. When he was nineteen, his opportunity for *Oz* came along.

"A barber named McConnell, in Seymour, subscribed to a Hollywood magazine, and Sonny had a shoeshine booth in the barber shop," Vierling says. "McConnell read they were gettin' midgets from all over the country for this movie, and he sent a photo in of Sonny."

Sonny hopped a train headed for California, worked as a Munchkin villager, and returned to his parents' home in Indiana afterward. At the end of the next summer, when the film premiered in a local theater, he became a local celebrity, pointing himself out to his family.

Just ten years later, Arnold Vierling died on June 11, 1949, of a venereal disease he contracted "years later after *The Wizard of Oz*," his brother explained. Sonny was only thirty years old.

CARL "KAYO" ERICKSON was one of the tiniest of the midget men, alongside Karl Kosiczky and Major Mite. The three tiniest men were chosen to portray the Munchkin trumpeters who traipsed out of the town hall in yellow tights to herald the arrival of Dorothy. Kayo also wore a pink bonnet nightie as one of the Sleepy Heads emerging from a giant nest egg.

Born on a farm near Corson, South Dakota, in 1917, Carl was a tiny baby just fitting in a shoebox that actually served as his first crib. At an early age, one of his young relatives nicknamed him "Kayo"—derived from a character in the longtime syndicated newspaper comic strip, *Moon Mullins*, created by Frank Willard. The name seemed to fit little Carl and it stuck.

Kayo's father worked out of town frequently and his mother did her best to raise four kids in the one-room housing shelter, a poor existence at best. Eventually, Kayo's mother became seriously ill and bedridden, and was no longer able to care properly for the children. Arrangements were made for the family to be split up and raised by other relatives. Kayo stayed with his mother and helped care for her, despite the fact that his growth had suddenly arrested at age four. Eventually he relocated and was raised by an aunt.

Kayo reached the height of thirty-nine inches and stopped growing completely. Because of this abnormality, his parents and guardians did not allow him to enter school until 1925 when he turned eight years old. Still, he was no taller than a toddler, and life seemed destined to be a major challenge. When he entered first grade, special accommodations were made by his teacher: chalkboards were occasionally lowered and an attached sewing spool low on the door worked as a makeshift doorknob for him to easily reach. Winters were always the toughest time for Kayo, as the snow made it difficult for him to maneuver. When his father was home, he would walk ahead of Kayo to cut a path, otherwise his sister Agnes

Kayo Erickson in the mid 1950s. One of the tiniest of the male Munchkins, he stood just thirty-nine inches tall. (Courtesy of Margaret Pellegrini)

would help him through the deep snow.

It wasn't until his early teens that Kayo underwent his first medical examination, whereby the doctor diagnosed him as a midget who would probably remain a juvenile and fail to mature physically. (The lifelong inability to achieve puberty and mature is typical in a good percentage of male and female midgets.) The doctor was correct in his prediction, but not necessarily his diagnosis. Whether the doctor determined the cause was the pituitary gland is not known. At that time, hormonal treatments were purely experimental, and Kayo wanted nothing to do with that.

In 1934, Kayo entered Washington High School and insisted on struggling with the average-sized desks, mostly sitting on his knees in order to work properly on the desktop. Kids were cruel to Kayo, however—they would trap him in metal lockers and the make him the butt of their practical jokes. Eventually, his skin began to thicken and his attitude grew dark. He was embittered. He despised the treatment he received and wanted to lash out. And the embarrassments had no boundaries at school.

Sporting a cap as the town's littlest newsboy, Kayo took a job selling newspapers on the street corner, yelling out in his high-pitched voice, "Get your *Argus-Leader*!" He was a curiosity in the town, actually. "So many people treated him like a child," says his cousin, Ray Erickson. "He had a feisty temper and he'd get mad. People weren't as accepting back then. He started smoking cigarettes about that time because he thought it would make him look older, and of course he had some people looking twice at him because all they saw was this child on the corner smoking cigarettes. I think some of them came up and yanked the cigarettes out of his mouth."

In 1938, Kayo was discovered by the Harvey Williams midget troupe which was touring through his area. They invited Kayo to travel to California with them to appear in a motion picture called *The Wizard of Oz,* and Kayo leapt at the opportunity. From that moment on, his surviving relatives agree, his demeanor forever changed. Because he was around other little people, he became accustomed to his own stature and even proud of himself. He was able to afford some dapper tailored suits and hats and was finally treated as an adult. Kayo routinely traveled with a lightweight suitcase which doubled as a booster chair on road trips.

According to his relatives, the filming of *Oz* was a physically uncomfortable experience for him. Using the common utilities and furniture in hotels was a struggle, and during filming, he claimed to have received rough treatment. "He said that when he was lifted onto the props,"

Yvonne Moray, one of the Lullabye League, as she looked in the 1950s. (Courtesy of Jerry Maren)

noted his sister, Alice, "they would pull Kayo by the arms and not lift him by the waist, even after he requested it."

Kayo returned home and graduated high school in 1939, the same year *Oz* was released, and the film created a stir in his hometown. He left South Dakota once again and toured a while longer with the Dolly and Henry Kramer midget troupe, traveling across country as well as into Mexico and Canada. Years later, Kayo attempted to settle in the Phoenix area and he searched for work. "At that time, he lived in a little trailer," says fellow Munchkin Margaret Williams Pellegrini. "He stayed with my husband and me for more than a month when we lived in Chicago and we even got him some work. All he traveled with was this big steamer trunk. When he moved to Arizona, we kept in touch and I didn't see him that often, but I remember when he got sick and his sister came out to Phoenix and found him. I think he was too far gone by that time. She told me that when she went to see him, she knew he was near death."

Kayo fell into a depression while residing in Phoenix and he continued to look for work. He developed pneumonia in early 1958 and was bedridden and malnourished, barely able to step out of his tiny trailer. He was eventually discovered, weak and frail, and rushed to the hospital, where his relatives say he appeared to have aged fifty years; he died a few days later, on March 28, 1958, at the age of forty. Kayo's body was shipped back to South Dakota and he was buried in a cemetery just outside Sioux Falls.

YVONNE MORAY BISTANY played the delicate Munchkin Lullabye Leaguer on the right. A brief studio bio noted that Yvonne Moray was born on January 24, 1917, in Brooklyn, New York. At the time of *The Wizard of Oz,* she was forty-two inches tall and weighed forty-nine pounds. She had one brother, who was six feet tall. She worked in Earl Carroll's Vanities

Munchkin Elsie Schultz and her husband, Ray, in 1986. (Courtesy of Dorothy Sadue)

vaudeville extravaganza and danced in other stage productions during the late 1930s. Yvonne's biggest show business break, perhaps, was portraying Nancy Preston, the attractive female lead and love interest of clean-cut Billy Curtis in *The Terror of Tiny Town* (1938). According to friends, she died in the 1970s.

ELSIE SCHULTZ was a Munchkin villager in *Oz.* During her stay in Culver City, she was hit by a car while mailing some Christmas packages back home to her husband, Ray Schultz (also a little person), and two daughters.

Elsie (née Reinking) was born on December 7, 1892, in Germany and emigrated to the United States with her parents when she was young. Elsie died in New York on July 11, 1987, at the age of ninety-four. Her husband, Ray, who also performed with some midget troupes, died in 1993.

NICHOLAS "NICKY" PAGE, one of the city fathers in the mayor's entourage, died on August 18, 1978, in San Francisco. Page was a longtime member of Singer's Midgets.

FRANZ "MIKE" BALLUCH and **JOSEFINE BALLUCH,** brother and sister, both returned to Vienna sometime during the early 1940s. They were originally brought to the United States by Leo Singer. Josefine died in 1984, and Mike died on January 24, 1987.

WALTER MILLER, who played a Munchkin soldier, was born on February 26, 1906. Walter died on October 26, 1987, at the age of eighty-one in Long Beach, California. According to Munchkin Hazel Resmondo, Walter was the Winged Monkey who swooped down, grabbed Toto, and carried the pooch off into the dark sky.

A Different Kind of Munchkin

In the film they're barely seen. Look closely in the background and in the windows of the Munchkin huts. That's them.

Who else could match the size of the Munchkins but children? The studio decided to audition and cast nearly a dozen youngsters to play Munchkins, so areas of Munchkinland wouldn't appear sparse. After all, this was supposed to be a whole city, and the number of midgets was not as great as MGM had hoped for.

BETTY ANN BRUNO (née Cain) was born in Honolulu but raised in southern California. At the time of *Oz,* she was an eight-year-old student of the Bud Murray Dance Studio. She had already appeared briefly in *The Hurricane* with Dorothy Lamour in 1937. Her mother brought her to the audition for *The Wizard of Oz,* and she was chosen by the dance director. ("We used to call him Cowboy," she says.)

"I was delighted to find people who were older than I was and shorter than I was," says Betty Ann Bruno of her experience as a child Munchkin. "I'd run around and measure myself against the midgets sort of surreptitiously. I'd put my hand even to the top of their head and, hopefully without them knowing it, bring it over to my ear. I guess it gave me a sense of stature."

Betty Ann went on to major in political science at Stanford University, and now in her early sixties, she is a retired television news reporter. In Oakland, California, she worked for KTVU-TV for twenty years as an on-camera personality, reporting on a variety of stories ranging from hard news to human interest. During the celebrations for the golden anniversary of *The Wizard of Oz,* Betty Ann became a human interest story herself. Newspaper columnists and reporters from rival stations asked for interviews with the former Munchkin.

"I remember the beauty of the set most of all," she says. "It was like going to a fairy land every day. And the gorgeous, big plastic flowers. The colors and the vividness. It was magic. I was in awe of that."

Rehearsal for the children first required learning some easy dance steps and a few of the simpler songs, all apart from the midgets. The children were measured for wardrobe just like the other Munchkins. Except for age, the biggest difference between the children and the midgets was their working hours. The children were allowed to work only four hours per day; then it was off to the school for tutoring.

Eight-year-old Betty Ann Cain was cast as a Munchkin although she was not a midget.

Today, Betty Ann (Cain) Bruno and her husband, Craig, work in the television field.

One of the children who played Munchkins, Priscilla Montgomery (left) poses with her little friend, Margaret Williams, a Munchkin in her teens. (Courtesy of Margaret Pellegrini.)

"I hated the school because it was so boring and it was never the same things we were doing in our regular school," Betty Ann remembers. "We always worked on those yellow paper tablets, and I wasn't used to that. The teacher was Mrs. Carter, and as it turned out later, one of my college roommates was her daughter. Funny how little circles turn around."

Betty Ann also recalls her costume. She wore a gray felt skirt and a little rosebud vase on her head. "I envied everyone else's clothes because they were brighter colors," she says.

Betty Ann's mother, Mary Ann Kalama, had the delightful experience of going to the studio every day with her daughter, passing the many midgets while they were getting their makeup applied and downing coffee before the day's shooting. Kalama recalled in 1988, "There were about nine youngsters selected to fill in the midgets. The girls were well taken care of on the set.

"They didn't allow us mothers on the set," she pointed out, "but they had two nurses who accompanied them to lunch and the rest room and helped dress them. It was a very strict rule that the mothers didn't interfere. And the studio treated us mothers nicely. They paid for all of our lunches."

Kalama said she attempted to avoid becoming the stereotypical stage mother, so she fully trusted the studio nurses, and her little Betty Ann seemed to enjoy the whole unusual experience, including her absence from her regular school.

"I do remember this one little girl . . . because her mother was really a pushy stage mother," Betty Ann adds. "Her mother made [the girl's] hair look like Shirley Temple's with curls and dyed it blonde. We'd always look at [her] roots. I've always wondered what happened to her."

The memory Betty Ann has stamped most indelibly in her mind is that of a midget who approached her in a pleasant manner one morning. "There was this little guy who kept asking me out to lunch and asking my mother if we could eat together," she remembers laughingly. "My mother would quickly clutch me to her side. One day he asked me what my favorite candy bar was, and I told him it was an Oh Henry! bar. After that morning, we'd kind of muster in a room and then go back to the stage as a group. The midgets would always file by our group, and this one would find me and hold up this Oh Henry! bar, waving."

Certainly, being a Munchkin was no ordinary thing, and these were no ordinary circumstances. And even more extraordinary was that Betty Ann and the other girls were wide-eyed children at the time.

"I've always loved the memory of being on the set and being a Munchkin," she confides. "About fifteen years ago people at work found out. It was like I had achieved a separate status. It's a very special thing, and I've just begun to get a glimpse of that. I feel very privileged to have been a part of it."

JOAN BERNHOFT (née Kenmore) was only seven years old when she was cast as a Munchkin. Born November 3, 1931, she says she vaguely remembers being in the little huts on the set.

"We used to bring our little lunch boxes and eat in those little huts," Joan says. "One time a little friend and I didn't want to come out of the hut for the scene, but a little midget in the hut with us said he was gonna snitch on us, so we went."

Joan, a cousin to former child star Jackie Cooper, was a member of the Thomas Sheehy Dance Studio when she was cast in *Oz.* "Many of us little kids got the parts because we knew someone," she speculates.

"Over the years, my parents didn't really talk to me about this subject, so I didn't find out the truth until I called an aunt—by marriage—one of the few still alive in my mother's generation.

"She told me the facts," Joan says. "About how my Italian grandmother used to read the theatrical papers and learn of the 'cattle calls' for children. She found auditions and parts for Jackie Cooper, my brother Roger, and finally me. And my dancing teacher also put in a fantastic word for me about my dancing ability for a seven-year-old."

Remaining in southern California, Joan eventually married and raised a family. She revels in her memories of *Oz.* "I remember we got paid eight dollars and nine cents each day," she says. "We'd go through a little booth like the extras and pick up the money. I remember this because my mother put the eight dollars away and always let me keep the nine cents in my pocket for candy."

VIOLA BANKS (née White) was eight when she became a Munchkin. "*The Wizard of Oz* stands out as the most glamorous thing I've ever participated in," she said.

As a young girl she sang and danced, winning prizes in amateur contests in small towns in Iowa, where she grew up. After she and her parents moved to Hollywood, she began working as a stand-in for child actress Juanita Quigley, "better known as Baby Jane," Viola said. "I was her stand-in in several movies with Mickey Rooney, Deanna Durbin, Bobbie Breen, and others. I also worked in an *Our Gang* film, but I don't remember the name of it."

At age eight and a half, she was a student in the Bud Murray Dance Studio when she tried out for *Oz.* "One thing I remember is that a little blonde girl and I were supposed to

Child Munchkin Joan Kenmore at age seven. (Courtesy of Joan Kenmore)

Viola White Banks, a child Munchkin in *Oz.*

Child Munchkins Betty Ann Bruno and Joan Kenmore appeared on a segment of the short-lived TV game show *3rd Degree!* with host Bert Convy, January 1990. (Photo by Craig Scheiner)

be up in those eggs, dressed in the bonnets, and one of the little midgets—the one who played a toe dancer dressed in pink and danced ballet—she pitched a fit because [the midgets] had contracts and we worked by the week."

Although most of the little girls hired to be Munchkins were simply placed in the background, Viola insisted that she was not merely decoration. "I was only a few feet away from the witch when we all hit the floor," she said. "I can pick myself out in the picture. The camera shows me as Dorothy was riding in the carriage, and I can see myself when she dances out of Munchkinland waving good-bye."

After *Oz,* Viola and her parents moved back to the Midwest, where she eventually starred as "The Little Sunshine Girl" in a local, fifteen-minute radio program on KFNF in Shenandoah, Iowa. "When I was twelve I became ill with rheumatic fever and had to quit show biz," she said. Viola

White Banks died of emphysema on January 8, 2000, in Omaha, Nebraska.

Like all the Munchkins, neither Betty Ann, Joan, nor Viola became rich from her work in the film. Nor were any of them fortunate enough to keep anything from the film, such as their costumes. MGM didn't allow that. They just have their memories to enjoy.

"I tried many times to get an autographed picture from Judy Garland," says Betty Ann. "It was frightening. I'd go up to her trailer and knock on the door and ask for a picture. I remember screwing up my courage every day. When I asked, she'd look down at me with those great big eyes, and she'd say, 'I'm sorry, I don't have a picture today. Can you come back?' That was very emotional. I did finally get her signature in a little autograph book."

MAYOR MANIA

The mystery of who actually portrayed the mayor of Munchkinland has caused an uproar among Ozologists, and the ballots have had to be closely examined. However many candidates there may have been for the highly coveted role of mayor of Munchkin City ("in the county of the land of Oz"), there was only one bona fide mayor. Hopefully this will once and for all circumvent any further mayoral misrepresentations.

For decades the actual identity of the little man who held office as the prized Munchkin officer had remained widely a riddle because of several factors: conflicting claims in the news media, misreports, and a lack of available MGM documentation. The man who played the green-suited, whiskered, chubby Munchkin who sported an oversized gold pocket watch died in relative obscurity in the late 1960s in Oakland, California. His name was Charlie Becker, a German midget, and he stood three feet nine.

Seemingly the most popular of the inhabitants of Munchkinland, the mayor has received enormous amounts of media coverage in the past twenty years—press that would have made Becker green with Munchkin envy—because unfortunately, the news reports never connected his name with any of it; countless articles in newspapers and tabloids around the country involved others who claimed to be the jolly, waddling welcomer of witch quenchers. Perhaps the imposters felt that nobody would ever know the difference because there were so many little people in the movie. The real mayor, however, is unmistakable. Charlie Becker was probably cast in the role because he was, for many years, Leo Singer's right-hand midget.

Becker was born on November 24, 1887, in Muschenheim, Germany (a small town near Frankfurt) and given the name Karl Becker. There were already two midget children in the Becker family when Charles was born. By age five, little Charlie was only three feet tall and weighed thirty-two pounds. He was the size of a boy of three, and his father "was crushed," Becker revealed in an early interview about his life.

Authors Bodin and Hershey discuss Becker in their 1934 book *It's a Small World*. When he was sixteen, Charlie's father "took him into his shop and taught him the meat-slicing trade with the aid of curses and blows. He looked like a child of six. He was too small to wield the cleavers and rapier-like butchers' knives. His fellow workmen tormented him. He was a neighborhood butt. There was not a bright spot in the misery that surrounded him. His life was unmitigated hell."

Around the age of nineteen his salvation arrived when he joined a midget troupe that toured southern Germany, Austria, the prairies of Hungary, and the Balkans. In 1913 Becker quit and moved to Vienna where he was

Buster and Hazel Resmondo visit with friends Charlie and
Jessie Becker in the early 1950s.

Charlie and Jessie Becker, newlyweds in 1940.

Charlie and Jessie Becker in their Wichita, Kansas, home in 1962. Inset: Jessie in costume for *Oz* in 1938. (Courtesy of Margaret Pellegrini)

In a 1962 *Wichita Eagle and Beacon* newspaper article, Charlie reflected on his immigration to America: "We didn't really want to leave London where we were performing, but war broke out, and because we were German midgets they wanted to put all of us in a concentration camp." Outside of two brief return trips to Europe, the Singer Midgets remained in the United States and toured steadily. "Once we got over here, we weren't sorry we came," Becker added.

In his early days in America Charlie and the other midgets became famous; Singer's midgets met Presidents Wilson and Harding, visited Charlie Chaplin on the set of one of his silent films, and performed on the vaudeville bill with George Burns and Gracie Allen. "George and I used to play checkers backstage before the performance while Gracie sewed in the dressing room," Becker told the *Wichita Eagle and Beacon* reporter. "Knew Will Rogers, too. Shame he's dead. He was a very nice fellow. Whenever we came to a town and he was there ahead of us, he always came down and helped us unpack our 120 trunks."

Becker appeared in only a handful of motion pictures outside of *Oz*, including the silent film *Spangles* in 1926, and as Otto the cook in *The Terror of Tiny Town* (1938).

When asked about his *Oz* costars, Becker said, "Of course Judy Garland was the real star. She became a favorite of mine." Charlie traveled the country, played fairs and circuses, and was the saxophonist in Singer's all-midget band before accepting the movie role that would give him immortality in a little green suit.

It was on the set of *The Wizard of Oz* where Charlie met a pretty blonde Kansas farm girl, slightly taller and slightly younger, who would become his second wife. She was also slightly married. Jessie Kelley, armed with a beautifully natural smile, came to California with the Kramer troupe of midgets. She played a Munchkin townsperson in the film. During the

recruited by Leo Singer. A year later the war broke out, and a tour of Europe was impossible, so Singer's Midgets crossed the ocean to make their debut in the United States. In America, the troupe toured and entertained and prospered for two decades.

The Unluckiest Munchkin

Jakob Hofbauer was a little Austrian fellow with a pleasing, wide grin, inconspicuous in nature, who came to America in 1928 with Leo Singer's group. He was thirty years old when he played a soldier in *The Wizard of Oz;* in reality, he was quite a trouper, drawing sympathy and special care from Singer himself.

In 1931, while traveling with the troupe, an unfortunate mishap in a hotel in Olean, New York, would change Jakob's life. The little fellow was just crazy about radios, it seems.

Says his pal Karl Slover: "The first thing he would do when he got into the hotel is he'd open the window and hang the aerial outside. This time he lost his balance and fell three flights."

Jakob toppled out from the window, cracking his head on a fire escape landing. Everyone was looking for Jakob because it was time for the little people to gather for the parade in town heralding their appearance at the theater. A maid came to work and found him laying there with his head split wide open, Slover says.

According to a news report, Jakob stayed in a hospital for three months, and his recovery was declared a miracle. He sustained a deep gash on his forehead, leaving an unsightly scar, but he returned to the midget troupe. In the film *The Terror of Tiny Town,* he portrayed the saloon bartender, with a slicked flip-curl of hair combed in such a way to masquerade the scar above his right eye.

After the fall Jakob's demeanor was never the same, although according to those who knew him he was still just as pleasant as ever. Jakob suffered from seizures thereafter that caused him to blank out on occasion, so his fellow performers seldom left him alone.

According to Karl Slover, an uncommon means of treatment was prescribed by the doctor. "At certain times, the scar would open up, and little bits of bone would come out," Slover recalls. "The doctor told us to take a cotton swab, clean that away, and then blow a little powdered sugar on that open sore, and that would heal it up. That's exactly what we did. Sometimes Mike Balluch or Freddie Retter would take care of him; even I had to do that with the powdered sugar once or twice."

Nobody quite knew whatever became of Jakob; it was rumored that he died in the late 1950s. "The last I heard," says Karl Slover, "is that he lived in Berkeley, California, and worked as wine steward in a hotel restaurant."

Eddie Buresh, Jakob (with the tambourine), and Karl Kosiczky, circa 1944. (Tod Machin collection)

Four of Singer's troupe: Jakob Hofbauer, Carlos Manzo, Sandor Roka, and Margie Raia in front. Raia, it was discovered, was only ten years old when she was making *The Wizard of Oz,* and MGM forced Singer to release her from the production midway through the job.

production of *Oz,* Jessie was in the process of a messy divorce from Charley Kelley, who was also within the group playing a Munchkin. Once her divorce was final, she and Charlie Becker began a courtship and eventually married in 1940. (Charlie Becker already had a son from his first marriage.) On July 23, 1943, the moment made news when Charlie stood in front of a judge in Oakland, California, and became a U.S. citizen through the proper naturalization procedures. According to the *Oakland Tribune,* when a reporter asked what he thought of Adolf Hitler, Becker responded, "Ugh, I don't want to even hear his name!"

Becker was known by the other midgets as a terrific cook, and he was a favorite of his boss. With his usual trunk of wardrobe and show business paraphernalia, Charlie also hauled along his own assemblage of pots, pans, and assorted cookware, and he routinely set up in the theater dressing rooms and cooked up a storm for the other midget performers: beef stews and goulashes were his specialty. Being the company cook, Becker was given the role of the cherubic cook named Otto in the movie *The Terror of Tiny Town,* a role which had him chasing a goose in one comical scene. And being a competent actor and performer, but not an aspiring one, he was comfortable filling the role as the mayor of Munchkinland although, according to an August 1939 *Good Housekeeping* article about the production of *Oz,* Charlie Becker had prepared himself for an engineering career. When writer Jane Hall visited the movie set during production, Becker remarked to her, "Nobody takes an engineer seriously these days. I mean if he's also a midget."

After Jessie and Charlie left the midget circuit, they lived in southern California for a while where both of them worked as stand-ins for children in motion pictures. The two reportedly appeared in one film together, *My Life With Caroline* (1941) starring Ronald Colman. Charlie tired of touring and performing and took up a sausage business and worked as a butcher; Jessie also sewed and ran a re-weaving shop. The couple eventually moved back to Jessie's home state of Kansas for a time in the early 1960s, living in a comfortable, doublewide mobile home. Eventually, they would return to the West Coast and begin full retirement.

Although he was a standout in the midget entertainment world for most of his life and a longtime veteran of the famed Singer Midgets, when Charlie Becker died of a stroke in an Oakland, California nursing home on December 28, 1968, he was given no celebrity funeral. There was no television coverage. He was eighty-one and a widower. But the spirit of the mayor of Munchkinland refused to die, and for years to come, false news stories about this favorite *Oz* character continued to pop up everywhere.

Out of nowhere, the Associated Press released a story on its wire service on June 23, 1984, that was picked up by virtually every major newspaper in the United States. "Mayor of Munchkinland, Dead at 84" headlines read. The only problem with the story was that the actor who actually played the mayor had already been dead for fifteen years. The man who died in 1984, Prince Denis, was a midget from the Pyrenees Mountains of France who worked in sideshows and circuses, including Ringling Bros. and Barnum & Bailey. True, Prince Denis had been a Munchkin, but not the mayor.

Denis was a widower who lived in a Phoenix nursing home where for many years he boasted to nurses, friends, and even the press that he had portrayed the mayor of Munchkinland. His chubby appearance, like that of Becker, would have made even the most experienced Ozphile look twice. Nobody questioned his claim.

"[Mervyn] LeRoy chose me for the mayor's role because I was the heaviest character of the bunch. He thought I appeared the most distinguished," Denis told a Phoenix newspaper in 1980.

Jessie and Charlie in 1964. (Courtesy of *Washington County News*)

In actuality Denis played the hefty sergeant-at-arms in a bright red military uniform. His character was quite visible, leading the Munchkin soldiers and waving to Dorothy from atop a hut when she skipped to the border of Munchkinland at the close of the scene. If you look closely, you can see that Dorothy even gave "little Denny," as he was known, a friendly wave in return. The mayor he was not, yet fans of *Oz* mourned the mayor's passing when Denis's death was publicized.

"I knew he wasn't," says Margaret Pellegrini, fellow Munchkin and longtime friend to Denis and his wife, both of whom retired in Phoenix. "But I didn't want to be the one to point the finger and say he wasn't. He told me he was the second choice for mayor, but he knew he didn't play it. We all knew Charlie Becker for years. I was a roommate with his future wife, Jessie, when we made *The Wizard of Oz,* so there's no mistaking who played the mayor.

"Denny received a lot of attention that made him feel very good during his last years," Pellegrini offers. "But I didn't like covering up for him. I avoided the subject in interviews. Once I had to tell people at the TV show *60 Minutes* not to come out to interview us when they called me because I didn't want to lie about the mayor."

The claims of midget Prince Denis were not without peer; additional reports appeared that placed the "real" mayor alive and well and living near Atlanta. Reporter Susan Laccetti of the *Atlanta Journal* quoted a little Gwinnett County, Georgia, man in 1985, a former schoolteacher named Dennis Binion who stood three feet six. "I was the mayor," he told the reporter. Binion said he was paid a thousand dollars for the role he was awarded after six weeks of acting school. Besides the tall tale of an exorbitant salary, most preposterous was the part about his age. Binion, then sixty years old, claimed he was twelve when he worked in the film. Watch the movie again; that's no teenager welcoming Dorothy most regally to the Land of Oz.

And there were more impostors: prolific midget actor Billy Curtis was one. Although he had worked in more than fifty motion pictures (*The Terror of Tiny Town, Saboteur, April Showers,* and *High Plains Drifter* among them), for some reason he found it necessary to claim the role that Charlie Becker played. Curtis was a prominent Munchkin townsperson, a city father donning yellow hair, a tall pointed hat, and an elaborate blue costume with tails. In

Actress Myrna Loy visits the lavish set and meets the tiniest of all the Munchkins, Olga Nardone, who was only about fifteen years old at the time.

The Lost Munchkin

For me, writing this book ended up being a deceptive blessing. The pleasure was relishing the challenge of searching for—and uncovering—the surviving little people from *The Wizard of Oz*. The torture was wondering if there wasn't just one more Munchkin, hidden somewhere in suburbia, who I had failed to locate. I merely *assumed* any individual who took even the slightest part in this special film would embrace the experience. It's unthinkable that any person would not enjoy sharing such a fascinating encounter in his or her life.

Imagine my surprise when, long after this book was first published, I found out that the tiniest of all the Munchkins was alive and well and living on the East Coast. For personal reasons, this little person had eluded all the media coverage and ballyhoo surrounding the golden jubilee of *The Wizard of Oz* in 1989.

It took a bit of detective work to find her; the winding trail involved a Munchkin who knew someone, who knew somebody else, who had the telephone number of a relative of an individual who supposedly worked in the movie. I couldn't believe it when I finally reached Olga Nardone on the telephone in 1992. Through the decades the littlest of the little has remained entirely reclusive—and prefers to keep it that way.

All of the other midgets clearly remembered her and affectionately called her "Little Olga" because she was so tiny and fragile—even to them. On film Olga is one of the first Munchkins to carefully emerge from the greenery and curiously greet this Dorothy Gale from Kansas. Little Olga looked like a china doll with short brunette hair, cute bubble cheeks, and fingers as dainty as a baby's. Obviously, her quaint size and innocent face made her a perfect Munchkin; you can spot her in various shots of Munchkinland.

Olga was also one of the Sleepy Head Munchkins in the giant, pink satin-lined nest egg. And maybe her most memorable and most endearing moment arrives when she appears as the middle toe dancer in the Lullabye League—the dainty trio that blows a kiss to Dorothy at the close of its sweet refrain.

Because Little Olga stayed in touch with none of her coactors after the film, a common assumption among them was that she had passed away. During my research there was not a single lead. None of the little people could rally even as much as a rumor about her history or existence, so Little Olga remained in obscurity.

I finally found her. This timid, engaging voice on the other end was the "lost" Munchkin stranded in my imagination. Only this was now reality, and I knew I probably would have just precious minutes with which to explore her *Wizard of Oz* experience. Miraculously, I caught her at just the right time, and she didn't mind talking.

I knew she was one of the youngest—if not the fledgling of the group—which might explain why she had little to reveal.

According to a few of her relatives, Olga remained very tiny in stature (estimated at just shy of three feet), and has lived with her family since making the movie more than fifty years ago. Even among scattered relations, she has lived a relatively private life. Her father was an Italian, and her mother was Belgian, said Olga, who was the only little one in a family with four children. Now in her seventies with naturally dark hair, Olga, who never married, reportedly looks very much the same as she did when she took her trip to *Oz*. "I don't like my picture taken, not anymore," Olga said with a slight laugh. "Even at Christmastime."

Her story is a simple one. Olga's dancing teacher, Mildred Sacco, recommended her for a role in *The Wizard of Oz* and made the arrangements through Leo Singer. Sacco accompanied Olga and her older sister, Linda, on the cross-country venture. After *Oz,* Olga continued performing ("tap-dancing and toe-dancing") and retired soon thereafter from show business, never to appear in another motion picture.

"There's not much I remember," she said of her two months at MGM studios. "Everybody was so nice, the directors and everybody. It was like a family.

"Judy Garland used to sit there and wait for her turn," Olga said. "There was a lot of waiting and standing around."

There were definitely some nostalgic undertones in her shyness. After all, she mentioned meeting such dignitaries as Myrna Loy and Norma Shearer. But in Olga's relaxed voice there was also indifference.

Although she explained she was not the type to reflect on the past, she did seem genuinely interested to know that the other ladies who danced alongside her in the Lullabye League had both died. When she received the original edition of this book as a gift, she said she thought "it was nice," still opting not to activate old acquaintances or draw any attention to herself. "The ones I want to know where I am and who I am, well, they know. They're my family," she said.

Olga professed to never having missed the movie on television, aware, she said, of the phenomenon it has become. Yet she prefers to maintain no contact with any of the other little ones and wants nothing to do with fans. For some unexplainable reason, she denies even the simple pleasure of an autograph. The conversation was all so paradoxical and surreal and quick. Mostly disappointing. I could only imagine this miniature lady on the other line, while I desperately tried to comprehend her solitude. Of course, I was grateful for the time we shared and assured her I would respect her wishes.

"I don't go out, and I don't have anybody in," she said. "I just stay home. I don't want to be in touch with any of [the Munchkins]. But I admit, I'd be curious about the whole thing."

one shot Curtis jumps out of a group of Munchkins and into the foreground and melodically chimes in, "And oh, what happened then was rich!" That was Billy Curtis.

For years before his death in 1988, Curtis told reporters and fans alike that he was the mayor and signed autographs as such, and really, no one questioned it.

Tommy Cottonaro of Niagara Falls, New York, for many years claimed to have been the Mayor Munchkin. Yes, he was a Munchkin villager in the film, but not the mayor.

In the past decade, imposters (midgets, dwarfs, and average-sized people) have continued to poke their head out and claim involvement in *The Wizard of Oz*. Why do they do it? If only for some recognition, some profit perhaps, or a bit of adulation, that's why these imposters make these wild claims.

Yes, there are still tall tales within the tiny community.

A MUNCHKIN GENEALOGY

by Jay Scarfone and William Stillman

With these words, Dorothy Gale first encountered the inhabitants of Munchkin Country, the region of the land of Oz where her house had settled after being carried away by a Kansas cyclone. In *The Annotated Wizard of Oz,* Michael Patrick Hearn suggests the origins of the name "Munchkin" may be traced to several sources: *Münchhausen,* an eighteenth-century German baron; a children's nursery rhyme that gives names to each finger on a child's hand; and "kin" as a suffix referencing the small stature of the country's natives are all speculative possibilities.

Author L. Frank Baum was whimsical in his description of the little people who would

While she stood looking eagerly at the strange and beautiful sights, she noticed coming toward her a group of the queerest people she had ever seen. They were not as big as the grown folk she had always been used to; but neither were they very small. In fact, they seemed about as tall as Dorothy, who was a well-grown child for her age, although they were, as far as looks go, many years older.

—L. Frank Baum,
The Wonderful Wizard of Oz, 1900

W. W. Denslow's depiction of Munchkins in Baum's original book, *The Wonderful Wizard of Oz* (1900).

befriend Dorothy before she began her epic journey:

> They wore round hats that rose to a small point a foot above their heads, with little bells around the brims. . . . The men were dressed in blue, of the same shade as their hats, and wore well-polished boots with a deep roll of blue at the tops. . . . The men, Dorothy thought, were about as old as Uncle Henry for two of them had beards.

In creating the first American fairy tale, it would seem that the Munchkins were Baum's answer to the gnomes, elves, and sprites of European fairy tales. But unlike the magical deities of Grimm and Anderson, the Munchkins are devoid of any supernatural powers. They are instead practical and hard-working. Baum describes the Munchkins as "good farmers . . . able to raise large crops." Indeed, the Scarecrow was stuffed and put together by a Munchkin farmer in order to keep crows out of his cornfield, the Scarecrow's hat and clothing being Munchkin discards. (In the 1933 *Wizard of Oz* radio program, the Scarecrow's clothing and hair were blue.)

Munchkin dwellings were also consistent with the style of their dress: "The houses of the Munchkins were odd-looking . . . round, with a big dome for a roof. All were painted blue, for in this country of the East, blue was the favorite color." While Baum's vision of Munchkin homes was similar to those that appeared in the MGM screen adaptation, the omnipotence of blue was not a consideration for the expensive Technicolor film. (Imagine the countless brilliant hues of this scene reduced to a monochromatic wash.)

Oz illustrator John R. Neill took the color coordination a step further when he wrote *The Wonder City of Oz* (1940). In this *Oz* installment, the inhabitants' region and clothing color also match their food, skin, and eyes.

Dorothy is hailed by the Munchkins when

The Royal Historian of *Oz* himself, L. Frank Baum, was a storyteller supreme who loved to enchant a group of children with his tales.

her house plummets and destroys the Wicked Witch of the East. She has also inadvertently further endeared herself to the Munchkins, as evidenced in this exchange from Baum's original book, *The Wonderful Wizard of Oz*:

> When Boq saw her silver shoes he said, "You must be a great sorceress."
>
> "Why?" asked the girl.
>
> "Because you wear silver shoes and have killed the wicked witch. Besides, you have white in your frock, and only witches and sorceresses wear white."
>
> "My dress is blue and white checked," said Dorothy smoothing out the wrinkles in it.
>
> "It is kind of you to wear that," said Boq. "Blue is the color of the Munchkins, and white is the witch color; so we know you are a friendly witch."

When Dorothy and the Scarecrow rescue the Tin Woodman, they learn that he was at one time in love with a beautiful Munchkin maiden. He explains that the girl lived with an old woman who kept her in a slavelike existence. The old woman made a pact with the Wicked Witch of the East to enchant the Woodman's ax. With each successive swipe it cut off his limbs, which he had replaced by a skilled tinsmith until he was made entirely of tin. He longs for a heart to fill his empty chest so that he may feel a passion he believes he no longer possesses.

In 1902, when *The Wizard of Oz* was translated into a musical comedy for the stage, Dorothy's meeting the Munchkins was one of the few plot elements retained from Baum's original text. Scene Two of the stage production transformed the Kansas set into "The Country of the Munchkins." The logistics of recruiting midgets to play Munchkins were unfeasible, impractical, and likely unacceptable. Instead, the Munchkins were more fashionably portrayed as a parade of more than two dozen chorus girls in tights. This asset wasn't overlooked in publicity for the production, which highlighted "more pretty girls than ever seen together on the same stage . . . a battalion of beauty-brights." Although a few actors augmented the shapely chorus, the most charismatic of the girls assumed male speaking roles such as Tom Piper and Peter Boq (a Munchkin name in the original book). Others portrayed Munchkins with names suggesting comic alliteration: Antonia, Sophronia, Premonia, Malvonia, and Semponia.

The Tin Woodman's motivation to seek a heart also survived the transition from book to stage. This time the metal man was given the name of Niccolo Chopper. His story received romantic embellishment when it was revealed that his betrothed was an ingenue named Cynthia. Niccolo was transformed into a man of tin by the wicked witch "because he dared to make love to a beautiful Munchkin girl." (Cynthia appeared in the Munchkin Country scene to sing "Niccolo's Piccolo," a number about her lost lover's musical abilities.)

The success of the stage production prompted an unauthorized song entitled "Dorothy" to be published in 1904. The lyrics allude to yet another Munchkin tryst:

A lad who lived in Oz was one day sighing
And pining for someone for whom to care
While far away, down in the state of Kansas,
There lived a little maiden, sweet and fair.

But one day came a cyclone dark and stormy,
And took this little maiden up above;
And to the land of Munchkins took her safely,
Where the lad could sing to her this song of love.

L. Frank Baum followed his original Oz book with thirteen sequels about the mythical kingdom of Oz. Prior to *The Patchwork Girl of Oz* (1913), the Munchkins were only referenced incidentally, usually when accompanied by an explanation of the color-quadrant geography of the land. But *The Patchwork Girl* gave star billing to a resourceful young Munchkin lad named Ojo. (In 1933, Ojo resurfaced in a book of his own, *Ojo in Oz*, written by Ruth Plumly Thompson.) Judging from John R. Neill's sketches for the book, the Munchkins were no longer diminutive. The book also provided a more detailed description of customary Munchkin attire:

[Ojo] wore blue silk stockings, blue knee-pants with gold buckles, a blue ruffled waist, and a jacket of bright blue braided with gold. His shoes were of blue leather and turned up at the toes, which were pointed. His hat had a peaked crown with a flat brim, and around the brim was a row of tiny golden bells that tinkled when he moved. This was the native costume of those who inhabited the Munchkin Country of the Land of Oz.

In 1914 Ojo was impersonated with pantomime coyness by actress Violet MacMillan in Baum's silent film version of *The Patchwork Girl*. Billed as "the Daintiest Darling of them all," MacMillan's costume mirrored Neill's *Oz* book illustrations.

When Baum wrote *The Tin Woodman of Oz* in 1918, the Tin Man retained his stage name, being known as Nick Chopper. He also retained his desire for his lost love. This time the beautiful Munchkin maiden was named Nimmie Amee. In the intervening years, however, she had taken up with—amazingly—a man made up of some of the Tin Woodman's old human parts!

Ruth Plumly Thompson's *The Royal Book of Oz* (1921) offered a nostalgic trip to the Munchkin cornfield where the Scarecrow had at one time presided. Stalking his ancestral roots, the Scarecrow "made . . . his way down the yellow brick road that ran through the Munchkin Country. For he had determined to return to the Munchkin farm where Dorothy had first discovered him and try to find some traces of his family." Along the way, "He was treated everywhere with the greatest courtesy and had innumerable invitations from the hospitable Munchkins." When the Scarecrow arrived at "the little Munchkin farm," he was greeted warmly by the Munchkin farmer who had made him. "Why it's you!—Come right in, my dear fellow, and give us the latest news from the Emerald City." Thompson acknowledged that "The farmer was very proud of the Scarecrow. . . . when [he] had run off with Dorothy and got his brains from the Wizard of Oz . . . the little farmer had felt highly gratified."

The text of the 1928 *The Giant Horse of Oz* noted "the blue Munchkin Country is governed by a King of whom nothing much has been heard for many a long year." One isolated portion of the country is populated by the Ozurians. As Thompson explained, "The Ozurians number one thousand and seven and are a tall fair haired race of Munchkins. In olden days they were the happiest, most carefree people in Oz."

The placement of Munchkin Country on the map of Oz is a point of conjecture. In *The Wonderful Wizard of Oz*, Baum is clear in orienting his readers to the lay of the land. Munchkin Country is east; the Munchkins had been enslaved by the Wicked Witch of the East.

Winkie Country is west, as ruled by the Wicked Witch of the West. Confusion arose with the publication of *Tik Tok of Oz* in 1914. The full-color endpapers for this book display a map of Oz with the Munchkin and Winkie Countries reversed. This contradiction was adhered to intermittently through many of the later *Oz* books, creating inconsistencies in cartography that, if nothing else, serve to delight and perplex readers.

In the years prior to MGM's interpretation of *The Wizard of Oz*, the Munchkins received a recognition that only paralleled their proportions. Ojo and his Munchkin uncle, Unk Nunkie, were included with more than four dozen other entities in *The Oz Toy Book,* a 1915 paper doll novelty issued by the publishers of the *Oz* books. Ojo was also featured on the Munchkin Country portion of the playing board for Parker Brothers' The Wonderful Game of Oz—an elaborate game, circa 1921, which remained on the market for nearly twenty years. Ojo's adventures with the Patchwork Girl were featured in a comic strip series, "The Wonderland of Oz," and the stories were issued in comic book form between 1938 and 1940. ("What will Princess Ozma do to Ojo? Will Dorothy help him? There will be another 'Wonderland of Oz' story in the next issue of Funnies.")

Early screen adaptations of *The Wizard of Oz* deleted the Munchkin episode entirely. Silent versions produced in 1910 and 1925 bypassed the Munchkins in favor of focusing on the antics of the Scarecrow and Tin Woodman. A 1933 Technicolor cartoon short begins Dorothy's adventures in Oz when she and Toto fall from the sky and land directly on top of the Scarecrow!

The overwhelming success of Walt Disney's *Snow White and the Seven Dwarfs* (1937) no doubt changed Hollywood's perspective of film fantasy. Public reception of Snow White's dwarfs—Dopey in particular—was a motivating factor that prompted other studios to seek similar properties featuring wee folk. The trend continued with the 1939 release of Max Fleischer's animated *Gulliver's Travels*. Lilliputian Gabby became popular and was featured in several of his own cartoon shorts.

When MGM began developing *Oz* for the screen, the Munchkinland sequence was emphasized not only for the shift to Technicolor, but to highlight the charms and comic appeal of the scene's miniature actors. The musical portion of the Munchkinland setting was intended to be lengthier than what appears in the completed film; Dorothy was to be greeted by the Munchkin Navy, Fire Department, and Mother Goose Club. In imitation of several scenes in *Snow White,* this sequence was scripted largely in rhyme. Also in concession to Disney, individual Munchkin personalities were to have been further defined. Included in the colorful parade were to be a town braggart and a "deaf townsman with ear trumpet." Early concepts for Munchkin costumes and makeup echoed the *Snow White* dwarfs with Baum's descriptions.

Playing up the midget angle in promotion of *The Wizard of Oz* locally was a publicity bit encouraged by the studio campaign:

> It is probable that one or more of the Munchkin midgets, collected by Leo Singer from all parts of the United States, is from your city. If so, the stunt possibilities are limitless and obvious. If not, you should be able to hire a midget or dwarf to work as a barker in front of the theater during the run. The tiny folk are loaded with feature story material.

Many of the initial reviews for *The Wizard of Oz* compared it favorably with Snow White and the Seven Dwarfs for capturing and sustaining an elusive element of childhood fantasy. Few reviewers singled out the Munchkins, and some who did were unsupportive. "*Oz* has dwarfs, music, Technicolor, freak characters,

Garland singing 'Over the Rainbow' did something extraordinary . . . in that moment she gave the film its heart, and the force of her rendition is strong and sweet and deep enough to carry us through all the tomfoolery that follows, even to bestow upon it a touching quality, a vulnerable charm.

—AUTHOR SALMAN RUSHDIE

and Judy Garland," commented Otis Ferguson in the *New Republic*.

Time declared, "Its Singer Midgets, most publicized of all the picture's cast, go through their paces with the bored, sophisticated air of slightly evil children."

Happily, the Munchkins in *The Wizard of Oz* have transcended any stuffy reviewer's pen to receive deserved recognition for a film sequence that is often imitated and fondly remembered. Sixty years later, the Munchkins are as equally revered, celebrated, and merchandised as their fellow Ozian counterparts. If their appeal wasn't on par with Snow White's dwarfs in 1939, today they have equaled—if not surpassed—that distinction.

Jay Scarfone and Bill Stillman are coauthors of *The Wizard of Oz: The Official 50th Anniversary Pictorial History* (with John Fricke; Warner Books), *The Wizard of Oz Collector's Treasury* (Schiffer Publishing), and *The Wizardry of Oz* (Gramercy Books).

Lines and Tidbits and Errors— Oh My!

The Wizard of Oz is magical indeed, but nowhere near perfect. There are gaffes, goofs, and film faux pas to point out, and the movie swirls with trivia to intrigue any true fan. So whip out the remote control, and prepare to press "pause." Here're a few brain teasers to test your trivia wizardry.

- Despite popular belief, the sinister Miss Gulch does not curse at Aunt Em, threatening to "bring a damn suit that'll take your whole farm!" The words are "damage suit."

- After the Wicked Witch has blown out of Munchkinland in a fiery billow, Glinda takes Dorothy by the arm and warns her never to let those ruby slippers off her feet for a moment. Watch as Glinda, surrounded by Munchkins, raises her wand and knocks it into her crown. Listen closely and you can even hear the "clink" as it strikes.

- Eye the implausibly rotund Mayor Munchkin during his scenes. On several occasions, actor Charlie Becker "lifts" his tummy stuffing. It's most noticeable at the end of the Munchkin scene when he jets out, tells Dorothy to "follow the Yellow Brick Road," and pulls up his padding.

- At the invitation of the Good Witch, the Munchkins emerge to meet Dorothy. One little man (Harry Doll) sporting a corncob pipe emerges from a manhole on the Yellow Brick Road. If you'll heed, you'll see the manhole cover has vanished from the brick road in the next shot.

- The shiny, black bird that lands on the Scarecrow's shoulder in the cornfield is not a crow, but a raven. Interestingly, this fact was revealed by Elizabeth Cottonaro, wife of Munchkin Tommy Cottonaro. When she was a child, she met the bird's owner and trainer, Curly Twifard, in 1940. "It was at a tent show in Los Angeles where the bird was on display," says Cottonaro, "and part of his spiel was about *The Wizard of Oz* and this bird. I was fascinated with it."

  Famed animal trainer Frank Inn, who gave us *Benji*, was friends with Curly Twifard. Inn said recently, "The raven's name was 'Jimmy the Raven.' Curly owned him for more than thirty years and let him fly loose in his house." Twifard also supplied animals and exotic birds for the film *Enchanted Forest* (1945) and his raven, Jimmy, also appeared in Frank Capra's Christmas classic, *It's a*

It's amusing to follow Toto's curious antics throughout the movie. During the Tin Man's song and dance solo, you'll see Toto flinch in shock when the Tin Man toots his funnel.

Notice Dorothy's wavering pigtails when she encounters the Scarecrow. Her hair length varies from short to long and back again.

At the moment when Dorothy is appalled at the lion's behavior and slaps him, closely examine Judy Garland's facial expressions. She snuggles Toto close to her face in an attempt to cover up her own giggles at Lahr's blubbering. Director Victor Fleming once noted this scene was difficult to capture because Garland kept breaking up.

Wonderful Life. According to Inn, his pal Curly died in the early 1950s; whatever became of Jimmy the Raven may remain a mystery forever.

- Do you recall in Emerald City when the Tin Man cracks a piece of pottery with his axe and presents the Lion with a makeshift crown? Keep your eyes on the crown, because it eventually falls off the Lion's head and bounces on the hard floor.

- Poor Toto. During the scene where the Wizard is exposed, pay no attention to the man behind the curtain. Look at the dog. He's literally attached to the curtain by his collar. Toto is obediently dragging it open toward his trainer, who is located off to the right side.

- A Spark of Trivia: When syndicated newspaper columnist Paul Harrison visited the set one day while the Wizard's throne room scenes were being shot, he witnessed a mishap. Harrison reported:

  > The Wizard himself was sitting in a portable sound booth behind the camera and was speaking in quite a normal tone. But the words were amplified until they shook the rafters. From then on the interview was punctuated with fancy pyrotechnics. . . . There were lightning flashes from carbon arcs, more steam, puffs of colored smoke, and occasionally sheets of flame would curtain the whole throne. All these manifestations came through a maze of pipes and wires hidden behind the scenes.
  >
  > During one take, the sheets of gas flame, puffing clear up into the catwalks overhead, got a little too hot. "Cut!" yelled Victor Fleming, the director. "I believe the throne's on fire." And so it was; the upholstery was blazing briskly. Croaked the disembodied voice of Frank Morgan, "Ah—the hot seat!"

- The character costumes, albeit uncomfortable and hot, were quite unique: The Tin Man's metallic-looking encasing was actually made of stiff silvered leather. (Costumers experimented with sheet metal, but could not calm the clanking.) Bert Lahr's leonine get-up (there were two made) was tailored from real lion pelts. His tail was held and twitched by a thin wire leading to a fishing pole manipulated by a prop man on the catwalks above.

- Green Around the Gills: Writer Paul Harrison made an additional observation in a 1939 newspaper column:

  > An incidental but ironic fact is that the technicolor cameraman on [*The Wizard of Oz*] is made ill by

Bound for Glory: In an interview long after *Oz,* Judy Garland remembered, "They decided my bosom was too big, so at first they tried to tape it down. Then a woman turned up who was called the Cellini of the corset world. She made me a corset of steel and I was laced up in that . . . I looked like a male Mary Pickford by the time they got through with all the alterations."

RAY BOLGER,
WHO LIKES TO
SMOKE, SET HIM-
SELF ON FIRE
WHILE WEARING
HIS "SCARECROW"
COSTUME FOR
"THE WIZARD OF OZ."

some of the sets. Everything in the Emerald City is supposed to be green. Metro has provided some variety with different intensities of green and shades of blue-green. But the cinematographer, perched on a swinging camera crane and squinting at all this for days and weeks, has been giving way to attacks of seasickness.

- Don't be gullible enough to buy into the silly—but popular—rumor about a dead Munchkin hanging from the rafters in the haunted forest scenes. How this ridiculous notion ever started is anyone's guess, but it deserves dousing. This urban legend, which began circulating in the late 1980s, perpetuated a tale that someone committed suicide on the set during production—and that it can be seen in the background during certain scenes. False. It never happened, nor can anything so ludicrous be spotted in the film. The only unusual things to be spotted in the background are during the apple orchard scene: Look for exotic birds such as a crane, a pheasant, and a toucan.

- Those *Oz* afficionados who own the laser disc or DVD version of the movie will appreciate this one. Fast forward to the scene where Dorothy and the Scarecrow harvest some fruit from the rude Apple Trees. At the end of the scene, the Scarecrow tells Dorothy, "I'll show you how to get apples," and makes a face at the talking tree. In response, the angry tree pelts the Scarecrow with apples. Here is where you pause the film and "still step," frame by frame, the action. Look closely at Dorothy's feet—she's not wearing the ruby slippers! Judy Garland didn't think her footwear would be seen in this shot and in just a few frames you can clearly see she is wearing her dark brown comfy slippers.

It's a quickie, but in one scene Judy Garland's brown slippers can be glimpsed.

Entertainer Danny Kaye hosted the annual CBS presentation of *The Wizard of Oz* from 1964 through 1967.

Oz Bides Its Time: The Television Renaissance

I t really was no miracle; what happened was just this: television. The tube made this motion picture a phenomenon. A masterpiece it always was. A successful masterpiece and a cultural icon it became.

Despite popular reports that the film bombed when it premiered in 1939, fact is, the reviews were mixed, with a plethora of raves. True, MGM didn't begin recouping its nearly three-million-dollar investment until years later. Its arrival on television in 1956 took *Oz* to a technically unexplainable journey into the outer stratosphere—to quote a Wizard.

It's been estimated *The Wizard of Oz* has been watched more than a few billion times—and viewed by more people than any other film in the annals of the medium. The explosion of television allowed everyone to experience its inimitable, unmistakable charm. Television may very well be the reason it is labeled the most popular film ever made. It was, in fact, among the first motion pictures ever to be presented on television.

The video age has enabled us to view *The Wizard of Oz* at will. Remember the olden days when we had to wait for the film to be televised annually? It was all schoolchildren could whisper about the day of its arrival. "*The Wizard of Oz* is on tonight." Imagine—children today will never experience the thrilling anticipation that went along with it all.

It's hard to believe the film has transcended

"It's like a toy. You get a new generation all the time because of television. The film didn't bowl anyone over when it first came out. It was never the big smash hit that television made it."

—Jack Haley,
New York Times

Oz alums Margaret Hamilton, Jack Haley, and Ray Bolger reunite for television in 1969. Ray Bolger put it beautifully: "The one thing that we will be known for, no matter what we've done any place else in the whole world, will be *The Wizard of Oz*. We don't get any residuals, but we have better . . . a kind of immortality and a pride in being part of a great American classic."

Candied Photo: The Lollipop Kid remains one of the most memorable of all Munchkins. Here, Jerry Maren strikes a familiar pose.

Florida's Munchkins reunited in 1989 for a *People* magazine story. The giant tree was part of a colorful miniature golf park and served as a unique background for the photo shoot. Clockwise from bottom: Nita Krebs (seated), Jeane LaBarbera, Gus Wayne, Tiny Doll, Meinhardt Raabe, and Karl Slover.

the decades, airing on television more than forty consecutive years, more than any single presentation on prime-time television.

Ironically, it all happened by chance. Originally CBS requested *Gone With the Wind* from MGM's vast library, but somehow leased *Oz* instead. The Wizard first performed his magic on television audiences on November 3, 1956, as CBS's finale for its *Ford Star Jubilee* program. The competition on the other networks offered a *Lawrence Welk Show*, a Sid Caesar variety show, a long-forgotten program called *Masquerade Party*, and George Gobel's comedy show. *Oz* ranked fourth that Saturday night, but nonetheless, nearly thirteen million sets were tuned in to Dorothy. In the years to come television would enable it to gather greater audiences and evolve into a bona fide American institution. There's probably not a child in America who doesn't recognize the characters.

Over decades a metamorphosis took hold of L. Frank Baum's identity as the writer of chil-

dren's books. More popularly he became known as the man who created the characters for which a wondrous movie was fashioned. Which was perpetuated by the television perennial. For which a top-selling home video-cassette was marketed. Which begot a successful laser-disc boxed set.

Writer Allen Eyles noted, "The film has almost entirely by itself sustained the interest in Baum's books. They are measured against the impression left by the film—not the other way around."

For all intents and purposes, the movie has not left the networks since (nor have Baum's books vacated libraries and bookstores). As rampant as it appears, however, *Oz*'s television ratings have rollercoastered over the years.

Without getting overly statistical, consider this: In its eighth showing in January 1966, *Oz* ranked number one in its timeslot and

Larry King welcomed Munchkin Margaret Pellegrini to his live CNN show on June 19, 1989, to discuss *Oz* and take callers.

Macy's "Tap-Oz-Mania" gathered a record-setting five thousand tap dancers to strut their stuff along New York City's 34th Street in 1989. Posing in the center of a group of dancers is special guest Munchkin and grand marshall, Mickey Carroll—himself an ol' hoofer from way back.

Dick Van Dyke brought along his children, Barry, Stacy, and Chris (seated) for a segment introducing the CBS network telecast of *The Wizard of Oz* in 1961.

Munchkin Mickey Carroll joked, "We're too old to trash the place this time." Munchkin Rendezvous 1997 reunited six of the surviving little people for a special Halloween event at the Culver Hotel—where many of the Munchkins resided while making *The Wizard of Oz*. The extravaganza was later listed in the special year-end issue of *Entertainment Weekly* magazine as one of "The Best of 1997" and was the topic of a *New York Times* feature story. Forming a conga line in front of the hotel are Jerry Maren, Margaret Pellegrini, Mickey Carroll, Ruth Duccini, Clarence Swensen, and Karl Slover. (Photo by Andy Cassimatis)

remained in the top ten for the next several years. In 1972, during NBC's brief period of optioning the film for air, *Oz* slumped to number nineteen in the ratings timeslot that Sunday evening (up against *The Mod Squad, The Glen Campbell Goodtime Hour,* and *Hawaii Five-O*). While still at NBC in 1975, it fell to number twenty-six (up against *The Six Million Dollar Man* and a *Waltons* special). One clever NBC print ad for the film read: "Somewhere over the rainbow there may be a more captivating movie—but don't bet on it."

When CBS gambled with high stakes and reclaimed *Oz* the next year, Dorothy, the Tin Man, Lion, and Scarecrow soared back to number three in the ratings on Sunday, March 14, 1976. Finally, someone at CBS must've decided, "There they are, and there they'll stay."

In the interim the networks invited special guest hosts to appear before (and during) the presentation and to introduce it in a variety of methods. Comedian Red Skelton and his twelve-year-old daughter, Valentina, hosted the second telecast in 1959. Richard Boone (of TV's *Have Gun, Will Travel*) took the chores a little more seriously in 1960 and filmed wraparound segments while on location for his TV series in Apache Junction, Arizona. Popular CBS star Dick Van Dyke and his children guest hosted some lighthearted segments for the 1961 and 1962 airings of *Oz*; entertainer Danny Kaye assumed the responsibilities in 1964, serving as host for the next three years.

When Judy Garland died in June 1969, distinctive plans were made for the next broadcast (the following March 15, 1970) to pay tribute to the legendary entertainer. The Singer Company launched a publicity campaign, spending nearly two million dollars on the whole event. The film's surviving stars (Bolger, Haley, and Hamilton) appeared in interviews around the country and were featured on covers of countless local television-guide supple-

Fifty years after they traveled cross-country together in 1938 en route to the West Coast for *Oz,* Munchkins Gus Wayne and Jerry Maren found themselves once again on a bus excursion promoting the film in 1989.

Margaret Pellegrini was a guest on Geraldo Rivera's talk show.

One of the largest gatherings of Munchkins took place in Judy Garland's hometown of Grand Rapids, Minnesota, in 1989 .

The Munchkins gather for a press conference in Minneapolis in 1989. This was the morning they had all reunited after fifty years.

A representative from the Disney/MGM theme park in Orlando, Florida, gave the Munchkins a special viewing of an actual pair of ruby slippers, which, during the 1990s, were on display at the park.

The Munchkins make this little boy and his parents very happy during a visit to a children's hospital in the Midwest in 1989.

ments. Opening the broadcast was a heartfelt speech by Gregory Peck, recapping Garland's life and legend.

Skipping ahead, the year 1996 marked the fortieth airing of *The Wizard of Oz* on prime-time television. CBS re-aired a star-studded documentary hosted by Angela Lansbury and produced by Jack Haley Jr. (which was originally prepared for the film's fiftieth anniversary in 1989). Time and again, some of the surviving Munchkins were interviewed in their respective hometowns around the United States, with just as much enthusiasm as ever. Evident in every interview was the fact that they are proud to be Munchkins of Oz.

After more than half a century, most of the little people admit that the enormous pleasure *Oz* has given them has far outshadowed any lack of residuals or recollections of the grueling schedule they adhered to when they made the film. They may have gotten the short end of the stick when they received their paychecks, but as clichéd as it may sound, they continue to echo: The residuals are the fans. "Today is today," says Munchkin Mickey Carroll in St. Louis. "I wouldn't trade it for anything."

ON THE ROAD AGAIN

The fiftieth anniversary of *The Wizard of Oz* in 1989 hit America like a twister touching down without sirens. All of a sudden, it seemed, *Oz* was everywhere, loud and clear; for more than a year's duration the golden anniversary of *Oz* was toasted. In print ads, in television commercials, on TV talk shows, in touring stage versions, in video stores, on the bookshelves, on radio talk shows, in print periodicals, charity events, Halloween parties, and even glistening ornaments adorning our Christmas trees. From Downy fabric softener commercials to a Pfizer Laboratories ad for arthritis patients (featuring the Tin Man painlessly clicking his heels in the air). You name it, and it was somehow in

After fifty years the Lollipop Kid, Jerry Maren, is reunited with one of the Lullabye League, Nita Krebs, in 1989. (Photo by Dan Thome)

Munchkins Jerry Maren and Margaret Pellegrini attended an extraordinary exhibit in 2000, celebrating the centennial of Baum's *The Wonderful Wizard of Oz*. Displayed for an extended period at the Los Angeles Public Library were selected museum-quality pieces from the Willard Carroll Collection.

This surviving pair of Munchkin maiden footwear, handmade mostly of felt, has fetched thousands of dollars at auction.

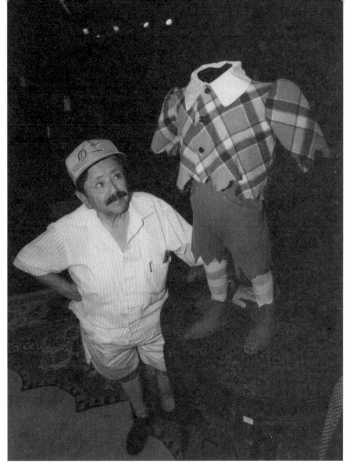

Jerry Maren examines his original costume from the film.

The Munchkins reunite in Grand Rapids, Minnesota in 1989.

Oooooohhs and Oz

✳

Additional tributes to the world of Oz during the anniversary:

- Westin Crown Center in Kansas City, Missouri (September 1989). A swirling Yellow Brick Road led a record number of fans into a massive exhibit on display. Unfurled were rare *Oz* books as well as a spectrum of original props and rare memorabilia from the motion picture. Munchkins Margaret Pellegrini and Fern Formica were the Munchkin guests, there to sign autographs, take pictures, and meet the crowds on specified days. (The Oz exhibit eventually moved to Kansas City's Toy and Miniature Museum and remained on display into 1990.)

- It was "Oz-Time at Macy's" department store where several floors were lavishly decorated with an array of Oz characters; special Ozzy offers, Macy's Oz products, and a calendar chock full of events lasted several weeks, beginning August 13, 1989. Kicking off the event was "Tap-Oz-Mania," involving no fewer than five thousand dancers, all in matching ruby spats and yellow shirts, tapping their hearts out down Seventh Avenue. Macy's highlights included appearances by: Jack Haley Jr. (son of the Tin Man Jack Haley), Lorna Luft (Judy Garland's daughter), Jane Lahr (daughter of Cowardly Lion Bert Lahr), Hamilton Meserve (son of Wicked Witch Margaret Hamilton), and Munchkins Mickey Carroll and Meinhardt Raabe. Aesthetically, Macy's gargantuan balloon displays and perfectly re-created Oz entryways throughout the store were more opulent than any other Oz fest of the year, bar none.

- Annual conventions held in Chittenango, New York (the birthplace of L. Frank Baum), and Chesterton, Indiana (outside of Chicago), went all out for the fiftieth anniversary of *The Wizard of Oz.* Both towns hosted huge parades, and a variety of events throughout their weekend-long Oz adventures. In each town thousands of tourists flock to celebrate with the Munchkin celebrities. The Yellow Brick Road Gift Shop in Chesterton, owned and operated by Jean Nelson, welcomes tourists year round. "It's a fantasy museum as well," she says, "like a grown-up toy shop."

- A large-scale traveling production of *The Wizard of Oz*

Macy's in New York City promoted the golden jubilee of *The Wizard of Oz* with grand style with a month-long celebration in 1989.

Munchkins Gus Wayne, Fern Formica, and Margaret Pellegrini make an appearance in St. Louis celebrating the fiftieth anniversary of the film. (Photo by John Kropf)

(an adaptation of the film, not the stage version) made its world premiere March 22, 1989, at New York's Radio City Music Hall. The indoor arena show sponsored by Purina Dog Chow and Downy Fabric Softener toured the United States through the end of the year. Specially licensed products and tie-ins were merchandised: a souvenir program, dolls, pennants, a coloring book, a digital watch, and playsets.

- As the events of 1989 and 1990 wound down, the little people vowed to stay in touch with each other, and that's exactly what has happened. In the ensuing years more reunions have brought them closer together, in proximity and in their personal relationships. Sadly, however, annual Oz reunions are not gauged anymore by an increasing number of midgets in attendance, but rather the diminishing number who are able to appear.

The Munchkins are virtually the only cast members of the film left. As one of the Munchkins observed during the anniversary, "This is something Judy [Garland] should have been here for . . . it's a shame she didn't get to see all of this."

cahoots with the Wizard. One company even manufactured a gadget that, when installed in a toilet paper dispenser and activated, played a musical rendition of "Over the Rainbow." An incredibly creative commercial for Heinz catsup depicted an army of animated red ants hauling off picnic hot dogs, chanting "Ohhh-eeee-ohhhh."

Even Uncle Sam got in the picture with the unprecedented release of United States postal stamps paying tribute to classic films. Naturally, *Oz* was a primary choice; a beautifully designed and painted close-up image of Dorothy and Toto by artist Thomas Blackshear II was released for the licking. The twenty-five-cent stamp became one of the most popular philatelic pieces ever produced by the United States Postal Service.

During the golden anniversary period, with the introduction of so many new toys, products, and all the hoopla, serious collectors of *Oz* memorabilia were either in heaven—or in bankruptcy proceedings.

For the little people, the anniversary season meant memorable reunions, *Oz* festivals, parades, newspaper and television interviews, special theater screenings of the film, exhibits, and more fans than anyone was prepared to calculate. Most of the Munchkins had never participated in festivities such as these; they were totally unprepared for the love displayed by masses of *Wizard of Oz* aficionados who trekked from all points of the globe to see them.

People magazine reunited six Munchkins in the Florida area for a photo spread and feature story. On a sweltering day with humidity at an all-time high, the little people braved the oven temperature to pose at a miniature golf park in front of a huge cartoonish carved tree with colorful bug eyes and a gaping mouth. It was a fascinating angle for the frustrated magazine photographer, who attempted to keep their attention on his lens. A frail Nita Krebs, age

eighty-three, kept peering at curious others with cameras, smiling until she tired. The *People* photographer pleaded, "C'mon, Nita, act like you're in show business again!"

Nita shot back, "Vell in show business, ve got paid to smile!"

Mini-reunions for the little people gradually led to larger, more widely publicized gatherings. The state of Minnesota hosted a biggie for

At an MGM *Oz* celebration in August 1989, Munchkin Margaret Pellegrini posed with Jack Haley Jr., Lorna Luft (Judy Garland's daughter), and Lorna's son—Judy Garland's only grandson—Jesse. Below, Lorna and Jesse meet Munchkins Fern Formica and Mickey Carroll in 1989. Jesse was the height of the Munchkins when they made *The Wizard of Oz* with his grandmother.

Jerry Maren and Karl Slover peer at the glass-encased pair of ruby slippers that were featured in the Smithsonian Institute's traveling exhibit in Los Angeles, 1996.

Ruth Duccini judges a costume contest in Chesterton, Indiana, in 1993.

Mickey Carroll talks about his experiences in *Oz* on TV's *Good Morning America* with Joan Lunden, June 8, 1989.

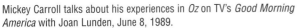

Familiar Sight: The Munchkins in an airport waiting for a flight. Margaret Pellegrini and Jerry and Elizabeth Maren, 1994.

Under the Rainbow

✳

If there is any one thing responsible for grossly inflating and perpetuating the rumors of drunken Munchkins, this movie is it. Set in Culver City around 1938, *Under the Rainbow* takes a comical peek at the welcoming of more than one hundred little people to Hollywood for the production of *The Wizard of Oz.*

Starring Chevy Chase, Carrie Fisher, Eve Arden, Adam Arkin, Pat McCormick, and Billy Barty (playing a little Nazi spy posing as one of the Lollipop Guild), this film is a feeble attempt at humor, although a few gags turn out funny. With some lame subplots involving Japanese tourists and Nazi spys, coupled with the riotous behavior of the little people taking over the hotel and running amok in the studio back lot, the whole thing adds up to a terrible movie.

Predominantly, dwarfs were cast as the Munchkin actors rather than midgets, who constituted almost the entire cast in the 1939 *Oz* motion picture classic. Less than a dozen midgets appeared in *Rainbow,* however, and only two were from the original film: Jerry Maren and Ruth Duccini. For some reason, their presence was not publicized in the film's promotion. Agreeably, Maren and Duccini felt the movie was awful and noted that it grossly painted an unclear picture of the Munchkins and what went on in 1938. Granted, *Under the Rainbow* was intended to be a parody, but it furthered the rumors about the Munchkins being uncontrollable; to this day fans of the Munchkins connect them with *Under the Rainbow* and assume it was an accurate portrayal.

Movie critic Leonard Maltin labeled *Under the Rainbow* a "bomb." Maltin stated, "Even by today's standards, this is an astoundingly tasteless and unfunny comedy. . . . Is this film the Wicked Witch's revenge?"

A cast of little people in the ill-fated film *Under the Rainbow.* (Courtesy of Billy Barty)

Under the Rainbow relied heavily on rumors that the Munchkins wreaked havoc in their hotels and trashed the establishments during the filming of *Oz*.

Munchkin Jerry Maren returns to MGM's Soundstage 27 and is interviewed on film for the BBC documentary *In Search of Oz,* in 1993.

the Munchkins. It was the first time thirteen of the little Munchkin actors reunited, for a Judy Garland Festival in Grand Rapids, Minnesota, the birthplace of Garland. This 1990 event became one of the largest *Oz*-related gatherings of the little people since the film itself.

The place: a huge hotel lobby in Minneapolis. The time: approximately 6 P.M. The purpose: a press conference. To say the least, it was a sight.

There was little Jerry Maren, the famous Lollipop Kid, with a replica sucker in hand, heading straight toward Nita Krebs, the oldest attendee of the group. Krebs was one of the Lullabye League. They hadn't seen each other since 1938. Jerry leaned down to the frail, dainty Krebs sitting in a wheelchair. He gently kissed the tiny lady on her cheek.

"I'm Jerry Maren. Do you remember me?"

Krebs knew exactly who it was. "You're still a good-looking man," she told him, placing her hand on his face.

Little by little, a spectacle took form as the press conference grew near. They came out of elevators and from around corners and rushed to each other in the lobby near a large stone fountain. With the sound of a mild waterfall in the background, the Munchkins anxiously hugged and laughed and marveled at each other, seeing who had grown taller and who had grown older. A few of them still had their accents. There were tears of nostalgia among them, too. Cameras flashed. The mood was electric.

The tiniest of the bunch was "Little Jeane" LaBarbera—almost at kneecap level—who had traveled from Tampa, Florida, with her six-foot husband, Robert Drake. The tallest Munchkin was probably Lewis Croft, over four feet, there from Idaho with his wife, Eva.

MGM in Culver City invited a group of Munchkins to once again converge at a a huge bash thrown on the studio lot on Saturday afternoon, August 19, 1989, for employees and their families. A large hot-air balloon with "Dorothy" aboard ascended from the grounds while the Munchkins cut a giant Ozzy decorated cake with some of the children of the original cast, Jack Haley Jr., and Lorna Luft. The huge blow-out was also a public relations tool to introduce the new fiftieth anniversary *Wizard of Oz* videotape distributed by MGM/ UA Home Video in conjunction with Turner Entertainment. Yes, the videocassette had a beautiful cover and was a great addition to any *Oz* collector, but it was a product that aggravated a few of the Munchkins.

Several little people made it known publicly that they were embarrassed at the studio's heavily touted home video release. The video box invited you to see "*Oz* as it was originally released in 1939—painstakingly reconstructed from a brilliant Technicolor print, and featuring the Kansas scenes in warm sepia tone." This was all capped by additional rare footage, a theatrical trailer, and a special thirty-two-page

The 1973 Tournament of Roses Parade featured Munchkins from the MGM film: Billy Curtis, Hazel Resmondo, and Jerry Maren. The float featured intricately detailed giant heads of the Cowardly Lion, the Tin Man, and the Scarecrow, all of which moved by independent animation systems. The entry earned the Governor's Trophy in the competition. (Courtesy of Jerry Maren)

illustrated booklet that, somehow, neglected the Munchkins—except for negative commentary. (Plenty o' monkey pictures in the booklet, but not a single shot of the Munchkins.) Moreover, the brief mention they did receive was further tripe regarding "off-set problems with late-night partying and altercations." As humorous and trivial as it may have seemed, that kind of memorialization in the most widely released authorized product from the studio itself was a slap in the face. Think of it: Millions upon millions of these videotapes were sold over the years, and countless millions of buyers who browsed the booklet were provided only this dubious impression of the little performers.

MGM/UA Home Video was not the only party to keep the rumor mill running at a steady pace. The television media was hungry for live personalities to exploit, thus the Munchkins were in demand for interviews. Some shows were kinder than others. Every popular news program and talk show invited a Munchkin. Little people guested on *Entertainment Tonight, A Current Affair, Larry King Live, Geraldo, CBS News Nightwatch,* and countless radio shows, including Tom Snyder's syndi-

cated ABC radio talk show. Exposés appeared in periodicals that ran the gamut from *Playboy* and *People* to the *Star* and the *National Enquirer.* Virtually every single story cited the same topic of supposed licentious conduct of the little people during the production. It was to be expected.

Complaints aside, the Munchkin survivors overlooked it, sometimes playfully battled it, and tried to have fun with it all while awaiting more pleasant activities. In that golden anniversary spell, the only reunion to match the magnitude of Grand Rapids was the Oztoberfest in Liberal, Kansas. Liberal's event gathered fourteen original Munchkins, one-upping Grand Rapids. The little people attending the Kansas extravaganza included Ruth Duccini, Lewis Croft, Fern Formica, Emil Kranzler, Nita Krebs, Jeane LaBarbera, Jerry Maren, Nels Nelson, Margaret Pellegrini, Karl Slover, Clarence Swensen, Meinhardt Raabe, Betty Tanner, and Gus Wayne. Joining the group was one of the children from the movie, Viola White Banks. That remained the largest gathering to date; if attempted today, this gathering would be an impossibility.

We're Off to Sell the Wizard

In spite of the Munchkins' charm on film, the majority of the vast merchandise tied to this film has been devoted to the four main characters in the movie. As the film gained popularity and recognizability over the decades, the Munchkins crept into toy stores. Agreeably, the Munchkin characters are essentially extras in the film, and to some marketing specialists they would be unlikely subjects to transform into purchasable playthings or ornamentation. But now, on the brink of a new millennium, the Munchkins are doing a solo on the Yellow Brick Road, as virtually the only known cast members to survive and tell about it.

The fiftieth anniversary of the film brought about a concentrated effort on *Oz* exploitation due mostly to a massive campaign orchestrated by Turner Entertainment. To the delight of masses of fervent *Oz* collectors around the world, this was no clinking, clanking, clattering collection of junk. The *Oz* onslaught capitalized on the little people's survival, and some of the more recognizable Munchkins characters were immortalized in various toys and collectibles. Usually the images employed were that of the Munchkin mayor, the Lollipop Kid, one of the Lullabye League, and maybe, just maybe, a Winged Monkey made it in there for good measure.

Oz (ŏz) n. An unreal, magical, often bizarre place: *regarded New York City as the Oz of the Northeast.* Also called *Land of Oz.* [After the fantasy land *Oz* created by L. Frank Baum in *The Wonderful Wizard of Oz* and other novels.]

—*American Heritage Dictionary of the English Language*

The Multi-Toy Munchkin dolls.

The Franklin Mint heirloom-quality porcelain collector dolls representing the Lollipop Guild and the Lullabye League. (Courtesy of Franklin Mint)

Hallmark has released some exquisite *Oz* Christmas ornaments over the years.

The Franklin Mint's series of four-inch porcelain statuettes premiered in
1989, along with a lineup of other characters from the film.

The Munchkinland Playset (Mego, 1976) featured Kansas on one side and Munchkinland on the other. *Oz* character dolls could be whisked between worlds via the "tornado transporter" in the center. (From the Scarfone-Stillman Collection)

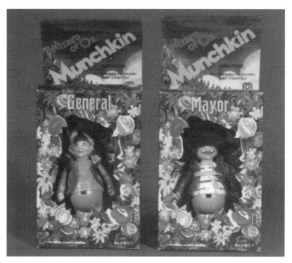

Mego's General and Mayor, two of four Munchkin dolls produced in 1976. (From the Scarfone-Stillman Collection)

A rare British picture puzzle, circa 1940. (From the Scarfone-Stillman Collection)

In a 1989 promotion for the Dunkin' Donuts "Munchkin" variety are Gus Wayne, Margaret Pellegrini, and Fern Formica.

In 1988 Multi Toys intended to issue six Munchkin character puppets to accompany their main character series. The Munchkins puppets were produced in limited supply and marketed only in Canada. (From the Scarfone-Stillman Collection)

Follow the Yellow Band Wiener
By Tod Machin

A story on the marketing of cold cuts in a book about Munchkins may seem a bit out of place, but upon closer inspection, Oscar Mayer Wieners have several *links* to MGM's 1939 film, *The Wizard of Oz*.

Little Oscar, the "World's Smallest Chef," has served as Oscar Mayer's goodwill ambassador since he was brought to life from an advertising cartoon character in 1937. Meinhardt Raabe, who stood just four feet six (or about thirteen wieners tall), portrayed the first Little Oscar. His unique employment came fresh out of college, where he had studied accounting at the University of Wisconsin.

Initially he worked in the accounting department during the week, but on Saturdays he would slip into a white chef's outfit and promote the company's products at local supermarkets. Five months later, Meinhardt was transferred to Chicago, and Little Oscar was equipped with "wheels." Not just any wheels, mind you, but a vehicle that was sure to draw attention and complement the novelty of the company's diminutive spokesman. The wheels became the renowned Wienermobile.

Meinhardt toured the Chicago area in the original thirteen-foot motorized sausage, gaining publicity and boosting sales for Oscar Mayer (M-a-y-e-r) until 1938, when his travels were temporarily curbed. When Metro-Goldwyn-Mayer (also M-a-y-e-r) was casting for *The Wizard of Oz* and searching for midget actors to play the inhabitants of Munchkinland, Oscar Mayer granted Meinhardt a leave of absence to appear in the movie. (No one knows whether or not that was an Oscar Mayer wiener Toto snatched from Professor Marvel at his campsite in the beginning of the film. A company spokesman said, "We haven't been asked yet.")

When *Oz* was released in 1939, Oscar Mayer capitalized on their little star's contribution to the film. Meinhardt made public appearances at theaters presenting *The Wizard of Oz* in the Midwest. With the Wienermobile parked out front, he would give a preshow demonstration and pass out food samples after the film's showing.

In 1946, Little Oscar gained a wife, Little Mrs. Oscar. Not coincidentally, Meinhardt was also married that year, with both roles going to Marie Hartline. While Marie's engagement with the meat company lasted only seven years, her real-life marriage to Meinhardt sustained, and the Raabes celebrated their golden wedding anniversary December 15, 1996.

Meinhardt Raabe, the original Little Oscar, posed next to a billboard outside a Chicago Theater, circa 1939. (Tod Machin Collection)

Jerry Maren as Little Oscar surrounded by the kiddies.

Little Oscar and another famous "frank." (Courtesy of Jerry Maren)

By the 1950s television was becoming a powerful force in the advertising world. The Raabes moved to Philadelphia, where Meinhardt introduced a series of Oscar Mayer television commercials. The national exposure of this successful advertising campaign had the "World's Smallest Chef" in popular demand. The company soon hired midgets George Molchan, Joe White, and Jerry Maren for their expanding staff of Little Oscars. Each actor worked a different territory of the United States, touring the local supermarket circuit and passing out plastic wiener whistles, plastic rings, plastic handpuppets, and other toys to children. (Today the company offers a Wienermobile Hot Wheels car made by Mattel and a child-size Wienermobile pedal-car for kiddies.)

Like Raabe, newcomer Jerry Maren also played a memorable role in *The Wizard of Oz*—the Lollipop Kid. While Jerry remained employed by Oscar Mayer for thirteen years, it was a job he sometimes hardly *relished*. Jerry recalls, "It was a tough grind to keep up that pace. We'd visit twenty to twenty-five stores in one day with no time for lunch. And that Wienermobile was always a problem and constantly breaking down—mostly on Saturdays when we were on our way home."

One of Maren's advantages, however, was his locale. He toured the West Coast region, which gave him access to the celebrities of Hollywood. Dressed as Little Oscar, Jerry had been photographed feeding hot dogs to the likes of Abbott and Costello, Charlie Weaver, Bob Hope, and Dorothy Lamour, to name but a few. It was all fun for Maren and great publicity for the corporation.

HOT DOGGIN' WITH LITTLE OSCAR

If you've never experienced a Wienermobile sighting out on the road, *frank*-ly, you've missed out. There's something about seeing an enormous hot dog cruising down the highway that makes you smile. They're outrageous, amusing, and really big! They have also become a symbol of the baby-boomer generation—a true classic among American popular culture icons.

In the beginning other modes of transportation were considered, such as a Wienerscooter and a Wienercopter, but in the end, it boiled down to a Wienermobile. Built in 1936, the first one was thirteen feet long with open cockpits in the center and the rear. Rarely would the Little Oscar protrude from atop the Wienermobile while traveling at highway speed. In the 1940s a glass box was installed to protect the riders from the elements, but with no air-conditioning, a sweltering afternoon could make this Wienermobile one *really* hot dog!

Short Order Cooks: The men who became famous as Little Oscar, "World's Smallest Chef," pose with the big man himself, Oscar F. Mayer, in the early 1950s. (L–R): George Molchan, Joe White, Meinhardt Raabe, and Jerry Maren.

Between 1950 and 1953, five more Wienermobiles were constructed. *Sandwiched* between 1953 and 1969, a futuristic bubble-nosed Wienermobile was designed by the late Brooks Stevens of *Excalibur* fame. His exceptional interpretation added buns to the chassis, and this 1958 design element is continued to this day. Two new models were introduced in 1969 (one was eventually retired to Puerto Rico), and a fiberglass and Styrofoam unit that now tours the streets of Spain was added in 1976. When mileage added up and they could no longer *cut the mustard,* they were retired and replaced by new models.

A renewed interest recently occurred when Honda cooked up an advertising campaign utilizing a Wienermobile. Television and print ads showed its Acura Integra parked beside a Weinermobile. The slogan states, "The second most fun car on the road."

The "Lamberwienie" of all Wienermobiles was unveiled in February 1995. Six slick, shiny new twenty-seven-foot-long hot rods feature a big-screen television, relish-colored seats, a computerized "condiment control panel," and a hot-dog-shaped dashboard. The state-of-the-art vehicle underwent stringent aerodynamic testing in the wind tunnel at the California Institute of Technology. Clocked at speeds in excess of ninety mph, the new Wienermobile can really *haul buns.* Another added feature is the external front and rear surveillance cameras that instantaneously turn this dog into a "watch dog" at the flip of a switch.

As Jerry Maren recalls, cruising around in the old Wienermobile could sometimes prove hazardous. "One of the Wienermobiles back East hit a kid," he says, "but it wasn't serious. The Wienermobile attracted so much attention, crowds of kids would gather around instantly. It became extremely difficult to maneuver around them."

Like *The Wizard of Oz*, Little Oscar's Wienermobile is another staple in American pop culture that's passing the test of time . . . and *that's* no b-o-l-o-g-n-a!

Special thanks to Sharon Rahn, Elaine Willingham, Geraldine Burke, Russ Whitaker, Tom Whitemarsh, and Sharon Dewey, and Becky Tousey from Kraft Foods, Inc. OSCAR MAYER and the Wienermobile are registered trademarks of Oscar Mayer Foods Corporation and are used with permission.

All Beef, No Turkey: Meinhardt Raabe pokes out of an early Wienermobile during the 1950 Thanksgiving Day parade in New York City.

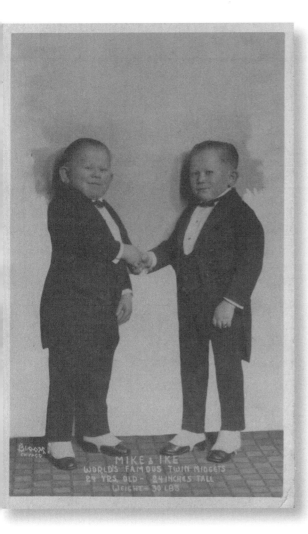

(Courtesy of Kevin and Marilyn Hoglund)

Mike and Ike: The Confection Connection

Genetically speaking, twins rare, and midgets are even more rare. *Midget twins* are almost unheard of. But there was a famous pair of identicals named Mike and Ike Matina who gained a reputation for causing a ruckus or two during their off-hours from production of *The Wizard of Oz.* You may not recognize their puffy faces. They're barely seen in the movie, especially under the makeup.

My quest was to trace whether the famous candy, which has been around since the early 1940s, was named for the famous midget twins who had been around since 1903. Haven't each one of us splurged on a sugar high and chewed some fruity, missile-like Mike and Ike candies just once or twice?

Their real names were Bela and Matjus Matina, but they were nicknamed Mike and Ike even before they left their homeland of Budapest, Hungary, in 1916. Even more bizarre, they had five midget brothers in the family. One of the brothers, Leo, also appeared as a Munchkin Villager in the movie. Mike and Ike each stood about three feet two, and their brother, who looked very much like them, had a few inches on them.

It is not known whether any more than three of the Matina midgets migrated to America. Mike, Ike, and Leo became U.S. citizens, "proud of having sold liberty bonds on New York's streets during the War," one newspaper article noted. In America the three Matina brothers were adopted by a thirty-six-inch midget lady, Mrs. Sybilla D. Rogers—a mother of six average-sized children. She was the wife of Tom Rogers, a showman of average height who died in 1925. The Matinas lived with Mrs. Rogers in Philadelphia for eighteen years, capriciously taking on the name of Rogers.

And so the question remains. Was the candy named for these Munchkins? Well, you decide.

A spokesperson at the Just Born Candy Company said no one could be sure. The company, which holds a patent on the Sanitary Square Suckers Machine (the suckers are "not touched by hand"), was founded by Samuel Born in Brooklyn, New York, in 1923. Get it? Just Born Sucker?

The candy company moved to Bethlehem, Pennsylvania, in the early 1930s, and today Just Born is one of the few family-owned giant confectioneries surviving in the U.S.

Interestingly, buried in the company archives is a peculiar piece of original, tattered sheet music. Titled "Mike and Ike (The Twin Song)," it was written by Dwight Latham and copyrighted 1937; at some point in time, the song was recorded by a musical group known as The Three Jesters. The lyrics make no reference to stature of the twins ("Mike and Ike, they looked alike").

We may never realize the sweet significance of the sheet music, the lollipop, and Mike and Ike. Maybe it's true. Maybe there *is* a sucker born every minute.

Munchkin friends: Ike Matina, Freda Betsky, Ruth Smith, and Mike Matina. (Courtesy of Beverly Smith.)

AFTERWORD
Some Final Thoughts From a Munchkin

by Mickey Carroll

My favorite part of *The Wizard of Oz* is Dorothy's simple words of wisdom: "There's no place like home." She was right. And yet, when I was just a teenager, I left my home to be a part of it all, never ever thinking it might have such a strong impact on my life.

My brother Bud and I left St. Louis in 1938 in a car traveling to Hollywood because I was going to be a Munchkin with Dorothy in a picture that has become one of the greatest fables. I was sixteen and had some schooling, but still I thought, "What is a Yellow Brick Road?" and "What the hell is a Munchkin?" "What is 'Ding Dong the Witch Is Dead'?" We were in these cockamamy costumes singing and dancing. I wasn't that familiar with the original book, but the chance to work in the film with Judy Garland seemed wonderful since I was an entertainer during those days. (I'm still an entertainer at heart.) Only who knew it would be so great?

I'll always remember my sister, Mary, taking me to tap-dancing lessons at the Fox Theater when I was a kid. My tapping eventually came in handy in Munchkinland. The Fox Theater is where I danced with Jack Haley (the Tin Man) back in 1932, years before *The Wizard of Oz* at MGM.

Later on I returned home, and Dorothy's famous words have stayed with me ever since, just like the film and the books have stayed with so many people. It never left me, and I never left the Midwest either. I've never married—I'm a devout coward. But I love children

Mickey Carroll with a couple of little fans dressed as Dorothy. (Courtesy of Linda Rosen)

dearly. Over the years I learned one thing: There really is no place like home.

It's amazing, but when I was a kid, I never dreamed I would be part of a legend like *Oz*. Kids and their parents stop me almost every day, whether it's in a grocery store or a restaurant, and ask about the movie. They don't let me go. Before I finish my breakfast I gotta sign twenty autographs, and more for the waitresses. They all know me here in St. Louis. You ought to see the mail I get. Kids ask, "Where does Dorothy live now?" or "Who was the mayor of Munchkinland?" "Do you watch the movie every year on TV?" Lots of questions. I think the author has answered most of them here in the book.

Yes, I do watch the movie each year. My mother did, too, every year until she died in 1981. She was ninety. Mostly I watch for Judy's song and for my scenes, and then I flip the channels. Since we didn't get our names in the credits, I don't usually wait around and watch the whole thing. Sure, the flying monkey—he got screen credit. Besides, I know how the movie turns out.

I did watch the entire film at the Museum of Art in New York City a few years ago as part of a fiftieth-anniversary celebration of the film. On that great big screen, in all of its glory, I stared ahead and enjoyed the film all over again . . . then got mobbed outside in the lobby afterward. But I loved it, I have to admit. (I don't think I'd ever seen such a breathtaking print of the film.)

The next day I led the Tap-Oz-Mania parade, consisting of thousands of tap dancers in matching gold shirts and hats, clicking our heels like a parade going past Macy's. We broke the record for the most tap dancers in one place. That was a sight. I was the only Munchkin there for the opening ceremonies. And again, my tap dancing came in handy.

I'm seventy-seven today. My phone won't stop ringing from people wishing me happy

One of many engraved yellow bricks located in the town center of Judy Garland's birthplace, Grand Rapids, Minnesota.

birthday and from people I don't even know. That's how much people love *The Wizard of Oz*! They all want to talk to a Munchkin. I'll always know that *The Wizard of Oz* will be enjoyed by millions of children when they see the movie or read the book, whichever comes first. The popularity of the movie continues to baffle me, but it makes me happy just the same. It just keeps going. And so do I because of the author of this book, Steve Cox. He got me out of the house. I'm so glad he's written this book. I'm very proud of it, and I know I speak for the rest of the Munchkins, too.

The story Mr. Baum wrote about a hundred years ago will be around for centuries to come, I'm positive. They say it's timeless. But is Oz really a story? Isn't Oz real?

Mickey Carroll

Mickey Carroll
Munchkin
"The Wizard of Oz"

St. Louis, Missouri
July 8, 1996

Metro-Goldwyn-Mayer presents
A Victor Fleming production

THE WIZARD OF OZ

The Cast

JUDY GARLAND	Dorothy Gale
FRANK MORGAN	Professor Marvel/Wizard/ Emerald City Gatekeeper, Carriage Driver, and Guard
RAY BOLGER	Hunk/Scarecrow
JACK HALEY	Hickory/Tin Man
BERT LAHR	Zeke/Cowardly Lion
BILLIE BURKE	Glinda, the Good Witch
MARGARET HAMILTON	Almira Gulch/the Wicked Witch
CHARLEY GRAPEWIN	Uncle Henry
CLARA BLANDICK	Auntie Em
PAT WALSHE	Nikko (head Winged Monkey)
TERRY	Toto

AND THE SINGER MIDGETS AS THE MUNCHKINS

Directed by Victor Fleming
Produced by Mervyn LeRoy
Screenplay by Noel Langley, Florence Ryerson, and Edgar Allen Woolf
Adaptation by Noel Langley
From the book by L. Frank Baum
Musical Adaptation by Herbert Stothart
Lyrics by E. Y. "Yip" Harburg
Music by Harold Arlen
Associate Conductor: George Stoll
Orchestral and Vocal Arrangements: George Bassman, Murray Cutter, Paul Marquardt, and Ken Darby
Musical Numbers Staged by Bobby Connolly
Photographed in Technicolor by Harold Rosson, A.S.C.
Associate: Allen Davey, A.S.C.
Technicolor Color Director: Natalie Kalmus
Associate: Henri Jaffa
Recording Director: Douglas Shearer
Art Director: Cedric Gibbons
Associate: William A. Horning
Set Decorations by Edwin B. Willis
Special Effects by Arnold Gillespie
Costumes by Adrian
Character Makeups created by Jack Dawn
Film Editor: Blanche Sewell

RUNNING TIME: 101 MINUTES

✳ The Munchkins of Oz ✳

NAME	ALIAS	CHARACTER	BIRTH DATE	DEATH DATE	NOTES
GLADYS W. ALLISON		Villager		Date unconfirmed	
JOHN BALLAS				Date unconfirmed	
FRANZ BALLUCH	Mike Balluch		September 8, 1913 Vienna	January 24, 1987 Vienna	Sibling
JOSEFINE BALLUCH	"Fini" Balluch	Villager	September 4 Vienna	1984 Vienna	Sibling
JOHN T. BAMBURY		Soldier		Date unconfirmed	
CHARLES E. BECKER	Charlie Becker	Mayor of Munchkinland	November 24, 1887 Muschenheim, Germany	December 28, 1968 Elk Grove, California	
FREDA BETSKY		Villager		Date unconfirmed	
HENRY BOERS				Date unconfirmed	Sibling
THEODORE BOERS	Teddy Boers			Date unconfirmed	Sibling
CHRISTIE BURESH		Villager	April 21, 1904 Domamil, Czechoslovakia	October 1979 Georgia	Sibling
EDUARD BURESH	Eddie Buresh		March 16, 1909 Domamil, Czechoslovakia	January 1982 Georgia	Sibling
LIDA BURESH		Villager	June 16, 1906 Domamil, Czechoslovakia	September 1970 Georgia	Sibling
MICKEY CARROLL	Michael Finocchiaro	Town Crier, Soldier, Fiddler	July 8, 1919 St. Louis, Missouri		
COLONEL CASPER				Date unconfirmed	
NONA COOPER	née Nona Appleby	Villager	Baltimore, Maryland	Date unconfirmed	
THOMAS J. COTTONARO	Tommy Cottonaro	Villager	March 20, 1914 Castrogiovanni, Italy	February 7, 2001 Niagara Falls, New York	
ELIZABETH COULTER		Villager		Date unconfirmed	
LEWIS CROFT	"Idaho Lewis"	Soldier	May 2, 1919 Shelley, Idaho		
FRANK H. CUCKSEY	"Cookie"	Gave bouquet to Dorothy	January 5, 1919 Brooklyn, New York	September 16, 1984 Sarasota, Florida	
BILLY CURTIS		City Father	June 27, 1909 Springfield, Massachusetts	November 9, 1988 Nevada	

Name	Also Known As	Role	Born	Died	Notes
EUGENE S. DAVID JR.				Date unconfirmed	Sibling
EULIE H. DAVID			April 10, 1921	September, 1972	Sibling
ETHEL W. DENIS		Villager	March 23, 1894	December, 1968 / Phoenix, Arizona	Spouse
PRINCE DENIS	"Little Denny" Denis Bernatets	Sergeant at Arms (Loft Munchkin)	January 26, 1892 / France	June 21, 1984 / Phoenix, Arizona	Spouse / Brother of Marie Winters
HAZEL I. DERTHICK	Hazel Resmondo	Villager	January 7, 1906 / Old Floris, Oklahoma	February 13, 1989 / Los Angeles, California	
JAMES D. DOYLE	"Major Doyle"	Villager	July 26, 1869 / New York, New York	October 11, 1940 / Spartanburg, South Carolina	
CARL M. ERICKSON	"Kayo" Erickson	2nd Trumpeter, Sleepyhead	October 12, 1917 / Corson, South Dakota	March 28, 1958 / Phoenix, Arizona	
JEANETTE FERN	Fern Formica, Johmie Fern McDill	Villager, Sleepyhead	January 17, 1925 / Drumright, Oklahoma	January 23, 1995 / Hemet, California	
ADDIE EVA FRANK		Villager		Date unconfirmed	
THAISA L. GARDNER		Villager		Date unconfirmed	
JAKOB GERLICH	Jackie Gerlich	Lollipop Guild (left)	September 21	Date unconfirmed	
WILLIAM A. GIBLIN	Bill Giblin			Date unconfirmed	
JACK GLICKEN		City Father (polka-dot vest)		Date unconfirmed	Dwarf
CAROLYN E. GRANGER		Villager	Ohio	Date unconfirmed	
JOSEPH L. HERBST		Soldier	April 7, 1908 / Joliet, Illinois	July 6, 1993 / Joliet, Illinois	
JAKOB HOFBAUER		Soldier	April 19, 1908 / Birkfeld, Austria	Date unconfirmed	
CLARENCE C. HOWERTON "Major Mite"		3rd Trumpeter, Sleepyhead	February 9, 1913 / Salem, Oregon	November 18, 1975 / Salem, Oregon	
HELEN M. HOY		Villager	Koenigsberg, Prussia	Date unconfirmed	Sibling
MARGUERITE A. HOY			Koenigsberg, Prussia	Date unconfirmed	Sibling
JAMES R. HULSE		Villager	March 16, 1915 / Circleville, Ohio	December 29, 1964 / Westerville, Ohio	
ROBERT KANTER	"Lord Roberts"	Soldier	New York	Date unconfirmed / New York	

Name	Alias / Spouse name	Role	Birth date & place	Death date & place	Relation
CHARLES E. KELLEY		Villager	Wellington, Alabama	Date unconfirmed	Spouse
JESSIE E. KELLEY	née Jessie Chappell	Villager	June 4, Mahaska, Kansas	Date unconfirmed, Oakland, California	Spouse (Later married Charlie Becker)
FRANK KIKEL				Date unconfirmed	
BERNHARD KLIMA	Harry Klima			Date unconfirmed	
EMMA KOESTNER		Villager	December 5, 1900	January 1984, New York	Sibling
MITZI KOESTNER		Villager	June 4, 1894	August 1975, New York	Sibling
WILLI KOESTNER	Billy Koestner	Soldier	December 29, 1908	November 1974, New York	Sibling
KARL KOSICZKY	("Karchy"), Karl Slover	1st Trumpeter	September 21, 1918, Hungary		
ADAM EDWIN KOZICKI	Eddie Adams	Fiddler	December 19, 1917, Wilkes-Barre, Pennsylvania	April 1986, Wilkes-Barre, Pennsylvania	
JOSEPH J. KOZIEL		Villager		Date unconfirmed	
DOLLY KRAMER	née Henny Fischer	Villager	June 23, 1904, Brooklyn, New York	July 9, 1995, Miami, Florida	
EMIL KRANZLER		Villager	December 1, 1911, Akaska, South Dakota	April 7, 1993, Arizona	
NITA KREBS		Lullabye League (left), Villager	October 8, 1905, Bodenbach, Czechoslovakia	January 18, 1991, Sarasota, Florida	
JEANE LaBARBERA	"Little Jeane," Jeane Drake	Villager	August 4, 1909, Italy	August 17, 1993, Tampa, Florida	
HILDA LANGE		Villager		Date unconfirmed	
JOHN LEAL	Johnny Leal	Soldier, Villager	February 26, 1905, Ventura, California	November 9, 1996, Ojai, California	
ANN RICE LESLIE		Villager	July 4, 1900, E. Greenwich, Rhode Island	July 27, 1973, Minneapolis, Minnesota	
CHARLES LUDWIG	"Prince Ludwig"	Villager	Thuringen, Saxony	Date unconfirmed	
DOMINICK MAGRO				Date unconfirmed	
CARLOS MANZO	Carl Manzo		1914, Yonkers, New York	Date unconfirmed	
HOWARD MARCO				Date unconfirmed	

Name	Stage Name	Role	Birth	Death	Notes
GERARD MARENGHI	Jerry Maren	Lollipop Guild (center)	January 24, 1920 Boston, Massachusetts		
BELA MATINA	Mike Rogers	Villager	1903 Budapest, Hungary	Date unconfirmed	Sibling (Twin)
MATJUS MATINA	Ike Rogers	Villager	1903 Budapest, Hungary	Date unconfirmed	Sibling (Twin)
LAJOS MATINA	Leo Matina	Villager	September 12, 1893 Budapest, Hungary	December 1975	Sibling
WALTER MILLER		Soldier, Winged Monkey	February 26, 1906 Worcester, Massachusetts	October 26, 1987 Long Beach, California	
GEORGE MINISTERI		Coach Driver, Villager	August 9, 1913 Boston, Massachusetts	January 29, 1986 Boston, Massachusetts	
HARRY MONTY	Hymie Lichenstein	Villager, Winged Monkey	April 15, 1904 Poland	December 28, 1999 Los Angeles, California	
YVONNE MORAY	Yvonne Bistany	Lullabye League (right), Villager	January 24, 1917 Brooklyn, New York	Date unconfirmed	
OLGA C. NARDONE		Lullabye League (center), Sleepyhead, Villager	Boston, Massachusetts		
NELS P. NELSON		Villager	November 24, 1918 Port Wing, Wisconsin	May 2, 1994 Los Angeles, California	Dwarf
MARGARET C. H. NICKLOY		Villager		Date unconfirmed	Divorced from Ike Matina
FRANKLIN H. O'BAUGH				Date unconfirmed	
WILLIAM H. O'DOCHARTY	W. H. O'Docharty	Villager, Carriage Footman	September 12, 1920 Texas	December 20, 1988 Corpus Christi, Texas	
HILDRED C. OLSON		Villager	Dassel, Minnesota	Date unconfirmed	
FRANK PACKARD				Date unconfirmed	
NICHOLAS PAGE	Nicky Page	City Father	May 2, 1904	August 18, 1978 San Francisco, California	
LEONA M. PARKS	"Duchess Leona"	Villager	April 10	Date unconfirmed	
JOHNNY PIZO				Date unconfirmed	Dwarf
LEON POLINSKY	"Prince Leon"	Villager	July 5, 1918	July 1955 New Jersey	
LILLIAN PORTER		Villager		Date unconfirmed	
MEINHARDT RAABE		Coroner	September 2, 1915 Watertown, Wisconsin		
MARGARET RAIA	Margie Raia	Villager		Date unconfirmed	Sibling, left film (underage)

Name	Character	Role	Birth	Death	Notes
MATTHEW RAIA				Date unconfirmed	Sibling
BILLY RHODES	"Little Billy"	Barrister (purple robe)	August 15, 1894 Lynn, Massachusetts	July 24, 1967 Hollywood, California	
GERTRUDE H. RICE		Villager		Date unconfirmed	Sibling
HAZEL RICE		Villager		Date unconfirmed	Sibling
FRIEDRICH RETTER	Freddie Retter	Fiddler, Villager	July 8, 1913 Austria	Date unconfirmed	
RUTH L. ROBINSON	Ruth Duccini	Villager	July 23, 1918 Rush City, Minnesota		
SANDOR ROKA			1899 Tatatovaros, Hungary	1957 Sarasota, Florida	
JIMMIE ROSEN			August 4, 1892 Russia	March 1973	
CHARLES F ROYALE	Charles Wojnarski	Soldier	Poland	Date unconfirmed Chicago, Illinois	Sibling
HELEN J. ROYALE	Helen Wojnarski	Villager	Poland	Date unconfirmed Chicago, Illinois	Sibling
STELLA A. ROYALE	Stella Wojnarski	Villager	Poland	Date unconfirmed Chicago, Illinois	Sibling
ALBERT RUDDINGER				Date unconfirmed	
ELLY A. SCHNEIDER	Tiny Doll	Villager	July 23, 1914 Stolpen, Germany		Sibling
FRIEDA A. SCHNEIDER	Gracie Doll	Villager	March 12, 1899 Stolpen, Germany	November 8, 1970 Sarasota, Florida	Sibling
HILDA E. SCHNEIDER	Daisy Doll, Daisy Earles	Villager	April 29, 1907 Stolpen, Germany	March 15, 1980 Sarasota, Florida	Sibling
KURT F SCHNEIDER	Harry Doll, Harry Earles	Lollipop Guild (right)	April 3, 1902 Stolpen, Germany	May 4, 1985 Sarasota, Florida	Sibling
ELSIE R. SCHULTZ	Elsie Reinking	Villager	December 7, 1892 Germany	July 11, 1987 New York	Left film on 12-21-38 (car accident)
CHARLES SILVERN				Date unconfirmed	
GARLAND SLATTEN	Earl Slatten	Soldier	February 17, 1917 Walters, Oklahoma	April 30, 1995 Pasco, Washington	
RUTH E. SMITH	Ruth E. Kline	Villager	November 24, 1895 Fairbank, Minnesota	September 5, 1985 Marshalltown, Iowa	Dwarf
ELMER SPANGLER			1910	Date unconfirmed	

Name	Also known as / née	Role	Birth	Death	Notes
PERNELL ELMER ST. AUBIN "Little Elmer"		Soldier	Canton, Ohio / December 19, 1922 Chicago, Illinois	December 4, 1987 Chicago, Illinois	Dwarf
CARL STEPHAN				Date unconfirmed	
ALTA M. STEVENS	Alta Barnes	Villager	August 28, 1913 Minnesota	September 3, 1989 Anaheim, California	
GEORGE SUCHSIE				Date unconfirmed	
CHARLOTTE V. SULLIVAN		Villager	April 15, 1906 Wisconsin	December 23, 1966 Los Angeles, California	
CLARENCE SWENSEN	"Shorty" Swensen	Soldier	December 29, 1917 Austin, Texas		
BETTY D. TOCZYLOWSKI	Betty Titus, Betty Tanner	Villager	February 5, 1916 Lynn, Massachusetts	November 8, 1994 Boston, Massachusetts	
ARNOLD J. VIERLING	"Sonny" Vierling	Villager	May 24, 1919 Seymour, Indiana	June 11, 1949 Seymour, Indiana	
GUS WAYNE		Soldier	October 16, 1920 Bronx, New York	January 23, 1998 Lakeland, Florida	
VICTOR WETTER		Captain of Army	June 11, 1902 Metz, France	December 8, 1990 New Brunswick, New Jersey	
GRACE G. WILLIAMS	née Grace Gould	Villager	Italy	Date unconfirmed California	Spouse
HARVEY B. WILLIAMS		Soldier	Minnesota	Date unconfirmed California	Spouse
MARGARET WILLIAMS	Margaret Pellegrini	Sleepyhead, Villager	September 23, 1923 Sheffield, Alabama		
JOHN WINTERS	John Maroldo, Johnny Winters	Commander of Navy	November 19, 1905	February, 1985 San Diego, California	Spouse
MARIE WINTERS	Marie Maroldo	Villager	September 14, 1901 France	March 1979 San Diego, California	(Sister of Prince Denis)
GLADYS V. WOLFF		Villager	August 13, 1911 St. Louis, Missouri	May 14, 1984 St. Louis, Missouri	
MURRAY WOOD		City Father (long blue robe)	June 12, 1908 Halifax, Nova Scotia	September 25, 1999 Miami, Florida	

INDEX

ABOUT THE AUTHOR

Steve Cox graduated from Park University in Kansas City, Missouri, with a B.A. in journalism and communication arts in 1988. In 1993 he worked closely with Buddy Ebsen as researcher and editor for the actor's autobiography, *The Other Side of Oz*. Cox has written for *TV Guide, The Hollywood Reporter,* and the *Los Angeles Times,* and has appeared on numerous television shows including *Larry King Live, Good Morning America, Geraldo, Maury Povich,* and *CBS News Nightwatch* with Charlie Rose. The award-winning author has also contributed as a researcher, writer, or producer on more than twenty television documentaries and specials that have aired on CBS, A&E, Turner Classic Movies, MSNBC, and E! Entertainment. Cox is a freelance writer residing in Los Angeles.

He is five feet six.